Sacred Language, Ordinary People

Sacred Language, Ordinary People

Dilemmas of Culture and Politics in Egypt

Niloofar Haeri

First published in 2003 by PALGRAVE MACMILLAN™
175 Fifth Avenue, New York, N.Y. 10010 and
Houndmills, Basingstoke, Hampshire, England RG21 6XS.
Companies and representatives throughout the world.

PALGRAVE MACMILLAN is the global academic imprint of the Palgrave Macmillan division of St. Martin's Press, LLC and of Palgrave Macmillan Ltd. Macmillan® is a registered trademark in the United States, United Kingdom and other countries. Palgrave is a registered trademark in the European Union and other countries.

ISBN 0-312-23898-3 hardback
ISBN 0-312-23897-5 paperback

Library of Congress Cataloging-in-Publication Data
Haeri, Niloofar, 1958–
    Sacred language, ordinary people : state, religion and modernity in Egypt / by Niloofar Haeri.
        p.   cm.
    Includes bibliographical references and index.
    ISBN 0-312-23897-5 – ISBN 0-312-23898-3
    1. Arabic language—Dialects—Egypt.   2. Arabic language—Variation—Egypt.   3. Arabic Language—Social aspects—Egypt.
    4. Diglossia (Linguistics)—Egypt.   5. Language and culture—Egypt.
    6. Arabic language—Religious aspects—Islam.   I. Title.
    PJ6773. H34   2002
    492.7'70962—dc21

                                                    2002074880

A catalogue record for this book is available from the British Library.

Design by Letra Libre, Inc.

First edition: January 2003
10 9 8 7 6 5 4 3 2 1
Printed in the United States of America.

For Abdullah & the blue flame

Contents

Preface

When I was a child, my mother used to gather us around regularly and ask us to read parts of the Qur'an out loud. She did not demand any recitation talents but simply correct pronunciation and fluency. I remember that the Qur'an we read had line by line translations in Persian. The Arabic was set off by a beautiful and thick calligraphy with little circles, dashes and curly lines above and below the letters. The Persian in contrast was in a plain ordinary type-face. While reading, my brother and I would glance quickly at the Persian to try to get some idea of the meaning of the verses. My mother would gently correct us, pause once in a while to explain the significance of what we had just read, and scold us when we giggled because some of the Arabic words sounded like Persian ones for extremely mundane objects. Her emphasis was on our recognition of the diacritic marks and the necessary liaisons between the ends of some words and the beginning of others. Eventually, she and my father taught us the five obligatory daily prayers (*namaaz* in Persian, *il-ṣalaa* in Arabic). In time, we memorized all of them, and learned the correct body movements that serve to mark different parts of the prayers. My parents also tried to teach us special prayers for particular occasions—those for important Islamic dates or for times of personal crises. My interest began to fade as I entered adolescence and left Tehran for Boston. But these experiences, along with my parents' love for the language of the holy book, stayed with me. As did countless childhood memories that are forever laced with the sounds of the Qur'an.

Many years later in graduate school in Philadelphia, I began to learn Arabic in order to do field research in Egypt. I studied the grammar of a language that I had first encountered in childhood as mere sounds and melodies. I found the chance to learn that language finally and become proficient in it exhilarating. Eventually, I went to Egypt to begin my first period of research in 1987–88, and was stunned to discover, like many researchers before me, that I was unequipped to have even a rudimentary conversation in the language. Of course I had been briefly told that the language I was taught was the language of writing and that it was different from the spoken language. But what I had not quite grasped was just how great the differences are. It was clear that in order for me to be able to do my research and have conversations with Egyptians, I had to devote time to the study of Egyptian Arabic as well.

Soon I realized that Egyptian schoolchildren and I have a somewhat comparable experience but in reverse: they start out knowing Egyptian Arabic because it is their mother tongue, and begin to learn Classical Arabic at school, since this is the official language and the medium of education. Why isn't Egyptian Arabic the medium of education? Most primary and secondary school teachers give their lessons in Egyptian Arabic—classroom interactions in general are in that language. So, unofficially, Egyptian Arabic is also a medium of education. But why not officially as well? The constitution of 1980, like those before it, declares Classical Arabic as the official language of Egypt. No mention is made of Egyptian Arabic. Why is citizenship in part defined in relation to a language that is no one's mother tongue? What does it mean to have a divine language as the official language of a state? These and similar questions motivated me to go back to Egypt for more field research in 1995–96.

Classical Arabic is the language of the Qur'an and of Islamic rituals such as the five daily prayers. It has been and continues to be the language of writing—used in textbooks, newspapers, magazines, fiction and nonfiction, and in bureaucracy. The language of daily exchanges and that of nonprint media is Egyptian Arabic, used in television, radio, theatre and film, but on the whole prevented from becoming a language of writing.

Many Egyptians told me that in order to learn Classical Arabic well, one had to study the Qur'an, whose language is the Word of God and the highest exemplar of Classical Arabic. If Classical Arabic is both the language of Islam and of the state, do Egyptians identify the two as the same? Or, as secular intellectuals believe, there has emerged a new form of Classical Arabic—a "third language"—over the past century and a half that is "modern"—a language that is independent of religion and in which "anything can be said"? If so, why do most other Egyptians find these claims so controversial, asserting, on the contrary, that there is only "one" Classical Arabic that is the language of the Qur'an and of Islam?

This book is an attempt at understanding the cultural and political implications of the divide between Classical and Egyptian Arabic. Since the nineteenth century, Egyptians set out to modernize and simplify (*tahdith* and *tabsiit*, respectively) Classical Arabic in order to make it more responsive to their needs and to the exigencies of contemporary life more generally. The central question that I pursue in the following chapters is: What does it mean to modernize a sacred language? I explore whether such an endeavor is possible, what kinds of limits it has and how it affects personal self-expression, cultural production and social and political relations in Egypt today.

So far, I have used the term "Classical Arabic" to refer both to the language of the Qur'an and to the contemporary written language. Some scholars may take issue with this choice, preferring instead to refer to the contemporary language of writing as "Modern Standard Arabic" or MSA for short. I resist this term for a number of reasons. First, there is no equivalent to this term in common usage in Arabic. The term MSA was coined by a number of linguists at Harvard University in the 1960s, according to the renowned linguist Charles Ferguson. In addition, its use implies that we understand the "modernity" of contemporary Classical Arabic and that the modernization of this language is now an accomplished fact. The term has allowed us to take the entire question of modernization for granted and hence has prevented inquires into the many complex issues surrounding it. The closest translation of the name of the language in Arabic—*al-lugha al-'arabiyya al-fuṣḥa*—is "the Eloquent Arabic Language." Egyptians often shorten this term to either *al-lugha al-'arabiyya* or *fuṣḥa*. I could have followed this usage throughout and used the term the "Arabic Language." But as non-Arab readers already need to be reminded that there is not just one "Arabic" language, and as many scholars writing in English use the term Classical Arabic, I have chosen not to do that. Finally, for those who write in English, it is common to refer to the non-Classical varieties of Arabic as "colloquial Arabic." I do not use this term because the modifier "colloquial" refers to a style of speaking or writing, and cannot characterize an entire language in which there are many styles of self-expression. I return to the issue of terms a number of times in the following chapters.

The entanglement of language and politics is not unique to Egypt or to the Arab world. In the United States, the English-only movement advocates a constitutional amendment to make English the official language, or more accurately, to make it officially the official language. There are many prominent politicians and celebrities who support this movement, including the Austrian-born actor Arnold Schwarzenegger, Senator Hayakawa of California and Newt Gingrich. Although love of the language could be part of the motivation for this movement, all of the reasons the movement offers are clearly political. Similarly, the heated debate about the use of African American English in the classroom (what came to be known as the "Ebonics" debate) and the many disadvantages that children speaking nonstandard varieties of English face, clearly illustrates just how political language issues can become. In Egypt and the Arab world, the language question has roots in religion, nationalism, colonial rule, secularism and interpretations over the heritage of Islam. Hence, it is also a highly sensitive topic. So much so that it is not only Arabs who often show this sensitivity but also non-Arab scholars who work on the region. I have had discussions with Iranian, European and American scholars who seem just as sensitive and defensive about the subject, and who have very strong opinions about what they think has been or is going on. I understand this sensitivity because there is a great deal at stake.

Writing this book has not only been a great challenge for me because of the complexity of the issues involved, but also because the very posing of the questions pursued seems to imply criticism. My hope is to contribute to an open dialogue that addresses some longstanding dilemmas in the Arab world and the region as a whole. I have tried to undertake as careful an analysis as I can without shrinking from following up some of its implications. In this task, I am in the company of a number of Egyptian and other Arab writers, past and present, who have been trying to call attention to the profound problems that the language situation exemplifies and creates. Generally, such writers are marginalized inside Egypt and are not read outside it. In the Middle East, external forces continue to bear responsibility for a variety of problems including disregard for national sovereignties and support for regimes that put their peoples' interests at the bottom of their priorities. But just as we need analyses of what is done to us, so we need to examine what we do to ourselves, in spite of the fact that the two may not always be easily separable. As hostility toward Muslims and even toward those who "look Muslim" grows in the West in the present political climate, the need for self-examination and critical thinking becomes even more pressing.

Acknowledgments

This book has benefited from the ideas and challenges of countless friends and strangers in the Middle East, the United States and Europe. In Egypt, I wish to thank all the members of the family whose linguistic practices and ideas about language form a major backbone of this book. They allowed me to come and go freely and frequently, admonishing me if I did not show up for a few days. Their warmth, friendship, insights, humor and patience made my research both possible and enjoyable. They introduced me to their neighbors, friends and kin to help expand my understanding. I am forever grateful to them and to their friends. I have changed their names and a few details of their lives to protect their anonymity. Two women whose friendship has always been crucial for me while doing research in Egypt are Zeinab Ibrahim and her mother Ragaa'. I thank them for the many kinds of support they have given me. I wish to thank Mahmoud Amin al-Alem, Magda Tahtawi, Madiha Doss, Cynthia Nelson, Iman Mirsal and Zeinalabdin Fu'ad. Were I to mention by name all the people I must thank in Egypt, the list would be endless.

I have had the blessing of inimitable interlocutors like Hanan Sabea, Ashraf Ghani, Tom Porteous, Abbas El-Tonsi, Lanfranco Blanchetti-Revelli, and Michel-Rolph Trouillot. I thank them for many sparkling discussions. I owe a great deal to Hanan for her help in all stages of my research. I continue to miss my friend, colleague and "boss" next door, Michel-Rolph Trouillot. Tom Porteous had the misfortune of having to listen to all my ideas. I have had the great fortune of having him in my life. I am grateful to Philip Khoury, Leila Ahmed, Steven Caton, Joel Kuipers, William Hanks, Bernard Cerquiglini, Dilworth Parkinson and Charles Briggs for their much needed support and for reading drafts of this manuscript and offering valuable ideas and suggestion. At Johns Hopkins, I thank Sara Berry, Ali Khan, Gyan Pandey, Veena Das, Kirstie McClure, Deepak Mehta, Murray Last and David Bell for taking the time to read and hear me and share their insights. Sara Berry made it possible for me to continue my career at Johns Hopkins after the near collapse of our department in 1998. I cannot thank her enough for what she has done for me. My other colleagues Sidney Mintz, David Harvey, Erica Shoenberger, Sonia Ryang and Donald Carter have all been generous in their support of my career needs. I thank Sharon Trader, Janet Freedman, Daphne Klautky and Lisa Emanuello for the smooth management of the day-to-day affairs of our department. I thank Matt for the basic work on Table 1.1 and I am grateful to Mahmoud al-Batal and Kirk Belnap for correcting many of the grammatical examples.

I would like to thank the students in my Social History of Languages courses and my graduate seminars in linguistic theory for some brilliant discussions that made me rush home and clarify my ideas. Two friends and graduate students who helped me with all kinds of tasks including library research, transcriptions, comments on my chapters and much more are Mulki Al-Sharmani and Maria Phillips. Maria's help and presence in the last stages of this book were essential to its completion. I owe her a special thanks, and one to her husband Franc Nunoo-Quarco.

I wish to thank Daryush Shaygan, Dr. Ehsani, Mohammad-Reza Haeri and Reza Haeri for their interest in my research and for discussions of the language situation in Iran. Shirin Haeri and my parents Behjat Altoma and Jamaleddin Haeri will be quite relieved to know that this book is finally finished. I am grateful to Shahla and Shokoofeh Haeri for many kinds of support and to Shahla for daily sessions of commiseration over our respective books.

I cannot enumerate the ways in which other friends have helped me in the course of writing this book but I would like nevertheless to mention their names: Brackette Willliams, Maria-Cristina Margotti, Siba Grovogui, Rula Ghani, and Carol and John Huppert.

A generous grant (# SBR9421024) from the National Science Foundation made the fieldwork for this book possible. I am grateful to the Bunting Program of the Radcliffe Institute for Advanced Study at Harvard University for a fellowship in 1999–2000 that released me from my teaching duties and allowed me to write. I thank Kristi Long, my editor at Palgrave, and the anonymous readers of this manuscript for encouragement and many helpful suggestions.

Notes on Transliteration

I have tried to use a simple transliteration system for the Arabic words that appear in this book. Most words make maximum use of English spelling. This includes the use of "sh" to represent the first sound in "shape," "th" to represent the initial sound in "thing," "kh" to represent the last sound in "Bach," and [gh] for a sound that is similar to the French uvular [r]. These choices make it difficult to transliterate accurately words in which such consonants are doubled. Instead of writing, for example, "khkh," I have decided not to represent the doubling of the consonant in these cases, to make reading easier.

For Arabic consonants that do not exist in English, the transcription system follows the most commonly used symbols. For example, Arabic has a set of consonants that are "emphatic" or pharyngealized. A dot under a symbol indicates an emphatic consonant. A number of phonetic distinctions that exist in Classical Arabic are absent from Egyptian Arabic. Hence where the transliteration represents Egyptian Arabic, it will not reflect those distinction either. A ['] indicates the glottal stop in Arabic, and a ['] indicates the pharyngeal fricative 'ayn. Double consonants are kept as they are, with the exceptions noted above. Because the term fusha appears very frequently in the book, it is important to note that it is pronounced as fuss-ha.

Contrary to a perception shared even by some specialists that "Arabic does not have vowels," all varieties of Arabic have long and short vowels. It is only that in Arabic *orthography*, short vowels are generally not indicated, or are indicated by diacritic marks. Long vowels have their own orthographic symbols in writing. In this book, long vowels are indicated by doubling the vowel. However, where a long vowel is part of a name or a frequently used word in English, e.g., *al-Ahram*, *hadith*, *Sura*, Qur'an, I write them with one vowel. This includes the term *'ammiyya*, which has a long vowel after the consonant *'ayn*.

The Arabic definite marker is written as "al-" when the word it is attached to appears mostly in writing or is in a quotation taken from written sources. The transliteration followed here also does not show the effects of the assimilation of the "l" of the definite article to its following phonetic context. The definite article is written as "il-" when what is being quoted is either clearly a word in Egyptian Arabic or the quotation is from an oral exchange. This is a compromise based on phonetic details and differences—it is not meant to imply that all such details are being captured by the transliteration choices here. The feminine marker is transliterated as "a."

Chapter One

Introduction

The first philologists and the first linguists were always and everywhere priests. History knows no nation whose sacred writings or oral tradition were not to some degree in a language foreign and incomprehensible to the profane. . . . [O]rientation [toward the alien, foreign word] is the expression of the enormous historical role that the alien word has played in the formation of all the historical cultures. It has played a role with respect to all domains of ideological creativity without exception, from the sociopolitical order to the behavioral code of daily life.

—Voloshinov 1986

Most world religions have produced exegetic traditions centrally preoccupied with the language of their holy texts. Among Muslims, the revelation of the Qur'an, and the recognition of its language as the Word of God (*kalaam allah*), turned every religious scholar into a linguist and made the mastery of the divine language the single most important prerequisite for intellectual and artistic accomplishments. Most classical languages have by now disappeared: Sanskrit came to be replaced by the local regional languages of India, and Latin eventually gave way to the European vernaculars, generation by generation, genre by genre, and domain by domain until even the Vatican stopped requiring it to be the language of prayers. But Classical Arabic (*al-lugha al-'arabiyya al-fusḥa*, "the Eloquent Arabic Language") as the language of the Qur'an continues to separate the sacred from the profane, writing from speaking, and prescribed religious rituals from personal communication with God.

In Judaism, there is also the belief that the language of the Torah is sacred—*loshn koydesh,*—"the Eternal" or "Sacred Tongue." Classical Arabic and Biblical Hebrew have proved to be "eternal" in that they did not die away once they ceased to be spoken as native languages. Valentin N. Voloshinov (1986) would consider both as examples of the "alien word." But their paramount religious, cultural and political significance makes any statement about their lack of "native" status (or their alienness) rather contentious, although Voloshinov has defensible reasons for this designation. On the one hand, these languages are native to Arabs and Jews in that they are not so to any other group in the world. On the other hand, both ceased to be spoken and used orally in daily life[1] and became "classical" languages, restricted to writing and religious rituals.

Linguistically, Muslim countries can be divided into two kinds: those whose national and official languages are not genealogically related to Arabic, such as Iran, Turkey, Pakistan, Indonesia, Senegal and Nigeria (among others), and those that speak various Arabic "dialects" or vernaculars related to, but quite different from, the Classical Arabic of the Qur'an. In both kinds of countries, regardless of native language, a believing Muslim must know some Classical Arabic in order to read the holy text, to perform the daily prayers and to carry out other religious rituals and obligations. In this sense, there is no Islam without Classical Arabic. There would also be no Classical Arabic without Islam—the language would not have survived in the way it has merely because it was the language of high poetry in Arabia. It has come to pass, and we are not clear about all the reasons, that the language and Islam are mutually constitutive. I say "it has come to pass" because there has been little systematic research on why religious obligations such as praying and reading the Qur'an must be done in Classical Arabic only, and we do not know how this requirement emerged in the course of the centuries following the rise of Islam.

In all Arab countries, in addition to being the language of religion, Classical Arabic is the official state language. Across the Arab world after the emergence of Islam, Arabic vernaculars emerged that mixed with the languages of the newly conquered, diverged greatly from the sacred language and became mother tongues (Ferguson 1959b, Versteegh 1997).[2] The Arabic vernaculars are all more similar to each other than any one is to Classical Arabic. In Egypt, Classical Arabic has existed for centuries alongside Egyptian Arabic, the mother tongue of the majority—referred to by Egyptians as *il-ʿammiyya* or *maṣri* ("the Common" or "Egyptian," respectively).[3] Regardless of class or level of education, it is Egyptian Arabic that is the medium of oral exchanges. Egyptian Arabic has social and regional varieties, like other languages, that show differentiation in lexicon, phonology and syntax on the basis of class, place of residence, urban versus rural residence, level of education, kind of schooling (private versus public) and gender. Cairene Arabic enjoys the most status representing the long-standing prestige of Cairo as a cultural and commercial center.

Classical Arabic is the de facto language of print for fiction, poetry, nonfiction, children's books and comic strips. On radio and television, the only regular program that is in that language is the news. There are also religious programs as well as debates on current issues in which participants use both languages. Egyptian Arabic dominates non-print media. Radio, television, film and theatre are overwhelmingly in Egyptian Arabic. There is a body of published poetry and plays in Egyptian Arabic, as well as highly culturally valued epics that continue to be performed. The main genres of writing in which Egyptian Arabic is accepted are poetry, plays, cartoon captions and short advertisements.

Classical and Egyptian Arabic are genealogically related, that is, they are in the same family of languages. They share cognates, sounds and many phonemes.[4] However, they differ on fundamental syntactic grounds. Classical Arabic has a case system of nominative, accusative and genitive that is absent from all the vernaculars; its canonical word order is verb-subject-object whereas in the spoken languages, it is subject-verb-object. Morphologically, personal suffixes, tenses, negation and so on are all different (see table 1.1). While the two languages share many sounds, their rhythms and pronunciation rules are distinct. To become proficient in Classical Arabic requires years of formal schooling.

This book explores a series of questions related to attempts to modernize Classical Arabic: What does it mean to modernize a sacred language? What do such processes look like? How do they intersect with political interests and official policies? And what is a modern language in the first place? Of course, the first question cannot be answered without some understanding of *why* the simultaneous preservation and modernization of Classical Arabic became and continue to be major preoccupations of diverse intellectuals, social movements and institutions.[5]

These and similar questions may be posed with regard to a number of other groups and societies. Hebrew led a "flickering but intense half-life . . . for two thousand years even as Jews made themselves at home in Romance, Germanic, Slavic, Arabic and other linguistic climates . . ." (Alter 1994:3). Attempts at revitalizing and modernizing the language then began in the late eighteenth century. Robert Alter observes, as others have done: "The unvoiced question hovering over every modern Hebrew text at least until after the First World War was: Why of all tongues Hebrew, when other, more natural alternatives beckoned?" (6).

Table 1.1 Examples of Grammatical Differences between Classical and Egyptian Arabic

	Classical Arabic *al-lugha al-ʿarabiyya al-fuṣḥa*	*Egyptian Arabic* *il-ʿammiyya il-maṣriyya*
Canonical Word Order	Verb-Subject-Object (VSO)	Subject-Verb-Object (SVO)
Examples:	kataba al-kaatib al-kitaab. *wrote the writer the book* akala al-walad al-ṭaʿaam. *ate the boy the food*	il-kaatib katab il-kitaab. *the writer wrote the book.* il-walad kal il-akl. *the boy ate the food.*
Cases		ʿammiyya does not have any cases. Form of the noun does not change.
Examples:	Nominative* al-kitaabu *the book* al-kitaabu jamiilun *the book is beautiful*	il-kitaab gamiil
Examples:	Accusative** (ʾan) yaktuba al-kitaaba. *(he) is writing the book*	No accusative. biyiktib il-kitaab. (he) is writing the book
Examples:	Genitiv*** dhahaba ilaa al-bayti. *(he) went to the house.* sayyaaratu al-waladi. *the car of the boy.*	No genitive raah il-beet *il-ʿarabiyya bitaaʿ il-walad the car belonging (to) the boy

(continues)

Table 1.1 *(continued)*

	Classical Arabic *al-lugha al-'arabiyya al-fuṣḥa*	Egyptian Arabic *il-'ammiyya il-maṣriyya*
Personal Pronouns		
	huwa 'he'	huwwa
	humaa 'they' (dual masculine)	humma 'they' (fem. and masc. plural)
	hum 'they' (masculine)	
	hiya 'she' (feminine dual)	hiyya 'she' (no feminine dual)
	humaa 'they' (feminine dual)	
	hunna 'they' (feminine)	humma 'they' (fem. and masc. plural)
	anta 'you' (masculine)	inta 'you' (masc. singular)
	antumaa 'you' (dual masculine)	
	antum 'you' (masculine plural)	intu 'you' (masc. and fem. plural)
	anti 'you' (feminine)	inti 'you' (fem. singular)
	antumaa 'you' (feminine dual)	(no feminine dual)
	antunna 'you' (feminine plural)	intu 'you' (masc. and fem. plural)
	anaa 'I'	ana 'I'
	nahnu 'we'	ihna 'we'
Relative Pronouns (e.g., "that" or "who" in English)		
masculine singular	alladhii	illi
masculine dual	alladhaani alladhaini	illi
masculine human plural	alladhiina	illi
feminie singular/all non-human plurals	allatii	illi
feminie dual	allataani allataini	illi
feminine human plural	allaatii	illi

(continues)

Table 1.1 *(continued)*

	Classical Arabic *al-lugha al-'arabiyya al-fusha*	Egyptian Arabic *il-'ammiyya il-masriyya*
Conjugation of Verbs		
Present Tense	'(he) writes'	
	yaktubu	biyiktib
	yaktubaani	
	yaktubuuna	biyiktibu
	taktubu	bitiktib
	taktubaani	
	taktubna	biyiktibu
	taktub	bitiktib
	taktubaani	
	taktubuuna	bitiktibu
	taktubiina	bitiktibii
	taktubaani	
	taktubna	bitiktibu
	aktub	baktib
	naktub	biniktib
Past Tense	'(he) wrote'	
	kataba	katab
	katabaa	
	katabuu	katabuu
	katabat	katabit
	katabataa	
	katabna	katabu
	katabta	katabt
	katabtumaa	
	katabtum	katabru

(continues)

Table 1.1 *(continued)*

	Classical Arabic *al-lugha al-'arabiyya al-fusha*		Egyptian Arabic *il-'ammiyya il-masriyya*
Past Tense	katabtii katabtuma katabtunna katabtu katabna		katabtii katabtuu katabt katabna
Future Tense	sawfa + present tense sawfa yaktubu OR sa + present tense sayaktubu	'(he) will write'	ha + present tense hayiktib
Negation			
Present verbal sentence Example:	laa + present tense verb laa yaktubu	'(he) does not write'	ma + present tense verb + sh mabyiktibsh
Past perfect verbal sentence Example:	lam + present tense verb lam yaktub		
Future Example:	lan + subjunctive lan yaktuba	'(he) will not write'	mish + present tense mish hayiktib

(continues)

Table 1.1 *(continued)*

	Classical Arabic *al-lugha al-'arabiyya al-fusha*	Egyptian Arabic *il-'ammiyya il-masriyya*
Negation (continued)		
Nominal sentence	laysa + noun	mish + noun
Example:	laysa kitaaban	da mish kitaab
	'it is not a book'	

Notes: This is a simplified representation of only some of the grammatical differences between the two languages.

*The nominative is the default case for nouns when they are the subject of the sentence. It is indicated by "u" or "un" at the end of the word.

**The accusative is used in several situations particularly when the noun is the object of the verb. It is indicated by "a" or "an" at the end of the word. Some of the instances in which it is used (e.g., as direct object or after *inna*) are given above.

***The genitive is used after prepositions and to mark the secondary terms in possessive constructions. Examples of its use after a preposition and after the second term in possessive construction are given above.

In Greece—one of the better-known cases of "diglossia"[6]—*katharevousa,* "purist" and *dhimotiki,* "demotic, popular" have co-existed for centuries, representing a multiplicity of profound societal divisions and disagreements. *Katharevousa* is a form of neo-Classical Greek that was "used until 1975 for most official purposes while *dhimotiki* was the 'ordinary spoken language' . . . in all its dialectal variety" (Herzfeld 1996: 280).

> This polarization of language, however, is but one realization of a deep ideological split which often took its symbolic form from the play of two opposed historiographies. The first of these, the "Hellenic," is neo-Classical, Western-oriented, formalistic, and aggressively referential. It is opposed to the "Romeic" theme—a nativisitic reaction historically predicated on the Byzantine and later roots of modern Greek culture, and stereotypically associated with informality and spontaneity and with disdain for the legalistic precision of 'pen-pushers' . . . (281)

In Greece, *katharevousa* was also the language of the New Testament, and, when in 1903 a translation in *dhimotiki* appeared, it "was the occasion for serious rioting" (Ferguson 1959a: 330). Rendering the holy text into the language of the masses was considered a grave insult.

Such long-standing examples of holding on fast to a language against all odds, drawing battle lines around it and untiringly cherishing it are deserving of close attention because they are not merely about language and narrowly linguistic issues. These language situations bring into particularly bold relief the ways in which ideas on language are inseparable from those about the self, national identity, inequality, group and individual rights, religion, culture, nation and forms of governance. In the case of Classical Arabic, its historical power is such that, in the nexus of state, religion and nation, it continues to stand at the center—used both to pull that triangle together and to push its constituents apart.

Since the nineteenth century, Classical Arabic was taken as the primary material out of which a "modern language" was to be developed. There can be no exact beginning date for a process such as the modernization (*tahdith*[7]) of Classical Arabic. Egyptian state institutions, individual writers, and various social movements have been involved in various ways and with different degrees of power in the modernization of the language. Following most historians, who see its initiation in the nonreligious and vocational schools instituted by the last Ottoman viceroy to Egypt (Muhammad-Ali 1805–48), we can say that the process is about a century-and-a-half old. The biggest impetus to this linguistic revival came first from the Nahḍa movement and later from pan-Arabism. The former is also known as the Arab renaissance, which began in the late 1800s and lasted into the early decades of the twentieth century. While accepting that the language of the Qur'an was a "miracle" (*mu'giza*) and that it had reached its perfection in that text (*al-namuuzag al-a'laa,* "the highest exemplar"), educators, journalists, writers and translators nevertheless wanted to simplify (*tabsiit*) and modernize the language to make it more suitable for modern functions. Although in the 1920s and 30s there were fierce disagreements about whether to allow Egyptian Arabic to become the main language for writing (Chejne 1969, Gershoni and Jankowski 1986), those in favor of the preservation of Classical Arabic prevailed.

In the nineteenth century, the desire for revitalizing Classical Arabic was part of a general movement for reform and change that were defined in different ways across a wide spectrum of ideologies. Many saw reforming the language as part and parcel of efforts to achieve social and political progress. There were significant debates among those who are often referred to as "Islamic reformers" or "modernists" on interpretations of Islam as a religion that was fully compatible with progress and change" (Hourani 1991: 307). Hence, language reform was seen as advancing alongside wider reforms.[8]

Historians, Western governments and media often characterize the state in Egypt since the nineteenth century as a "modern" state, in part because it has sought independence from the religious establishment. However, the selective integration of aspects of Islam by successive governments in domains such as law and education (Starrett 1998) should encourage modifications of this characterization. In the past century and a half, Egypt has seen very different governments during and after British colonial rule, but it seems that each considered such integration as beneficial to its interests. Generally, the dominant interpretation of such acts is that the state is pressured by the religious establishment and the "zealot masses" to give in. At present, official linguistic practices and educational policies show that the state's claims to religion and to its language are not merely a result of pressure. Public education is in Classical Arabic and textbooks emphasize the links between it and Islam without any discussion of modernization efforts. Even after the socialist revolution of Nasser in 1952 the state "chose" Classical Arabic as its official language. That is, it chose a language in which a minority were/are proficient and one whose most primary affiliation is with Islam. In contrast, when socialists came to power in the 1970s in Greece, one of their major goals was to elevate *dhimotiki* to the status of a written, official language. The "elitist" *katharevousa* was pushed aside in favor of the mother tongue— the "language of the masses."

But the 1950s in Egypt and the rest of the Arab world were the heydays of pan-Arab nationalism—a movement in which many non-Muslim Arabs participated and one that was expressly aimed at including Arabs of every faith. The language that all Arabs share is Classical Arabic, not the local "dialects" that are different and therefore "divisive."[9] Pan-Arabism's explicit efforts in defining an Arab as anyone who speaks "Arabic" as a native language was meant to remove religion and race as bases of an Arab identity. Non-Muslim Arabs welcomed this shift and seem to have contributed to its emergence as well. The definition also follows a long-standing and major ideological division among Arabs (and other Muslims): Is Islam a culture or a religion? The question continues to polarize Muslim societies. Secular Muslims insist on considering Islam as a culture and emphasize its humanistic achievements. Believing Muslims argue that all those achievements are due to the powers of Islam as a religion, which, as a way of life, is also of course a culture. With respect to language, pan-Arabism seems to have hoped for at least a parallel constitutive relationship such as the one existing between Classical Arabic and Islam. But there were (and are) also many who hoped to *supplant* that relation altogether and replace it with one between the language and the movement. Hence, many of its proponents, for example, pointedly locate the origin of the language in the time *before* Islam and not with the appearance of the holy book, as is commonly held.

The high reverence for Classical Arabic and the idea that it must be preserved, however, long predate not only the pan-Arab movement but also the short-lived French occupation of Egypt (1798–1801) and the much longer British colonial rule (1882–1952). Unlike the French in the Maghreb, the British did not set out to eradicate Classical Arabic completely. Elementary education was left in Classical Arabic, as was the study of humanities. But most higher education in medicine, law, engineering and so on under their rule was in English or French, as were many important components of their bureaucracy. In these ways, the spread and development of Classical Arabic was discouraged. One of the major consequences of colonial rule was a further reinforcement of allegiance to Classical Arabic. The language became the central trope through which opposition to that rule was articulated. At the same time, the use and spread of English and other European languages in Egypt during colonial rule undermined the historical image and status of Classical Arabic as the "perfect language" (Eco 1995). Egyptian intellectuals, educators and high bureaucrats, particularly those who acquired their training in European languages inside and outside of their country, came to regard Classical Arabic as too literary and flowery and as lacking in modern vocabulary needed for the sciences and for technology. Although such deficiencies became prevalent preoccupations, most believed that systematic attempts to enlarge the vocabulary and simplify its grammar were not only worthy but also attainable goals (Chejne 1969, Altoma 1969, 1970). Egyptian Arabic, in contrast, was considered to be a "weak" language (*rakiika*), and lacked status and merit for becoming the language of writing.[10]

A focus on language situations that involve, albeit in distinct ways, the use of a sacred language leads us to inquire into our assumptions about what makes some languages "modern." How do we know a modern language when we see one? Introductory textbooks in linguistics state that Ferdinand de Saussure founded "modern linguistics." Briefly put, what was modern was that de Saussure's new conception of language discouraged prescriptive studies and, more importantly, showed that the reason human language is at all possible is that the relation between form and meaning is arbitrary (de Saussure 1983).[11] Muslim Egyptians explicitly hold that the relation between the linguistic forms of the Qur'an and their corresponding meanings is *nonarbitrary* because the text reflects the words of God. One of the most frequently voiced statements in this regard is that the *forms* of the language of the holy book matter greatly and cannot be translated. Hence no satisfactory translation is possible and all attempts are mere interpretations (*tafaasiir,* pl., *tafsiir,* sing.).

If we study a community that explicitly holds the relation between form and meaning to be nonarbitrary, what are we to do with that knowledge? I suggest that we take it seriously and try to follow its implications. Orientalist scholars paid exclusive attention to the textual heritage of Islam in the Middle East (Said 1978) and the lion's share of anthropological research on the region has gone to small, rural communities where the roles of writing, literacy and print are rarely discussed (Abu-Lughod 1989).[12] Moreover, the strength of the idea that written languages are "artificial" and that in their analysis one might slip into the old prescriptive ways, has generally resulted in a bias against the study of written languages.[13] But what happens between the world of texts and that of small communities? Where daily life does not involve regular reading and writing—whether in the city or in the village—does a written language still play a role in people's lives?[14]

The language situations in the Arab world, Greece and Hebrew inside and outside of Israel have a great deal to offer because they provoke questions with implications beyond these groups and societies. For example, does the existence of a modern and secular political system *require* the existence of a "modern language"? How would Europe be different today had Latin remained simultaneously the language of the Church and of government, writing, education and bureaucracy?[15] Apart from historical linguists and lexicographers putting dictionaries together, few use the term "modern language." Even so, it is clear that we have ideas about languages in this respect: we make implicit distinctions between Sanskrit and Hindi, Latin and French and Biblical Hebrew and modern Hebrew, among others. We do not think of the first languages in these pairs as modern languages. Why not?

Before we go on to answer that question, I would like to explain my use of the terms "modern," "modernization" and "modernity." In relation to language, I will define below what I mean by a modern language. In so far as the second term is concerned, when it is used to describe processes of change that a language has undergone, the term becomes somewhat meaningless. The reason is that if we set out to "modernize" a language and state that we mean the addition of new vocabulary, the simplification of grammar and basically any other changes that can be interpreted in these ways, then by definition whatever change that the language goes through can be characterized as modernization. There is not necessarily a problem with this circularity as long as we do not automatically equate a modern language with a modernized language. The most problematic term here is "modernity." Among the current preoccupations of anthropologists and other social scientists are debates about the definitions, histories and politics of modernity.[16]After defining what a modern language is according to a set of criteria, I use the term modernity to refer back to such criteria—e.g., the modernity of such and such a language. Beyond language, wider applications of the term in this book appear generally in the form of quotations from other scholars' works. In the concluding chapter, I replace this term with another, which I hope will have a clearer content.

Returning now to an exploration of our generally tacit assumptions about modern and not-so-modern languages, let us consider the idea that perhaps the antithesis of a sacred or classical language is what we consider a vernacular: a spoken language that is contemporary with its speakers (though it precedes them), that grows up with them and, crucially, that changes with them. Egyptian Arabic is such a vernacular. Changes in Classical Arabic have been historically resisted and fought against with ideologies of purity, appeals to the sacred origin of the language and by institutional means. Indeed, at times proposals for reform and change have been construed as immoral acts aimed at undermining religion, especially if proposals came from non-Muslim Arabs or from foreigners. By comparison, Egyptian Arabic like other vernaculars may change and transform far more freely, unfettered by the constraints of its (absent?) civilizational status and religious origin.

The nonarbitrary relation between the forms and meanings of the Qur'an is articulated in strikingly similar ways by educated and uneducated people from widely different social and generational backgrounds. It is argued that the form is as important as the meaning and that since form cannot be translated, the text is untranslatable.[17] There are hundreds of "interpretations" of the Qur'an (all of which are also in Classical Arabic) that can be consulted—so the argument continues—to help one understand its meaning better. Often, when in my interviews I used the term "translation" (*targima*), people immediately corrected me: "You mean *interpretation* (*tafsiir*), not translation." But the same belief is not held with regard to Egyptian Arabic, so that in one case meaning and form are inseparable but in the other they are not.

Is this what lies behind our conception of a "modern" language? If form and meaning are viewed as separable so that texts written in one language can be translated into any other, are we then dealing with a "modern" language?[18]

We might recall in this connection that de Saussure's thesis of the arbitrariness of the relation between form and meaning came centuries after the Reformation. That is, centuries after translations of the Bible into the European vernaculars had in effect made it clear that if that text can be translated into *any* language then that relation must be at least somewhat arbitrary.[19] In this way, the spirit of de Saussure's thesis had been already around, so to speak, long before he articulated it in his courses in the last years of the nineteenth and the early years of the twentieth century.[20]

The "origin myth" of vernacular languages is in the realm of humans (however mythologized and romanticized), whereas sacred languages have divine origins. This is perhaps why they cannot be *owned* by anyone— believers are their *custodians,* not their owners. How does one modernize and hence necessarily change a language one does not own? There seem to be different ideas with regard to property rights for sacred and nonsacred languages. To further elaborate on these ideas, it is worthwhile to use a passage from Umberto Eco's discerning historical novel *The Name of the Rose.* In this passage, an abbot contrasts the "word of God" with the "vulgar tongue":

> down below in the great settlements, where the spirit of sanctity can find no lodging, not only do they speak (of laymen, nothing else would be expected) in the vulgar tongue, but they are already writing in it, though none of these volumes will ever come within our walls—fomenter of heresies as those volumes inevitably become . . . it is up to us to defend *the treasure of the Christian world, and the very word of God,* as he dictated it to the prophets and to the apostles, as the fathers repeated it without changing a syllable, as the schools have tried to gloss it, even if today in the schools themselves the serpent of pride, envy, and folly is nesting. . . . And as long as these walls stand, *we shall be the custodians of the divine Word.* (Eco 1980: 36–37, emphasis added)

We find, in the abbot's words, a claim over the custodianship of the "treasure of the Christian world." Christians, even those who are high up in the church's hierarchy like the abbot, are not the owners of the "very word of God," only its keepers. The question of whether Arabs are the custodians of Classical Arabic or its owners is one that lies at the heart of some of the major contemporary ideological battles. But these are not battles that are primarily between Arabs and non-Arabs but among Arabs themselves and within each individual language user.

The abbot also asserts that those who speak the "vulgar tongue" are "fomenters of heresies" and outside the moral community of believers. The term "vulgar" continues to have connotations of immorality, and "vernacular" is used to mean principally "profane," which stood in opposition to Latin. Hence, those who spoke, and worse still, wrote in the "vulgar tongue" were not quite as moral as those who wrote in Latin. There are very similar constructions of Egyptian Arabic in Egypt—it has historically been referred to as *rakiika*, "weak," linguistically and morally, as showing *fisaad*[21] "corruption," and as lacking in integrity because it accepts too many foreign words. Of course, at the same time as vernaculars are thought of as belonging firmly to the profane world, they are used in many cultures in spiritual and mystical poetry. Still, vernacular languages, or "vulgar tongues," generally are not constitutive of or exclusively attached to any particular religion.[22]

According to these criteria, it seems that any vernacular spoken as a mother tongue by some community is modern. The criteria developed here will be used throughout this book and will be elaborated further with examples. Not all vernaculars are equally modern. English, Persian and Haitian Creole, for instance, are all mother tongues, but English is considered more modern because it is intimately linked with the West, industrialization, technological advances, certain political systems and ideologies and so on. What the criteria make clear is that the modernity of a language does not merely have to do with historical time—namely, all that matters is whether a language is older or younger than another in terms of historical time. Modern languages generally also have a (standard) writing system and, ironically, languages that have acquired such a system in modern times, such as Somali for example, are not considered as modern as those that have had it for centuries.

When vernaculars become official languages of a state, a standard and codified variety is developed in which transformations are resisted through a variety of means and ideologies. The most remarkably frequent is an appeal to national unity—"One Language, One Nation"—used as a major rallying cry in places like Turkey, Iran, Tanzania, France, Spain and many other countries. There are also appeals to the inherent superiority of the standard language (e.g., Parisian French), bodies of revered literature and so on (Leith 1997, Achard 1980). But innovations and changes are not resisted through reference to the divine origin of the language or its sacred status. The state takes active part in defining permissible changes (e.g., through the training of various kinds of linguistic gatekeepers, textbooks, national exams, and language academies), but it does so not for keeping "God's Word" pure but rather for the "good of the nation" or, more accurately, for a particular reproduction of that nation. Moreover, depending on the political and economic organization of any given country, the market and the business world also play very important roles in these matters (see chapter 3).

In the literature on the emergence of modernity in Europe, some studies have analyzed the role of "vernacularization" as an integral part of those processes. In his famous book on the rise of nationalism and of the nation-state in Europe, Benedict Anderson explores the replacement of Latin—the language of Christendom—by European vernaculars: "Beneath the decline of sacred communities, languages and lineages, a fundamental change was taking place in modes of apprehending the world, which, more than anything else, made it possible to 'think' the nation (1991: 22)." Vernacularization is thus viewed by Anderson as one of the major defining features of modern political systems. More recently, Sheldon Pollock credits vernacularization with "ushering in early modernity":

> In the early centuries of the second millennium, wide areas of Eurasia, and most dramatically India and Europe, witnessed a transformation in cultural practice, social-identity formation, and political order with far-reaching and enduring consequences. I call this transformation vernacularization, a process of change by which universalistic orders, formations, and practices of the preceding millennium were supplemented and gradually replaced by localized forms. (1998: 41)

Pollock makes the point that in India, through the use of the vernacular, a different *place* was produced (51). Writing in Sanskrit meant "participating in a vast ecumene . . . extending from Central Asia to Sri Lanka to Afghanistan to Anam"—it was a claim to universality and to many varied places. He quotes an eleventh-century poet who had said: "Earlier, there was poetry in Sanskrit . . . but the Calukya kings and many others caused poetry to be born in Telegu and to be fixed in place . . . in the Andhra land" (ibid). Writing (and reading) poetry in Telegu could hardly evoke a non-Telegu speaking place. It made no claim to a "vast ecumene" but only to a place where Telegu was the mother tongue of the inhabitants.

A *pan*-Arab language like Classical Arabic was meant precisely not to evoke any *one* place in the Arab world, but all of it—that is, the Arab nation. In part through this powerful symbol pan-Arab leaders wished to effect radical changes in Arab societies, offer their own alternative visions of a modern political system (that is, alternative to the colonial version) and unite on the basis of a common language, not on the basis of the different faiths that could divide them. But language offers simultaneously both freedom and constraint, both understanding and misunderstanding. Language users are not completely free to do with it as they please. Just as we cannot all create our own individual grammars, so we cannot easily alter what a language comes to represent, evoke and signify. There are strong constraints on the creation and alteration of the worlds, visions and images that a language accumulates and comes to be associated with.[23] In part, both freedom and constraint have to do with the fact that languages are not "neutral" lacking owners, keepers and genealogies:

> there are no "neutral" words and forms—words and forms that can belong to "no one"; language has been completely taken over, shot through with intentions and accents. For any individual consciousness living in it, language is not an abstract system of normative forms but rather a concrete heteroglot conception of the world. All words have the "taste" of a profession, a genre, a tendency, a party, a particular work, a particular person, a generation, an age group, the day and the hour. Each word tastes of the context and contexts in which it has lived its socially charged life . . . (Bakhtin 1981: 293)

In the "tastes and contexts" of the "socially charged life" of Classical Arabic, religion dominates. This is an aspect of the debates on language that nonreligious intellectuals have seemed unwilling to recognize.

Yet, the lack of unlimited freedom in relation to language is true for all languages and linguistic varieties, not just for Classical Arabic. It holds both for sacred languages and for vernaculars. It is just that owners have more freedom than custodians. Writers and readers (speakers and listeners) of all languages face constraints in their creations and interpretations. Hence, the difference between languages in this respect is in the *degree* of freedom that users can have. The more codified and institutionalized a language becomes, the more it becomes enmeshed in cultural and political struggles and in ideas about the self and the other, the more authoritative its source(s), the stronger its associations with certain worlds and images, the more constraints there are. Hence, there are more constraints in the use of standard rather than non-standard varieties. When Latin was still the main language of writing, it offered less freedom than writing in European vernaculars; and when Hebrew was being revitalized by central European Jews in the nineteenth century, they felt more constraints in writing in Hebrew than in Yiddish.

The same can be said about Egyptian and Classical Arabic. The latter is regarded as arising from an "epic" time—that is, the early centuries of Islam when everything seems to have been perfect. In his study of literary genres, what Bakhtin says about epics is very similar to how those early centuries are viewed by believing Muslims:

> Epics are not simply set in a time that has receded, for epic time is best perceived as a value. What was in the past is automatically considered to be better, bigger, stronger, or more beautiful. In epic, someone is speaking about a past that is to him inaccessible, and he adopts the reverent point of view of a descendant. In its style, tone, and manner of expression, epic discourse is far removed from the discourse of a contemporary addressed to other contemporaries. Even though

both its singer and its implied listener are located in the same time and value system, the represented world stands on an utterly different and inaccessible time and value plane, separated by epic distance. (Bakhtin 1981: 287–88)

For Arab Muslims, the golden age of Islam was also a time when Classical Arabic was at its purest.[24] In the mirror of Classical Arabic—in its "epic time"—the dominant image of Muslim Arabs is triumphant, ascendant, at the forefront of scientific advances and humanistic refinement. The language belonged to a self (Muslim Arab) that was a member of an empire.

Mahmoud Taymour, a famous Egyptian playwright who wrote in the 1940s and '50s, had this to say in support of the preservation of Classical Arabic as the language of literature and of writing in general:

If the Arab Empire has failed in a political sense, it is, on the other hand, much in evidence in a linguistic sense that binds nations and peoples as it did in the past. In our overt and covert awakening, we are endeavoring to perpetuate our imperial bond by means of the Arabic language as if we were revivifying with this bond our bygone empire. [We are doing it] in a manner befitting our modern needs. Thus our faith in the literary language [fusha] is born out of our faith in that empire, which embodies our long-cherished glories. With this faith, we are upholding those things which are dear to us and to humanity at large. In this adherence, our natural instincts come forth to protect us in the battlefield of survival. (Taymour 1956)[25]

Writing in the 1960s, the Nobel Laureate Naguib Mahfouz likened Egyptian Arabic to "poverty and disease" along with other obstacles to "progress" (Dawwarah 1965).[26] Anwar Chejne, who has written one of the few social histories of Arabic, characterizes the views of many intellectuals with regard to Egyptian Arabic in the following terms: "[V]ulgar, deficient, devoid of any linguistic wealth for expressing thought . . . [the dialects] lack any literary tradition to speak of . . . they suffer from the major defect of not portraying the past in its full glory, and are inadequate for the political, social, and cultural needs of present-day Arab society" (1969: 164).

Like all cultural practices, linguistic usages give specificity to and help establish and define times and places. We do not usually think of linguistic usages in the abstract but as having particular contexts and users (i.e., where, when, who). It is impossible to read or hear "Thou Shalt . . ." and not think of the Bible, or at least of ancient times, or "the air nimbly and sweetly recommends itself" and not think of Shakespeare or of his time.[27] Words, particular ways of phrasing matters, certain grammatical constructions, sayings and so on create and are marked by particular times, places and types of persons. In short, different languages and different linguistic usages within them create and evoke "images," or as Bakhtin would say "images of man" (of the actual or imaginary user) in specific times, places, characteristics and so on. The image of man depicted and projected by the vernaculars is that of the Arab as "common" (*'aammi*,[28] from the same root as 'ammiyya), "backward" (*mutikhallif*), humble (*ghalbaan*)—a member, not of an empire but of a former colony who has perhaps never recovered.

Not everyone sees Classical and Egyptian Arabic in the dichotomous terms used above. Often, there are simultaneously contradictory characterizations of both languages whose worlds and histories in part overlap. For example, the "epic time" of Islam—its golden era—is also intertwined with images of pure but "primitive" and "tribal" Bedouins, at least from the point of urban Muslims residing in important cultural centers. Furthermore, there are many forms of writing in which the two languages are made to approach each other. Nevertheless, there is a general and pervasive reification of *two* languages, and it is frequently in these terms that their historical, political and cultural significance are characterized. On the whole, images projected through the use of Classical Arabic across the centuries have seemed far preferable, at least by scholarly and political elites, to those of vernacular Arabic.

In Egypt, opinions with regard to whether attempts at the modernization of Classical Arabic have succeeded vary greatly. Some firmly believe that there has emerged a contemporary or modern (or new) Classical Arabic (*fusha al-'asr, fusha al-hadisa*) that is significantly different from the language before the nineteenth century and that this variety has an *independent* existence from religious or "heritage Classical Arabic" (*fusha al-turaath*). To underline this point, some call contemporary Classical Arabic "the third" or the "middle" language (*il-lugha il-talta,* or *il-wusta*). They point to a large modern vocabulary and to the "reality" that it can be and is used for any and all purposes, not just religious ones. Often, when assertions are made by some that Classical Arabic has been modernized, there is also the concomitant claim that this new language is not exclusively or even primarily attached to Islam. This is generally the position of most nonreligious pan-Arabists. Many reasons are offered to substantiate these views—that the language was not born with Islam, but predates it; and that there is a vast body of scientific and humanistic literature written in that language.

There are others who equally firmly believe that, while the language has undergone changes, none of them are so substantial as to have cut off continuity with its past. Indeed, some people (scholars and nonscholars) cite with approval the fact that "we" can still read texts and use dictionaries that are centuries old precisely because the language has changed so little. They further argue that no author has managed to produce a text that rivals the power and beauty of the language of the holy text. Indeed, although pan-Arab writers have produced a vast body of fiction and nonfiction, none of this writing is characterized as marking the dawn of a kind of Classical Arabic exclusive to the movement and independent from the (linguistic) authority of the Qur'an. They also point out that it is only with the appearance of the Qur'an that the language gained its paramount status, whatever existed before that event. There are, of course, other views. For example, some find contemporary Classical Arabic a sign of numerous failures—of faith, of education and of knowledge more generally. And they routinely disparage it publicly, choosing to write in ways that others consider to be convoluted and archaic.

It bears emphasis that the complexities of the language situation both in Egypt and in the Arab world as a whole cannot be reduced to one of "modernists" versus "traditionalists" or "Islamists" versus "secularists." To begin with, what people think about the language situation is often not in a one-to-one relationship with their religious or political beliefs. It is not the case that if one is a believer, one is necessarily against the modernization of Classical Arabic or against making Egyptian Arabic the language of writing. And regardless of religious beliefs and political affiliations, most people that I talked to articulate various contradictions, whether or not they see them as problems. Moreover, dichotomies like those mentioned above hinder understanding rather than promote it. The positions of religious individuals and groups with regard to the language situation have been and continue to be far more consistent both with their religious beliefs and with their political ideologies.

For those who believe that Islam needs no reform and adaptation, Classical Arabic as the Word of God is clearly the language that must be perpetuated and taught, at the expense of Egyptian Arabic or any other vernacular. For Islamic reformers (and this itself is a large category), Classical Arabic must be kept alive and disseminated but it can be adjusted to move forward with the development of Islam under changing socio-historical conditions. If Islam, however interpreted, is to be the basis of social order, then its language must clearly be preserved. The language is the reservoir of religious knowledge and is a prerequisite for acquiring that knowledge. It provides continuity in a well-developed universe of discourse that spans many centuries—a continuity that is essential to informed debate. Since the early centuries of Islam, there were those who believed that it is the revelation of the Qur'an that is divine and not its language. Others argued that it is both the revelation and the language that are sacred. Scholars in the former category do not necessarily believe that the language must be used for any and all purposes, only that its thorough knowledge is necessary for theological debate and understanding. The point is that what different people think about the language situation should not be assumed to be known based exclusively on their religious and political ideas.

The position of secular Arabs (pan-Arab or not, and including Muslim, Christian and Jewish Arabs) in favor of preserving Classical Arabic is markedly more contradictory in this respect, as is the view of those who are religious but believe in the separation of religion from politics. To be sure, there have been and continue to be people in almost all such categories who reject the choice of Classical Arabic as the official language of Arab states. But at present, judging from their writings, and from my interviews with them, most secular Egyptians believe that the modernization process is complete and there is now a "modern" language that stands on its own, independent from the Classical Arabic of religion. It is simply a language of writing, so they maintain, that has emerged in the last century or so and it serves equally well all kinds of social and political orders and ideas. I will argue that this lack of acknowledgement of the continuing link between Islam and Classical Arabic has resulted in a number of profound dilemmas.

Where does the modernization process stand today? The various lines of inquiry begun here will be laid out in more detail in the following chapters.

Organization of the Book

The fieldwork and research for this book were guided by attempts to conceptualize *what* one needs to know and where one begins given the complexity of the issues involved. There are in fact many kinds of knowledge (and data) one needs and this book does not provide them all. But given a number of constraints, I chose a few basic sites of research that seemed to me to be fundamental. One of the most essential and most neglected requirements for understanding the language situation in the Arab world is an examination of how Classical Arabic has continued to survive across centuries in the lives of "ordinary," lay people. I use "ordinary" in opposition to "sacred," but within the category of lay people, of course there are all kinds of hierarchies. Given the disappointing absence of social histories of language in the Arab world, we are limited to examining the present situation.[29]

While there are a number of studies that contain descriptions of the views and practices of scholarly elites with regard to Classical Arabic, there are no comparable studies of those whose daily lives do not involve reading and writing in that language. I had originally planned to live with one or two families for several months in order to observe language use better. This did not prove to be an easy task. I was interested in the role of Classical Arabic in the lives of non-elite and less well-to-do Cairenes, but they generally live in very small apartments where there is barely enough room for their own family members. Every adult works and, excepting Fridays and holidays, during the day, the house is empty and there is little to observe. Therefore, I lived in a different neighborhood but spent a great deal of time in the course of several months with members of one family, their neighbors and friends. In addition to spending time at home, eating, chatting and watching television and videos, I went to their places of work, family gatherings and shopping excursions. Eventually, I carried out tape-recorded interviews with some of these individuals. I devote the next chapter to an ethnography of language among people who do not regularly engage in reading and writing and whose means of subsistence does not require high degrees of proficiency in the language. How does Classical Arabic enter their daily lives; for what reasons, and what are their views of the language situation? How do their experiences with the language compare when they use it for religious purposes as opposed to its use as a medium of education at school? Since both the language of Islam and that of the state is Classical Arabic, do they identify them as the same, or do they distinguish between the two? Are there two or more kinds of Classical Arabic for them? These are some of the questions that are addressed in chapter 2.

In order to have a better basis of comparison, I spent a few months in a public library in Cairo and interviewed a number of librarians there. These are individuals who have to read and write the language regularly and whose jobs require knowledge of Classical Arabic. I was also interested in how non-Muslim Egyptians view the language situation, and to that end, I interviewed a number of Egyptian Copts, at work, and in their church.

Classical Arabic is the language of almost all that is written. To understand its other roles, one has to examine written and print language—how it is produced, corrected and in general *regulated*. I studied the processes involved in publishing and interviewed writers, poets, publishers, journalists, correctors (similar to copyeditors), translators and editors. Texts can have a variety of impacts and implications whether they are read by a majority or not. (We cannot be sure that the Bible has been thoroughly read by every Christian, and yet, the impact of the Bible among believers and nonbelievers in Christian communities is undeniable.) In Egypt, as in many other parts of the world, nonprint mass media are the dominant channels of information and knowledge. But they also serve to familiarize people with religious and literary texts. The novels of Naguib Mahfouz are known to most Egyptians not through readings but through the movies that have been based on them (shown repeatedly on television). Hence, texts disseminated in a variety of ways and reaching large numbers of people, can have a significant impact without being read by everyone.

At the same time, a tremendous amount of writing takes place in Egypt every day: newspapers, weeklies, monthlies, literary and academic journals, works of fiction and nonfiction, children's books and so on. What is the language of such texts like and who watches over it? Chapters 3 and 4 are devoted to cultural practices involved in the production and regulation of written language. Chapter 3 examines what happens to a piece of writing from the time it is submitted for publication to the time it gets printed. I explore what kinds of regulation take place, who the regulators are, what forms of professional training they have had, what authoritative sources they consult and what kinds of institutions lie behind them.

I will analyze processes of text regulation as *cultural* practices. In the same way that the details of the performance of certain religious or other rituals (that also get regulated) are routinely characterized as matters of culture, how a society regulates its official language is also a part of its culture. Examining the regulation and regimentation of written language as cultural practices has implications for semiotic analyses. Reading and analyzing pieces of culture as "texts" has often been limited to what the text is in its final form, not to how it has come to be produced in that way. But texts are joint productions, especially if they are to be published and the process of their production is directly relevant to their forms, semantic contents and social meanings. In chapter 3 I bring together the sensibility of language historians—specifically print scholarship—with anthropological approaches. The processes that a written piece undergoes illuminate various "sites" of ideology as diverse professional trainings, political views, and authoritative sources negotiate and clash while preparing copy and readying the text for publication.

In chapter 4, the struggles of newspaper writers to develop forms of prose better suited to their needs and to new functions is followed through an investigation of the language of the oldest surviving daily in Egypt, *al-Ahram* ("The Pyramids"). Founded in 1875 in Alexandria, *al-Ahram*'s first complete issue was published in 1876. It is the most influential daily in Egypt and has the largest circulation—perhaps comparable to the New York Times in the United States. It is the main source for information both nationally and internationally. It is also generally referred to as the "semi-official" newspaper of Egypt since it is very closely connected to the government. The central question pursued in this chapter is what kinds of struggles with form did newspaper writers face. More specifically, how did they strive to render Classical Arabic into a language of *contemporary* life— an unaffected medium for the narration of events, views, scandals, commercial advertisements and so on?

I examine the development of language ideologies, newer forms of writing, the treatments of reported speech and the shadowy or explicit presence of Egyptian Arabic in the space of print. My aim is not to undertake a history of this particular newspaper, but to examine aspects of the development of nonliterary prose. I will argue that while the received wisdom among linguists and historians is that all major "changes" in Classical Arabic are directly a result of the influence of European languages such as French and

English, in fact most come from Egyptian Arabic (and other non-Classical varieties). The word "change" appears in quotation marks because there have been few *permanent* changes in the syntax of Classical Arabic. In any given period, some writers followed certain changes and some did not—their pieces appearing side by side in the same newspaper.

Chapter 5 is devoted to the views of contemporary writers, poets, journalists and publishers and to their dilemmas with regard to language. I explore their reasons for considering Classical Arabic "modern" and for choosing not to write in Egyptian Arabic. The chapter also is concerned with the politics of cultural productions and its implications. Hence the role of the state is examined as well. The story of the brief life of a journal devoted to poetry in Egyptian Arabic is followed in some detail because it illuminates the complex positions of diverse groups of intellectuals and of state cultural institutions with regard to the language question.

The conclusion returns to the question of what a modern language is, to the significance of vernacularization, and to why both are necessary for certain kinds of social transformation. I attempt to locate some of the main reasons for the ambiguous status of contemporary Classical Arabic. The central focus of the conclusion is on the kinds of cultural and political problems that the language situation helps perpetuate and gives rise to.

Chapter Two

Humble Custodians
of the Divine Word

Classical Arabic in Daily Life

How many lives do languages have? Do they remain vital only so long as they are mother tongues? Most people seem to believe so. But some languages continue to survive even after their function as a medium of daily expression and exchange has been replaced by another and relegated to other, more restricted spheres of activity. In fact, some languages persevere across centuries without native speakers—Classical Arabic and Biblical Hebrew are two prime examples, as was noted in the introduction. For many centuries now, Classical Arabic has not been spoken as a mother tongue, and yet it has not died away.

It would not be too difficult to imagine how this language has remained vital for scholars, writers and men of religion—it has, after all, been mostly a language of high culture, of the sciences and the humanities. Almost all that has been published in the Arab world since the founding of Islam is in Classical Arabic. But how has this language managed to continue its presence in the lives of "ordinary" people—in particular those without high levels of education whose daily activities do not involve regular reading and writing? Like Eco's abbot, we are used to assuming that it is only religious/scholarly elites who can be the custodians of the "divine Word." But a practicing Muslim needs to have some knowledge of Classical Arabic. Muslims define themselves in that way whether they are highly literate or not at all, whether they are from the lower or upper classes, whether they are Arabic-speaking or not.

One of the central goals of my most recent ethnographic research in Egypt was to explore the ways in which Classical Arabic enters the daily lives of ordinary Egyptians whose mother tongue—Egyptian Arabic—is very different from the classical language. I wanted to find out in what spheres of activity the language has been present; at what age people first *hear* Classical Arabic and for what reasons; who teaches them; what they think about the language and how they see its relation to Egyptian Arabic. To answer these questions, let us meet a number of individuals with whom I spent time in the span of several months. I use the example of their daily routines in order to consider the questions posed above.

Nadia and Her Family

I had met Nadia during a first period of fieldwork in Cairo in 1987–88 through my friendship with one of her daughters. I re-established contact with her in 1995 when I went back for more research. Nadia is about 60 years old and has four children—two daughters and two sons. She got married when she was around 20 years old and her husband died 10 years later. Nadia never remarried. One of her daughters lives in Saudi Arabia with her husband. Her youngest son is in his late 20s and his siblings are all in their 30s. Nadia's neighborhood has unpaved alleys that are lined with apartment buildings four to five stories high. The main street leading to the various alleys is narrow and unpaved. Most of the daily shopping can be accomplished within the neighborhood—there are grocery stores, a butcher, a video rental that has posters of kung-fu movies hung on its outside walls and several fruit sellers. Although this is a lower-middle-class neighborhood and trash collection is a major problem, it is a rather elegant area with harmonious buildings of stucco facade. Her small apartment has a foyer and two rooms at each end of a corridor. The front room leads to a balcony. Between the two rooms, there is a bathroom and a kitchen.

Unlike her own children and many members of her generation, Nadia did not attend a *kuttaab* ("religious school") before or in conjunction with attending a public elementary school. The first time she remembers hearing Classical Arabic was when her parents brought a reciter (*fī'ii*) to their house to recite some prayers. She learned the five obligatory daily prayers at school. She explained that students were given short manuals on *il-ṣalaa* ("the prayer") and *il-wuḍuu'* ("the ablutions, ritual washing and cleansing"), which precede each prayer. Most of her teachers were *shiyuukh* (sing. *sheikh,* graduates of religious schools, or clerics), and they explained the meaning of the prayers to the pupils. After Nadia finished the fourth grade, she went to a vocational school to learn tailoring. She explained that in her time, particularly in Upper Egypt (*il-ṣa'iid*), where her parents are from, girls did not continue school beyond that grade. Her family had moved to Cairo before Nadia entered elementary school and had settled in the neighborhood in which she lives now. She started to work shortly after graduating from the tailoring school by buying a sewing machine and working at home. After her husband's death, she began to teach tailoring and stopped sewing herself. What does a typical day in Nadia's life look like? How does it come to be marked by her use of Classical Arabic?

She wakes up everyday just before dawn with the loud call to prayer, the *adaan,* from a mosque that is within one block of her house. The dawn prayer (*ṣalaat al-fagr*) is the shortest. It has two *rak'a*s ("prayer cycles"). After doing her ablutions, she recites, beginning as every one of the five obligatory daily prayers do, with *al-Fatiha,* the opening *sura* ("chapter") of the Qur'an[1]

al-Fatiḥa	'The Opening'
bism allah al-raḥmaan al-raḥiim	In the Name of God, the Merciful, the Compassionate
al-ḥamdulillah rabb al-'aalamiin	Praise belongs to God, the Lord of all Being,
al-rahmaan al-rahiim	the All-merciful, the All-compassionate,
maalik al-yowm al-diin	the Master of the Day of Doom,
iyyaaka na'buduu wa iyyaaka nasta'iin	Thee only we serve; to Thee alone we pray for succour.
ihdina al-ṣiraaṭ al-mustaqiim	Guide us in the straight path,
ṣiraaṭ alladhiina an'amta 'alayhim	the path of those whom Thou hast blessed,
ghayr al-maghḍuub 'alayhim walaa al-ẓaaliin	not of those against whom Thou art wrathful, nor of those who are astray.[2]

After the dawn prayer, she can sleep for another hour or so before she wakes up again to go to work. I accompanied her one day to her place of work, which is housed in a large courtyard structure surrounded by other Ottoman-era mansions. Nadia's daughter had explained to me that at the initiative of Jihan Sadat, the wife of the former president of Egypt, some of the old mansions in this neighborhood had been converted into workshops and offices where individuals who had undergone job training would be employed. Nadia's studio was a large, beautiful room with very high ceilings, wood panels and stained glass windows. The light from the outside filtered through the colorful windows. On that day, only two students—women in their early 20s—came to class. The rest, Nadia joked, were "*lissa fil-agaaza*" ('still in their holidays'). While teaching about different kinds of skirts, collars, blouses, various fabrics and so on, Nadia's Egyptian Arabic was interspersed with many borrowings from Italian, French and English (we will return to her professional vocabulary below). Since it was the first day after a long holiday and few students had shown up, Nadia decided to end the class earlier than usual. By noon, the students were gone, and Nadia went to the prayer room for noon prayers at the sound of the *adaan*.

There are different styles for the recitation of the *adaan* as there are for recitations of the Qur'an (Nelson 1985). But all the styles are melodic and very evocative. The fact that the *adaan* is heard throughout every day of one's life makes it even more powerful and moving. In the prayer room, there were several other women who worked in the various offices housed in the building. All whispered their prayers so quietly that it was impossible to hear them—one could only see their lips moving. This is generally the case for women—they whisper their prayers (unless they are teaching their children, as I was told). Men pray out loud more often, particularly when they perform the dawn prayer. The noon prayer is twice as long as the one performed at dawn and is composed of four *rak'a*s (*raka'aat*, pl.). Beginning again with *al-Fatiha,* Nadia did her ablutions and stood to pray ṣalaat il-ẓuhr ("noon prayer").

When we came back home that day, her second daughter Fatima, who is also married, was busy doing household chores. Fatima has her own apartment in another neighborhood where she lives with her husband and two young sons. But they all spend much of their time at her mother's place. Fatima is in her mid-30s and teaches in an all-girl public high school. She attended a *kuttaab* and began to learn the prayers there. The learning of the prayers is a process that takes some time. The learner must not only memorize altogether 17 prayer cycles but also the appropriate bodily movements of standing, kneeling with hands on knees (*rukuu'*) and prostration (*sujuud*), each at the correct moment accompanied by the correct formulae. Children often learn the shortest prayer (recited at dawn) first and gradually master the others. Fatima's *kuttaab*, which was also attended by one of her brothers, was a particularly good one because in addition to the usual teaching of the recitation and memorization of sections of the Qur'an, it also served as a kindergarten where they were taught other subjects.[3] Like other children who enter the public school system, she was also taught how to pray in elementary school. She has a college degree in English and that is what she teaches seventh and eighth graders.

In her free time, Fatima reads the Qur'an, *ahaadis* (the sayings and actions of the Prophet), *tafaasir* (interpretations of the Qur'an), books for children's religious education and at times newspapers and magazines.[4] She reads newspapers and magazines more frequently than her mother, but not regularly. Her husband, who worked in Saudi Arabia for eight years, brought back some of these types of books at her request. Others she bought herself. In a day-long visit to her own apartment, I saw her collection of Qur'anic recitation cassettes. One of these played during the better part of the day while I was there. While she can name several fiction writers, she has not read their works and is not interested in reading fiction in general. Most of what she reads, in addition to the Qur'an, are texts about religion. She has now been praying regularly for many years.

Her brother Taher sings pop songs for a living in a mid-priced restaurant on the Nile. Taher is in his early 30s and attended the same *kuttaab* as his sister and speaks very fondly of the experience. He said that it gave him a head start for elementary school, where he did very well because in the first few years he had already learned the material at the *kuttaab*—to which he referred at times as *"hadaana"* ("kindergarten"). The first time he memorized a short *sura* ("chapter of the Qur'an") he was three years old. He began learning how to pray when he was five at the *kuttaab* and later at the school, with the help of teachers and small manuals published by the Ministry of Education, like *"Keefiyat al-Salaa"* ("How to Pray"). However, like many people, he started to pray regularly when he was a few years older. He attributes his success at the public schools to the fact that he learned Classical Arabic very well at the *kuttaab,* and also because he just loved the language. He got a high school diploma and chose not to go on to college.

Taher is more familiar with books of fiction than his sister. Most of his knowledge comes from installments of stories published in newspapers. He said that he picks up his sister's religious books once in a while and reads them. His favorite show on television is soccer *(koora)*. He does not very often watch the nightly news, which is one of the few programs in Classical Arabic. He realized from the time he was a teenager that he had a talent for singing and decided to pursue this career. One night I went to watch Taher's show. He has a great voice and sings with self-confidence. The audience was quite elated, participating with a lot of clapping and even accompanying him in some lines. Taher's songs, like those of the majority of Egyptian singers (Danielson 1997, Armbrust 1996), are entirely in Egyptian Arabic.[5]

Fatima's husband Mansour is in his late 30s. He went to a *kuttaab* when he was four and continued there until he was six-and-a-half years old, at which time he entered elementary school. The curriculum of his *kuttaab* was different from the one his wife and her brother went to in that he does not remember studying any subject other than the Qur'an. He was seven when he began learning how to pray, having learned the prayers in the same way as Taher and Fatima. Around the same age, he also began attending the mosque with his father and other relatives and there he watched and imitated the adults: "*kunna binruuḥ il-gaami' wa bina'mil zayy il-kubaar*," "we were going to the mosque and doing/acting like the grown-ups."

Mansour had ten siblings and left school in the seventh grade to search for work in order to supplement his family's income. He worked as a mechanic for several years and then found a job in Saudi Arabia. He spent eight years there, operating heavy machinery in the construction industry. He stayed for so long because he wanted to get married and needed money for the dowry and down payment on an apartment, and in order to help his three sisters get married.[6] He repeated several times "*rabbina karamni*" ("God was generous / good to me; I succeeded") because he accomplished all of these goals. He also explained that he was quite proud of his wife's far higher level of education and her secure job.

On Fridays—a day of rest for Muslims—there seemed to be a main familial routine. One of the men, either Mansour or Taher, would buy a newspaper (somewhat more often al-Akhbar ["The News"] rather than the main daily al-Ahram) and bring it home. Fatima would generally take the page on *hawaadis* (events, accidents, robberies, weddings, murders, etc.) and the men would read the sports pages. Nadia did not seem interested in any section of the newspaper, and no one took much interest in the front page or the editorials. Just before the noon prayer, the men would go to the nearby mosque to perform their prayers. Nadia and Fatima never went with them. The general religious obligation to pray at mosques on Fridays seems to be understood as applying mostly to men. After lunch, there are usually soccer matches on television and Taher's older brother would come and join everyone to watch the match.

Domains of Presence

For members of Nadia's family, Classical Arabic is chiefly present because of their performance of the five daily prayers. Even for those who attend schools and acquire college degrees, unless their daily routines and their occupations require them to read and write, their contact with the language is limited. Most such people do not use the language as a means of self-expression. For that, Egyptian Arabic is used—the language that dominates most people's daily exchanges. Some of the fundamental ways in which Classical Arabic is encountered in daily life are shared across educational levels, occupations and class lines. For example, as children, Muslim Egyptians first *hear* Classical

Arabic when professional reciters (*fi'ii*) recite particular prayers at the mosque or are brought home on special occasions, through the calls to prayer, through Qur'anic broadcasts on radio and television, through their male elders praying or through cassette tapes played at home. Of the four domains of religion, bureaucracy, schooling and mass media, it is the first that seems to have guaranteed the survival of Classical Arabic in people's lives.

No one with whom I talked mentioned their classes at school or their textbooks as their first encounters with the language. People's childhood memories of religious festivals, the celebrations and rituals during the fasting month of Ramadan, the first time they successfully memorized a chapter of the Qur'an or one of the prayers, the rhythms of their days marked by lunches and dinners that are defined in relation to the timing of noon and evening prayers—"after the prayer" or "before the prayer"—are all intertwined with the sounds of Classical Arabic. These kinds of experiences create many emotional bonds with the language. The Egyptian feminist historian Leila Ahmed, who is from the upper classes, describes one of her childhood memories from the month of Ramadan in her recent autobiography:

> It was grandmother who taught me the fat-ha [i.e., *al-Fatiha*][7] (the opening verse of the Qur'an and the equivalent of the Christian Lord's Prayer) and who taught me two or three other suras (Qur'anic verses). When she took me up onto the roof of the Alexandria house to watch for angels on the night of the twenty-seventh of Ramadan, she recited the sura about the special night, a sura that was also by implication about the miraculousness of night itself. Even now I remember its loveliness. It is still my favorite sura (1999: 122)

Muslims around the world are able to relate to such experiences. As we will see, such feelings of fondness are on the whole absent from people's experiences with the language in other contexts.

Moreover, members of Nadia's family, like all believing Muslims, read the Qur'an regularly at least on a weekly basis. They have copies of the Qur'an for reading purposes, copies that are just beautiful to look at, copies that are for taking on trips that often come bound in a leather case and are rather small, copies they give as presents to children or to other people and so on. Many families pass on the Qur'an used by the father, mother, or grandparents to younger generations. Hence, many homes also have copies that have great sentimental value. In these ways, the Qur'an becomes a highly endeared and beloved object and one develops a personal relationship with one's copies. I did not observe the kind of attachment and relationship with the Qur'an with any other book.

Nadia's job neither required her to know Classical Arabic in order to obtain it nor does she need it for teaching purposes. Some of the fashion magazines she uses are translated from various European languages into some version of Classical Arabic, such as *Vogue* or *Bourda*. But Nadia did not read them—she used the patterns and examined the pictures. Her daughter, Fatima, obtained a college degree and, although her major was English, she did have to learn Classical Arabic as many of her classes were in that language. I accompanied her to her school and was able to talk with a number of teachers of Classical Arabic, although I was not permitted to observe any classes. At her job, Fatima comes across different kinds of bureaucratic forms that are in Classical Arabic. Utility bills also arrive at the house and these are generally taken care of by Nadia's children or directly by the landlord. If they need to write legal letters, they would generally employ someone like the scribes that sit in front of offices to help people with such matters (Doss 1996). Hence, unlike her mother, Fatima comes into contact with the language for reasons other than religion.

At the same time, neither Nadia nor her daughter have any reason to regularly engage in active use of the language in writing or speaking. Fatima explicitly stated that she does not like to read books and does not regularly read newspapers. Being a singer, her brother Taher did not need any proficiency in Classical Arabic for his occupation. However, he said that he loves the language and reads regularly—newspapers, magazines and short stories. Fatima's husband did not complete high school and he did not need any knowledge of the language to become an operator for heavy machinery. He only likes to read about sports and does not pursue any other kind of reading material. None of these individuals use Classical Arabic as a means of self-expression. This is not surprising since that language is used mainly for writing and since the investment of time in gaining the required level of knowledge is for most people quite high.

Insofar as nonprint media are concerned, most programs on radio and television are in Egyptian Arabic. They all watched a great deal of television but what they watched were all programs in Egyptian Arabic. Nadia's family rarely watched the news or other special programs that were in Classical Arabic (see table 2.1). They did, however, watch and listen to Qur'anic recitations and interpretations offered on television as regular features. The most popular was a program anchored by an especially well-liked sheikh called Sheikh Sha'rawi. I watched some of his programs and asked both this family and others why they liked the sheikh so much. Many people said they liked him because he spoke "directly" (*'alaa ṭuul*) to them, "as if he were sitting" in their "living room." Sheikh Sha'rawi in fact offered interpretations of sections of the Qur'an in *Egyptian* Arabic in a very friendly tone, with broad smiles and much enthusiasm for his task. He clearly addressed ordinary viewers and not other religious scholars. His program was in fact talked about by many people and a professor of Classical Arabic commented that if one were to transcribe the sheikh's interpretations, one would have for the first time, a *written* translation of the Qur'an in Egyptian Arabic. Offering Qur'anic interpretations in Egyptian Arabic is probably not that unusual. But as many people commented on his use of that language, it does not seem to be very common either.

The programs in table 2.1 reflect the special programming that is reserved every year for the month of Ramadan and advertised in advance with much fanfare. There exist five channels but most homes do not receive all

Table 2.1 Television Programs on Channel One (al-Qanaa al-Ulaa)[6]

Time	Kinds of Program	Language
8:00	Good Morning Egypt	EA
10:05–12:09	Children's program, educational programs	EA
12:09–12:25	*Adaan* for Noon Prayer	CA
12:25–1:00	Health, The Woman	EA
1:00	News Summary	CA
1:05–3:11	Food of Ramadan, Arabic film	EA
3:11	*Adaan* for Afternoon Prayer	CA
3:30–4:30	Game show, serial	EA
4:30	News Summary	CA
4:45	Meeting Sheikh Sha'rawi	EA, CA
5:33	*Adaan* for Evening Prayer	CA
5:40–9:50	Children's serial, "Puzzles" game show, Sitcoms, Arabic music	EA
10:20	Religious serial "From the Stories of the Qur'an"	CA
10:35	The News	CA
11:00	Sheikh al-Azhar's Talk (Ḥadith Sheikh al-Azhar)	CA
11:10	With God (Ma'a Allah)	EA, CA
11:15–2:35	Serials, sports, caricature (karikaatir)	EA
2:35	Religious Serial "Jurisdiction in Islam" al-Qadaa' fil-islaam	CA
3:25	Wake up call for eating before dawn (il-musaḥḥaraati)	EA
3:30	Talk show	EA
4:35	Braodcast of Dawn Prayer from the Mosque of al-Sayyida Nafisa	CA

Television Programs, Saturday, March 2, 1996
EA = Egyptian Arabic; CA = Classical Arabic
Total programming time   20 hrs & 35 minutes
Approximate total time for Religious Classical Arabic   2 hrs & 17 minutes
Approximate total time for non-Religious Classical Arabic 45 minutes
Approximate total time for Egyptian Arabic   17 hrs & 35 minutes

and the most watched channel with the longest programming per day is channel one. Beside Ramadan and a few other special occasions, the proportion of programs in Classical Arabic to those in Egyptian Arabic is the same or even smaller.

Form and Variation

Although at present one often hears that the *kutttab*s no longer exist in urban areas, the majority of the Egyptians that I came across had in fact spent a part of their childhood attending classes at a *kuttaab* in their neighborhood. This included younger people as well—those who were in their 20s when I met them during my research. The duration of individuals' attendance varies—some have gone for a few months and some for up to three years (they continued their classes after entering primary school). Depending on the age at which people attend a *kuttaab*, they begin to learn the daily prayers there but generally master them all at public schools. This was a rather surprising discovery for me because when I went to school in Iran during the reign of the Shah, public (and Persian-language private) schools did have mandatory classes on religion, but prayers were not taught or discussed. Nor did a state publishing house publish manuals for prayers. One learned them either from parents or special teachers.

One of the implications of the situation in Egypt is that if someone does not attend a *kuttaab* or public school, he or she has to make a special effort to learn the prayers. For Egyptians, as for other Muslims, the correct pronunciation of the prayers, their meanings, the different postures of the body, the number of prayer cycles and their repetitions all must be formally taught. There are special prayers for the sick, the poor, the newborn, for weddings, funerals and particular events in the history of Islam (e.g., the revelation of the Qur'an). All these prayers are in Classical Arabic.

Nadia and other women of her generation and class explained to me that their mothers "prayed with al-Fatiha alone" (*salleyt bil-fatha bass*)—that is, only with the opening chapter of the Qur'an. Their mothers did not attend any kind of school and grew up in rural areas. Somehow they learned the opening chapter of the Qur'an—*al-Fatiha*—and at every prayer, they recited only that chapter. It is interesting that most people only mentioned this in connection with their mothers. But equally significant, no one seemed to think that there was anything terribly wrong with how their mothers (or other people in similar situations) prayed. So much so that there is an expression for doing so (*bitsalli* [fem.] *bilfatha* or *biyisalli* [masc.] *bilfatha*, "prays with the Fatiha"). One woman told me proudly that she not only taught her mother the prayers after she herself learned them at school but she "gave her a few more chapters [*suras*]" so that on different occasions, her mother could slightly vary parts of her prayers. Thus although the prayers are formulaic and largely the same across Muslim societies, their form is not perceived as wholly fixed and non-negotiable. If someone does not learn all the verses of prayers but only a part of them, they see nothing wrong with just reciting those parts. People seemed to believe that the intention to fulfill the obligation of daily prayers is more important than their exact performance. It is likely that such practices would be interpreted by some scholars as evidence of the "nontextual" nature of "popular" or "folk" Islam." If by nontextual is meant an absence of formalist orthodoxy generally associated with learned Islam, that certainly seems to be the case. But at the same time, it bears emphasis that there is an overwhelming consciousness of the *text* of the Qur'an, and of the fact that the oral prayers are always in reference to and based on that text.

The Tapestry of Everyday Language

How does one capture in writing the feel and texture of a language spoken by so many people in an imponderably large number of contexts for all kinds of purposes? An essential thread that defines the texture of Egyptian Arabic is that verses from the Qur'an are used frequently in greeting exchanges and politeness formulas, and for showing surprise, disapproval and a whole host of communicative purposes. The most common response to the greeting "How are you?" is: "*alhamdullilaah*," which is the third verse of the sura of *al-Fatiha*. In this exchange, it means "I am fine," "thanks to God." "*Bism allah al-rahmaan al-rahiim*" ("In the Name of God, the Merciful, the Compassionate"), the first verse of the same sura is used by many to mark the beginning of an activity and keep the evil eye at bay, such as when entering a house, wearing new clothes, eating, doing something dangerous or difficult, taking an exam and so on. It is also used to show disapproval at hearing something or to show surprise—in this context often only the first part is uttered accompanied with a loud voice: *bism allah!* There are many such examples of phrases that have religious origins and are a part of the resources of Egyptian Arabic used for all kinds of purposes, many of which are not religious. So much are these phrases a part of the language that one need not be a believer nor even a Muslim necessarily in order to use at least some of them (Ferguson 1967, Caton 1987, Badawi and Hinds 1986, Abboud 1988).

Vocabulary from Classical Arabic is used while speaking Egyptian Arabic not only when there are discussions on "formal" topics (as Latinate words would be used in English), but also for achieving humorous effects. Walking out of a cheap restaurant with rather bad food, a friend remarked: *il-akl kaan—raa'i'* ("the food was—splendid"). The adjective *raa'i'* is a word from Classical Arabic and the speaker exaggerated the trilling of the "r", lengthened the long vowel and heavily pharygnealized the last sound to mark the word and achieve a more humorous effect. Such effects are particularly successful when the speaker juxtaposes such grandiloquent and somewhat pompous words with slang from Egyptian Arabic in the same sentence. For example, some people use the Classical Arabic formulaic expression "*huna yuujad*" (or *"yuugad"* in the Classical Arabic of Egypt) "here find" or "there is," followed by slang words from Egyptian Arabic, for example: "*huna yuugad ḥittit juup*" "Here find a piece of skirt" or "check out (how great) this skirt is" where the word for skirt is a borrowing from French.[9]

As was mentioned earlier, Egyptian Arabic also has a large number of borrowings from other languages. During the day that I spent with Nadia at her class I found her work vocabulary replete with borrowings:

/mooḍa/	'fashion' > French
/jerzeh/	'jerzé' > French (from the name of the British island)
/lino/	'linen' > Italian
/fiskoz/	'viscose' > English or French
/batrun/	'pattern' > French patron? 'paper pattern for a dress' (Badawi and Hinds 1986: 52)
/baadi, istiritch/	'spandex' > English
/dikulteeh/	'decolté' > French (Badawi and Hinds: 298)
/sabrina/	'Sabrina' > English
/kerwaazeh/	'croisée' > French
/kol rivé/	'col rivé'?> French?
/kornish bliseh/	'pleated flounce' > French (Badawi and Hinds: 746)
/kiloosh/	'full skirt(ed dress)'> French (Badawi and Hinds: 762)
/il-mizuura/	'tape measure' > Italian (Badawi and Hinds: 821)

Similarly, Taher's trade vocabulary contained such borrowings as "*il-gitaar, il-draamz, il-org,*" all from English, and "*il-kamanga*" from Persian *kamaan* or Turkish *keman* (Badawi and Hinds: 763, 765). Taher referred to the members of his band as "*il-istaf*" and said that when they practice, they do not dress formally, but wear "bantalon jiins" (from French 'pantalon' and English 'denim jeans'). His brother-in-law, Mansour, told me that he operated three kinds of machines: *il-gireeder* ('grader' > English), *il-ḥaffaar* ('electric digger' > Arabic), and *il-bundoozer* ('bulldozer' > English).[10]

There are also a number of kinship terms that are mostly borrowings from French. Though the use of these terms is more frequent among the upper classes, it is not limited to them. Among these are "tante" and "oncle," meaning "aunt" and "uncle" respectively. The former is used also among the less well-to-do, whereas "oncle" is less commonly employed. "Tante" can apply both to a female blood relative and to older women who are close friends of the mother (or the family).

Egyptian Arabic, like other languages with large numbers of speakers, a long history and many kinds of contacts with speakers of other languages, has tremendously diverse resources. Some of these are in the form of borrowings from other languages—vocabulary and expressions. At the same time, it has many sayings derived from the Qur'an and the prayers, which infuse the language at times with a spiritual quality. The juxtaposition of borrowings from many different sources that occurs routinely in the course of conversations in Egyptian Arabic is not controlled or prevented. No one watches over them. While the language has ended up with many resources for self-expression, it is also for the very same reason considered "corrupt" and promiscuous in comparison to Classical Arabic.

Local Conceptions of Language

The great majority of Egyptians grow up speaking different varieties of Egyptian Arabic. This is their mother tongue, the language they learn at home without instruction, the one they are surrounded by, the one in which they learn to sing, tell jokes, insult their adversaries, make up slang—in short the language in which they acquire many kinds of social competencies. Like most aspects of culture, Egyptian Arabic is evaluated in simultaneously contradictory ways. There are a number of "official" or "party line" opinions about the language that rarely go unsaid: "it does not have a grammar" (*mal-haash qawaa'id*) and "it changes a lot." But Egyptian Arabic also and unquestionably defines an Egyptian identity and a national culture. Rarely did anyone wish, for example, that Egyptian Arabic should just die away and be replaced by Classical Arabic—a wish held by a number of intellectuals. People characterized Egyptian Arabic as "easy" (*sahl*) "light," (*khafiifa*) "full of humor," (*dammaha khafiif*) and "more beautiful than" (*ahla min*) other Arabic dialects; as "habit" (*ta'awwud*) and as the language of "*masriyiin*," "Egyptians." Equally significant, people feel at home in this language because their linguistic competence is not brought under question. No one seemed to know personally individuals, no matter how educated, who spoke in Classical Arabic—the spontaneous use of which in face-to-face interactions is considered pompous and can be a cause of ridicule. The true and "authentic" Egyptians—the true sons and daughters (*ibn* or *bint il-balad*)—have to speak Egyptian Arabic and not "philosophize" in *fusha* (El-Messiri 1978). But what is significant is that the relation between this language and an Egyptian identity is not articulated in opposition to people's identity as Muslims so that "true Egyptian Muslims" should stop speaking Egyptian Arabic.

Egyptian Arabic has layers of lexical borrowings, as we just saw, as well as other influences from many languages—Coptic, Turkish, Persian, Greek, Italian, French, English and Classical Arabic. Many of these borrowings are no longer marked as foreign as they have become completely integrated phonologically through time. As with other Arabic vernaculars, this shows explicitly the varieties of contacts with other languages. This is one of the main reasons for the historical malignment of the non-Classical languages by some intellectuals. Classical Arabic is considered to be "pure" and this purity extends beyond the language itself and is articulated also in terms of moral virtue. By contrast, lacking a historical relation with Islam or more generally with a nonmundane sphere of activity, Egyptian Arabic is criticized as too permissive, promiscuous, even, in comparison. Nevertheless, it is also the mother tongue of the very people who disparage it.

I interviewed at length a woman who was in her early 40s. Omm Hasan had attended a *kuttaab* while in elementary school. Every day after school, she would spend one or two hours with a sheikh at the *kuttaab* close to their house. She loved both experiences but her father took her out after she finished fourth grade (*kharragni min il-madrasa*). She was such a good student that her teachers used to stop her father on the street and try to shame him into letting her continue. But her father was ill and her mother did not work, and so Omm Hasan began to work as a maid. Through my frequent contacts with her and through long discussions, she made me understand better something that I had heard often from others. Omm Hasan is very articulate and provides careful answers to questions in addition to volunteering very many relevant details. In the process of discussing her favorite magazine and her love of reading, she stopped to explain the difference between Egyptian (*'ammiyya*) and Classical Arabic (*al-lugha al-'arabiyya al-fuṣḥa*) to me:

> There are differences. When I speak in *'ammiyya*, it is from me to you directly [*minnii liikii 'ala ṭuul*]. What is in the magazine is *il-'arabiyya il-fuṣḥa*, what I speak with you now is *'ammiyya*. The Arabic language is not difficult, but, well, *'ammiyya* is the dialect of life [*laḥgat il-ḥayaat*]. If I spoke to you in fuṣḥa, that takes time and it is not normal/reasonable (*mish ma'uul*) that we speak like that to each other.

"From me to you *directly*" is a rather precise conception of Egyptian Arabic because its oral use, as is the case with the use of all mother tongues in spontaneous daily exchanges, is the least mediated language variety. It is also described by many people as the language for face-to-face interactions, unlike Classical Arabic: "For when we sit in front of each other" (*'aa'diin uddaam ba'd*). Lack of mastery of Classical Arabic for oral interaction on the part of a majority of people "makes its use take time" and is not *'alaa ṭuul*. The expression "the dialect of life" has a tinge of irony in that what one uses for life is a dialect and not a language. A 45-year-old man who was a school teacher said: "The language of 'ammiyya is easier and faster and reaches the heart and the conscience faster than the Arabic language [fuṣḥa]" (from Haeri 1996: 211). But Classical Arabic is mediated through grammar classes, sheikhs and teachers, *kuttaabs* and schools and reading and writing. It is not *"ala ṭuul"*, direct, or from one person immediately to his or her interlocutor. And as we will see in the next chapter, its mediation goes even further.

Classical Arabic at School: Grammar and the Case Endings

Women and men of various backgrounds said that they feel they must know Classical Arabic *because* they are Muslims *(mafruud ni'raf al-lugha al-'arabiyya 'ashaan ihna muslimiin)*. At home, at the *kuttaab* and at school, people learn that *"al-lugha al-'arabiyya"* ("The Arabic Language") is the language of the Qur'an and *"kalaam rabbina"* ("the word of our God"). Everyone in Nadia's family told me that when they pray, they become calm *(mistirayyah)*, feel comfort *(raaha)* and peaceful *(haadi)*. Indeed, such feelings of well-being, comfort and peace run through many people's descriptions of their experiences while praying, reading the Qur'an or listening to its recitations. The father of a friend told me that as soon as he wakes up in the morning, he plays one of his cassettes of recitation so that as he goes about getting ready for work the sounds of the Qur'an fill his house. He said that this experience puts his mind at ease and gets him ready for the day ahead. In many people's descriptions of their feelings toward this language, they often mentioned that they find it very beautiful *(gamiil)* and powerful *(qawi)*, it moves them and makes them forget their daily problems.

It was therefore puzzling to find that so many people also spoke of their dislike and even hatred *(kiraaha)* of their language classes—that is, classes on the grammar of *al-lugha al-'arabiyya*. Nor did they like very much their literature classes, or reading books in *al-lugha al-'arabiyya*. Indeed, with few exceptions, even many college educated people made a point of saying that they do not like to read books or other "long texts" in *al-lugha al-'arabiyya*. Why? I interviewed two women in their early 20s who were librarians. They both obtained a college degree from Cairo University and were from a comfortable middle-class background. Both had also attended a *kuttaab* and heard their first explicit statements about the language of the holy book from their parents. Their degrees and their jobs involved knowledge of Classical Arabic, unlike most members of Nadia's family. I asked one of them:

Q: When you were little and listened to the Qur'an, did you have any idea what it was you were listening to?

A: Yes. We used to sit around and listen and we understood that this is something sacred [*haaga muqaddasa*]. My parents told us that this is the word of the Qur'an, [and] we must protect it and memorize it because it is the word of God. When I was a child, before reaching the age of prayer, I would watch my mother and try to imitate her. It was a fun game for me. I would grab one of her long scarves and put it over my head and stand to pray. The adults loved it. I would sometimes recite the one or two short chapters of the Qur'an that I had memorized and I could see the look on my mother's face. She looked so proud of me and when guests would come over she would ask me to recite for the guests. Then I would get big smiles and praise from everyone. I could tell that it was very important for my parents that I learn all the prayers well and memorize parts of the Qur'an.

Both of these women also described the same feelings of peace and calmness while they prayed and in general toward the religious uses of the language. And, just like members of Nadia's family, they disliked the classes on grammar and literature. In answer to why they liked the language so much but not learning about its grammar or reading literary pieces, one of the women said:

It was difficult because we were being taught in a very convoluted [*mi'a''ad*] way. There was beating, there was anger. We were supposed to memorize the rules [*il-qawaa'id*] so that when we come to write we [would] write correctly and when we come to speak, we [would] speak correctly, when we come to read the Qur'an we would know that, for example, something is in the accusative case and not genitive; [that] the case endings [were] necessary (*il-i'raab laazim*) so that we would not make a mistake.

Indeed grammar as a whole for most people comes to mean the case endings (*il-tashkiil, il-i'raab*).[11] Classical Arabic has a case system of nominative, accusative and genitive that are three short vowels—a high back [u], low front [a] and high front [I], respectively. In addition, depending on whether a declined word ends in a vowel, the phonetic shape of the endings change. There are a whole series of rather complex rules regarding the correct phonetic shape of the case endings (see Table 1.1 in Chapter 1).

Orthographically, these cases are represented by diacritics placed above the last letter of the item that is to be declined. There are no letters for their indication as Arabic orthography represents long vowels but not short ones.[12] The Qur'an is a fully voweled text and part of learning how to read it involves crucially the recognition of the diacritics and hence the correct pronunciation of the case endings represented by the diacritics. So long as people are only learning to read this text and memorize (generally the shorter) chapters, the task is never described as a very difficult one. It means recognizing that such and such a diacritic stands for the sound [a], for example. When, as children, people first begin to learn to read the Qur'an, they are not required to understand the case system and its various intricacies. They do not have to worry and be daunted by the fact that something is "in the accusative not genitive." Moreover, the Classical Arabic of the Qur'an and religious rituals is not presented nor seen as competing with Egyptian Arabic *in terms of self-expression.*

But then they go to school, where a great deal of time is spent on teaching them grammar. It is after elementary school when the intense and serious teaching of grammar begins, in the seventh and eighth grades (*il-a'daadi*), continuing in to the twelfth grade. Having previously learned to read and recite correctly short *suras* from the Qur'an without mastering the case system, they are suddenly expected to understand and decipher its minutiae. Neither their experience as native speakers of Egyptian Arabic nor their schooling in learning the Qur'an prepare them for such a task. Not only do they now have to understand the system insofar as their proficiency with the text of the Qur'an is concerned, but even more daunting is that they have to write and answer exam questions in Classical Arabic. That is, they have to learn to actively and correctly produce a grammatical system that is very different from Egyptian Arabic and their grades depend on how well they manage to do so.

Nadia's son, Taher, tutors his fiancée's sister, a high-school student. He told me that she had not done well on her history exam because she had used too many Egyptian words and sentences. For example, instead of writing "*thumma,*" she had put "*ba'deen,*" both meaning "afterward," but the latter is the Egyptian Arabic term. Taher explained that her answers were not wrong (*di mish ghalṭa tarikhiyya*) content-wise, but they contained linguistic mistakes. The family living above Taher had two girls in college and one in high school, as well as two boys, one of whom was also a high-school student. Their older brother had failed his final high-school exams *saanawiya 'aamma* (which qualify one for college entrance) two years in a row because of his bad performance on the Arabic language exam. Recalling his performance at the two exams, this young man asked rhetorically: "Can you believe I failed in the language of my country?" In a number of group discussions with this family about their school experiences—discussions that were quite excited, at times heated and always full of humor—they explained their problems with exam grades. They said that they had teachers who would not accept answers in Egyptian Arabic even if they were correct, others who did accept them and still others who took only partial points off. High-school students also mentioned choice of correct vocabulary as one of their major concerns.

The older generation seems to have had similar experiences. An Egyptian Copt who was in his 60s recalled his high-school days:

> I remember that in my time, the teacher [*il-mudarris*] would not wear a suit [*badla*] but the cape and the turban and so on. Our teacher one day entered the class and gave us a dictation. I wrote normally [*katabt 'aadi*], all of it correct but without the case-endings [*mish mitshakilla*], without the glottal stop and the vowels and I don't know what. He gave me a zero. But to those who wrote with mistakes but put the case endings, he gave them a high grade. Later I asked him why [*leeh kida*]? He said what you wrote is Egyptian Arabic [*kida lugha 'ammiyya*] and that won't go [*ma tinfa'sh*]: "I want the Arabic language [*ana 'aayiz lugha 'arabiyya*]." Okay, I began to understand and do the case endings [*ba'mil il-tashkiil*] and everything. At that time we were in the first year of high school [*uula saanawi*].

Dilworth Parkinson, who has spent a number of years researching Egyptians' language abilities and what they consider to be Classical Arabic, has administered detailed written tests to Egyptians of different educational backgrounds. In addition to finding that many educated people are "uncomfortable with the form," he also came to the conclusion that "Some even express resentment toward the form for its difficulty and the effect of the results of their Arabic school tests on their future career choices" (Parkinson 1991: 40).

Every time I asked about what specifically people found difficult, they would give examples of problems with case endings. It is difficult to exaggerate Egyptians' attention to and fear of the case system. There is an ever-present and an all-pervasive consciousness about them. Hence while everyone knows that the *tashkiil* are of utmost importance in reading the Qur'an, their active use in other contexts is feared and disliked, as in grammar classes or at exam and composition times. One hears over and over this dislike of grammar classes—something that I was already familiar with from my first fieldwork (Haeri 1996, ch. 6).

The fear of making mistakes in Classical Arabic is not only expressed by people with few years of schooling but even by those with college degrees or doctorates. A copyeditor who had spent his entire life correcting the grammar of other people's writings told me that when he is in the company of a learned cleric he finds himself full of trepidation: "[What] if I make a mistake and he'll say this man who is supposed to be a corrector does not know the language well enough?" As might be expected, such feelings are widely combated with humor and satire. The figure of the language teacher and the opacity and convolutedness of school Arabic are used in many jokes—both standard and on the spot. Some people refer to language teachers as "*il-ikhwaan il-nahawiyiin*" "the grammar brothers," perhaps on the model of "*il-ikhwaan il-muslimiin*" "the Muslim brothers" or "the Muslim Brotherhood," which is now an outlawed but still active Islamist political party.

What then can we say about how Classical Arabic comes to be experienced? On the one hand, it is a language that socializes people into the rituals and ceremonies of Islam, a language that affirms their identities as Muslims, that marks certain activities as belonging to the realm of purity, morality and God. A language, furthermore, whose aesthetic and musical qualities move its listeners, creating feelings of spirituality, nostalgia and community. This is particularly the case because as the language of religion, Classical Arabic is, for the most part, an *oral* language. The prayers are recited and not read from any text, children are taught to memorize (chapters) of the Qur'an and often when people read the text, they are reciting from memory. Moreover, the art of the recitation of the Qur'an is highly developed and people buy cassettes of their favorite reciters to listen to. In the context of religious rituals and learning, heavy and consequential expectations of the correct *use* of Classical Arabic are absent.

It is true that many people speak of the sternness of their Qur'anic teachers and even of beatings and so on. But the tasks they must learn to perform do not involve active use of the language in order to gradually replace Egyptian Arabic. A prayer would not be a prayer if it were performed in any other language. On the other hand, while no contexts arise in which their competence in their mother tongue—Egyptian Arabic—competes with their competence in Classical Arabic when this language is used for religious purposes, the schools confront pupils with an entirely different set of tasks. To learn to use Classical Arabic actively, to learn to express oneself in speaking and writing it, create anxieties and contexts where the differences between their mother tongue and Classical Arabic and their relative competencies in each are brought into sharp relief. To have to avoid using the language they have most mastery over, whether for answering exam questions or writing a composition, discourages most students from reading and writing beyond what is required at school. Since written self-expression in Egyptian Arabic is largely discouraged, many people are excluded from the domain of print.

So the Classical Arabic of schools, speeches, books and other print material is "difficult" (*sa'b*) and "heavy" (*ti'iil*) and creates fears and anxieties, but the language of the Qur'an is a "miracle" (*mu'giza*), making the reciter or the listener feel calm and peaceful. There seems to be, therefore, the Classical Arabic of religion on the one hand, and the Classical Arabic of everything else on the other.

Classical Arabic and "Classical Arabic": Arenas of Ambiguity

If experientially, there appear to be such antithetical and paradoxical encounters with the "same" language, do people therefore conceive of them as distinct and do they give them different names? On the whole, most people use the same terms to refer to both, namely, *al-lugha al-'arabiyya* or *al-fusha* or *(al-lugha) al-'arabiyya al-fusha*. The same terms are used in textbooks, the mass media and in public speeches by politicians and intellectuals. (See Parkinson 1991.) Most people insist that there is just one Classical Arabic (*fiih fusha waahid*). The contemporary and nonreligious uses of Classical Arabic, they say, are direct continuations of the language of the Qur'an. The older encompasses the historically newer forms and the latter never supersedes the former by any measure. I asked Omm Hasan whether the language that was in the magazine she was showing me was the same as the one in the Qur'an. She responded:

> No, there is a difference in that the Qur'an is written with case endings [*mit-shakilla*] with the nominative, accusative and genitive and you must, when you read it, take them into account [*ta'milii hisaabhom*]. And you must pronounce *all of them* in the Qur'an. But in the magazine, no, you write the word, but it does not have the case endings. But there are no differences except in this respect [*mafish far' illa fi tashkiil*].

As was mentioned earlier, the case endings of Classical Arabic are short vowels that are indicated orthographically with diacritics placed above and below letters. On the whole, nonreligious writings, particularly those intended for adults, do not indicate the case endings. One is supposed to be able to supply them correctly as one reads. It would actually be considered something of an insult to adult readers, and hence newspapers and magazines do not print their articles with case endings. So they are physically absent, as Omm Hasan explained. Yet, no Qur'an ever appears without full voweling. Hence religious and nonreligious Classical Arabic *look* very different in print. One main exception to this is books for children that often indicate some of the vowels. Moreover, the Qur'an is always printed in various calligraphic styles, not typeset or published with fonts that are used for other printed material. So what Omm Hasan says is true in two related respects: In the magazine she was reading, the case endings are physically absent, and, at the same time, magazines and newspapers generally adopt a style of writing whose understanding does not entirely depend on the readers' knowledge of the case system. (See chapter 3.)

This fundamental difference between the language of print mass media and the Qur'an was articulated by many people. Repeatedly, they characterized the difference in these terms. I asked whether such differences rendered the print mass media, for example, "easier." As it turned out, the question is rather opaque. The text of the Qur'an is not read, except perhaps when one is in a classroom, with the aim of some kind of transparent "understanding"—a word-for-word decoding of information. It is not a textbook, news story or informational manual. No religious text is. It is there to be read, recited, and pondered over, as much for its forms and sounds as for its meanings. So one cannot compare its language with other texts in terms of "ease" or "difficulty" particularly because these considerations only come up, as was just argued, when people have to produce (i.e., actively use) the language themselves, which is not the case in dealings with the Qur'an or prayer books, or the daily prayers that are memorized.

Is the language of print mass media and more generally nonreligious texts therefore something different from *al-lugha al-'arabiyya?* Most people responded in the negative. I insisted on this question, asking whether they had heard a number of terms used by some intellectuals, for example, "contemporary/modern fusha," (*fusha al-'asr*), "fusha of newspapers," (*fusha al-sahaafa*), and "simplified fusha" (*fusha al-mubassata*). They had not heard such terms. Again they repeated differences in terms of case endings, explaining that there are some kinds of writing that are "heavy" or "too complicated," especially due to their use of "difficult vocabulary" and there are others that are not—"but they are all fusha." "Do you mean the same fusha that is the language of the Qur'an?" I asked. A typical response was: "Yes, that is the origin [*il-asl*] of *al-lugha al-'arabiyya*, there is no other *fusha*." "Has fusha changed over time from what it used to be"? "No, it is the same, fusha does not change and it is not supposed to change. Whatever is written now is encompassed by and based on the fusha of the Qur'an."

As was mentioned in the preface, many Arab and non-Arab social scientists, including linguists, use the term "Modern Standard Arabic" or less often "modern Arabic"(in French *l'arabe moderne*) to refer to contemporary uses of Classical Arabic. Egyptian and Arab intellectuals who have also coined terms such as "contemporary Classical Arabic," "modern Classical Arabic," the "third" or "middle language" (*fusha al-'asr, al-lugha al-'arabiyya al-hadiisa*, or *al-fusha al-hadiisa, al-lugha al-thaalitha, al-lugha al-wusta*) wish to underline the fact that the contemporary forms of the language are not only *linguistically different* from that of the old religious texts, but they have an independent, nonreligious status. One publisher told me with some vehemence: "[T]his is modern fusha, it is like any other modern language like English or French; it exists, it is everywhere, there's not much more to talk about." In the introduction to the first comprehensive Dictionary of Egyptian Arabic, the authors make a distinction between the "linguistic vehicle of the legacy of Islamic high culture and religion," which they call *"fusha al-turath"* ("traditional" or "heritage" *fusha*), and the "vehicle of modern culture and technology," which they term *"fusha al-'asr"* (Badawi and Hinds 1986: viii).[13] Although most people do not use such terms nor do they make such a distinction based on different criteria, the ways in which "*al-lugha al-'arabiyya al-fuṣḥa*" is experienced in the context of religion and in other contexts are significantly different.

The active use of Classical Arabic is in the domain of writing, and such issues are viewed differently by writers, poets and journalists whose ideas will be discussed at length in chapter 5. But for now, what is important to note is that those who disagree with the existence of some "modern" or in any case distinct kind of Classical Arabic are people who have religious beliefs, some of whom do not find there to be a necessary opposition between "modernity" and religion. For the most part, however, those intellectuals who want a "modern Egypt," a secular country where the state would be based on the modern principles of citizenship, are the ones who make a great distinction between the Classical Arabic of Islam and Classical Arabic as the language used for all other written purposes today in Egypt. What is therefore at stake is the very definition of Egypt and of its future. A modern nation must have a modern language, so goes the argument. But which language defines Egypt as a nation, and is the state in Egypt "modern," where citizens by principle are treated as equals regardless of their religion, language, gender, class and so on? Of what does the "modernity" of contemporary Classical Arabic consist?

The Egyptian Constitution of 1980 defines "Classical Arabic" as the official language of the country (it also mentions Islam as its official religion and *shari'a* as the basis or framework for its laws). But which Classical Arabic? The one that is the Word of God, of the Qur'an and of Islam, or the "modern" version, or perhaps both?

This is a great arena of ambiguity that can be used and manipulated for a variety of political ends by many different groups and institutions, including those of the state. In the realm of cultural and political struggles, both overt and implicit, Classical Arabic has emerged as the prime channel for the articulation of many kinds of visions and worldviews. Insofar as the state's political aims are concerned, the ambiguity in the referents of "Classical Arabic" is expedient. Because of the existence of the *al-Azhar* religious educational establishment, which is the oldest in the country (founded in the tenth century), it is often assumed that what is outside of this system, notably the public educational institutions of the state, is "secular." For example, "traditional fusha" is said to be taught "within the Azhar system" whereas "contemporary fusha" is taught in "secular schools" (Badawi and Hinds 1986: ix). This is similar to the statement made in the Historical Dictionary of Egypt when it refers to the curricula of *missionary* schools as "secular": "[T]hey offered a high quality secular education to Egyptians" (1984: 270). But as we just saw, not only is religion a part of the curricula at state schools, but religious rituals are also taught there. Television and radio stations, all of which are controlled by the state, broadcast the calls to prayer and offer a number of other religious programs. Starrett's ethnography of the state educational system in Egypt, aptly titled "Putting Islam to Work," demonstrates that the curricula is far from "secular" (Starrett 1998).

The ambiguity of "Classical Arabic" also allows for constructions of nationhood that blur the boundary between "Egypt" and "Arab Egypt" (*il-miṣr il-'arabi*), as the official name of the country "The Arab Republic of Egypt" indicates. Historically, Egyptians have considered themselves as distinct from "Arabs" and even at present rarely do they make that identification in casual contexts; "*il-'arab*" as used by Egyptians refers mainly to the inhabitants of the Gulf states who are on the whole looked upon with some disdain. That Egypt's inhabitants spoke Coptic before the arrival of the Muslim armies, that the lengthy Pharaonic civilization flowered there, and, more important, the fact that unlike other Arab states Egypt has historically had the same territorial boundaries are all in part reasons for perceptions of a distinctly Egyptian identity. At the same time, beginning in the 1940s the political identity of "Arabs" as articulated through the vision of a pan-Arab nation standing united against colonialism, Israel and imperialism in general also began to be propagated in Egypt.[14] The language of this pan-Arab nation—one in which "Arab" was defined as anyone who speaks "Arabic" regardless of religion—is Classical Arabic. It was/is hoped, I believe, that this "Classical Arabic" would not be identified with the language of Islam but with the language of scholarship, of books and literature, so that it would not exclude non-Muslims. Historical and ethnographic analyses of how Egyptians experienced processes that were to turn them into Arabs *through the use of Classical Arabic* are sorely lacking. One of the few sources that sheds some light on this question is the autobiography of Leila Ahmed. Like most other members of the upper classes, Ahmed attended a private foreign language school (in her case English) and was taught Classical Arabic as a subject a few hours a week. In a chapter entitled "On Becoming an Arab," she describes an experience from her Arabic language class in high school just after Nasser came to power in 1952:

> The teacher called on me to read. I started haltingly. She began interrupting me, correcting me, quietly at first but gradually, as I stumbled on, with more and more irritation, leaving her desk now to stand over me and pounce on every mistake I made. She was an irascible woman, and I had not prepared my homework.
>
> "You're an Arab!" she finally screamed at me. "An Arab! And you don't know your own language!" "I'm not an Arab!" I said, suddenly furious myself. "I am Egyptian! And anyway we don't speak like this!" And I banged my book shut. (Ahmed 1999: 243)

To bring Egyptians to recognize and accept the reasons for the need to consider themselves as "Arab Egyptians" is therefore a process spanning a number of decades—the results of which are still not all obvious. The linguistic ambiguity, as I have suggested, both feeds into and is encompassed by whole fields of related ambiguities with diverse players.

I interviewed a number of Egyptian Copts and asked about their school experiences in some detail, as I had done with all other people that I talked to. Hatem, who was in his late 20s and worked in a state-owned library, recounted his school days in these terms:

> We were a few Christians, maybe around 8 or 9, and we took classes in religion and that is what made me learn a lot about Islam and memorize parts like Ayat al-Kursi and things like that. I still remember them. When we listened to the ayaat [verses], there was no difference that I am a Christian or a Muslim—the students, all of them, had to memorize the aayat that they were given in the class. They told us that those who do not know the Qur'an, do not know the Arabic language well. This made me dislike the Arabic language [*al-lugha al-'arabiyya*]. I felt that I was learning a language that has a specific religious purpose [*hadaf diini mu'ayyan*]. I felt that the teacher wanted to teach me the language through the medium of the Qur'an. This went against my self-esteem. To this day, I don't like this language.

Before Hatem told me about what he had heard at school—that "he who does not know the Qur'an, does not know the Arabic language well"—I had heard very similar assertions from many other people. A common saying that I heard in a number of contexts was: "[I]f you want to learn the Arabic language well, you must know the Qur'an." In other interviews with Egyptian Copts, including a group interview conducted at a church cum community center, I was told that they hear this a lot (*binisma' kitiir*). The link is problematic for non-Muslims because Classical Arabic is defined as the official language of Egypt. If, for example, Egyptian Arabic were the official language of Egypt and Classical Arabic were confined to the domain of religion, the link would not pose problems for non-Muslims. In Arabic language classes at state schools a non-Muslim Egyptian is confronted with a language that is both the official language of his/her country and at the same time said to be the language of Islam. Muslim pupils learn their prayers at public schools (in addition to other venues), as we saw earlier. But Copts learn their prayers at their churches and at home. Does the triangle of Classical Arabic, the state and Islam render tenuous the status of non-Muslims as citizens?

"The Language of My Country"

In a number of interviews with high school teachers, I was told that Egyptian Copts cannot become teachers of Classical Arabic in public schools.

There does not seem to be a law to this effect, but an implicit under-standing. Both the teachers who told me this and a few others with whom I spoke about it had exactly the same explanations for why this should be the case.[15] They all said that the most important text of Classical Arabic is the Qur'an and, since this text defines the highest level of linguistic achievement, it must be used for teaching purposes. One cannot expect non-Muslims, they argued, to know the Qur'an as well as Muslims. There-fore, non-Muslims should not become teachers of the language. Knowl-edge of the language is so thoroughly defined in terms of knowledge of the Qur'an that when I would point out that we were discussing teaching lan-guage rather than religion, I was told that "there is no difference here" (*mafiish far' hina*).

At the same time, the Bible that Copts read as well as their prayer books are all in Classical Arabic.[16] Do they also consider Classical Arabic the lan-guage of their religion? In the group interview mentioned earlier, everyone said that they found the style of the Qur'an harder than that of the Bible (*us-luub il-qur'an as'ab min usluub il-ingiil*). One young man, who was 17 years old, spoke at length about how "easy" the Coptic language is and that if it were taught at schools, everyone would learn it in a few years. But for a while the discussion centered on the difficulty of the language of the Qur'an (*gaamid, sa'b*). As if to balance the discussion, one young woman in her 20s said, "[T]here are probably people who like it very much, certainly it is very good in some respects (*fiih naas bithibbaha giddan, akiid hiya hilwa fi ha-gaat*)." Although they all use the same prayers books and memorize a few of their prayers, all of which are in Classical Arabic, they said that they "can pray in any language" if they want to. In comparing the relations between the two religions and the language, one man said: "There is a very big dif-ference. In Islam, there is a pressure to learn the language: 'Do this, memo-rize that.' But for us, we are not forced. You can be a Christian and not know the Arabic language." Some mentioned that the Bible can be in English or French. I asked the oldest member of the group who was in his 60s whether he agrees with that. He responded: "The relation [of the language] with the religion of Islam is strong but with respect to Christianity, it is not special ['*aadi*]." Another man added: "I believe that there is no Muslim who would agree to pray in English—that would be *haraam* [religiously forbidden] to read the Qur'an in English. [One] prefers to read it in the Arabic language."

Two members of this group had previously made a point of saying that they really love Egyptian Arabic. Having listened to views about the respec-tive relations of the two religions with Classical Arabic, I asked them what their reactions would be if someone would translate their Bible and all their standard prayers into Egyptian Arabic. The old man immediately re-sponded: "No. All our books are in fusha, no. My personal opinion is no. I have our Book in the Arabic language [*il-lugha il-'arabiyya il-fusha*] and

that's it, we are used to it and I pray in it and understand it and everything."
Another man added: "Writing in Egyptian Arabic [*il-'ammiyya*] is difficult.
Our Bible is 'The Good News' [*il-khabar il-tayyib*]. Our Bible is small [ges-
tures with fingers]—the New Testament. When you come to *'ammiyya*, it
might take 7 volumes whereas in the Arabic language, it is much shorter."
The youngest member joined in:

> The language of *'ammiyya* from a long time ago, you can no longer use it be-
> cause it changes a lot. Our Muslim brothers, they have the Qur'an—our Lord
> [*rabbina*] wrote that book, with the revelation [*bil-wahy*], right? We have the
> Bible which is considered written [*yu'tabar maktuub*] by our Lord with the
> hands of the prophets [*bi-yad il-anbiyaa'*] but with the revelation of the Holy
> Spirit [*ruuh al-qudus*]. And without that revelation it would not be the Bible
> because the Bible in essence is God's book and without limit [*gheyr mahduud*].
> And if the spirit of our Lord was not in it, it would have been a book like any
> other book and that is why it is called "The Book of Life" [*kitaab al-hayaa*].
> And this book, I can't change anything in it so long as it is the work of the
> Holy Spirit or Our Lord, there will not come a time when I'll say that I'll
> write it in *'ammiyya*.

Thus, on the one hand, there is general agreement that the relationship between Christianity and Classical Arabic is not "special"—not at all the same
as that between Islam and the language. But on the other hand, the Bible
should remain in Classical Arabic (now that Coptic versions are very rarely
used). In part, the general exaltation and respect for Classical Arabic and the
perceived inadequacies of Egyptian Arabic as a written language (it "changes
all the time," it "is not concise," etc.) are also shared by some Egyptian Copts.

But equally importantly, the ambiguity of Classical Arabic allows constructions of a "nation" whose language may be viewed as standing removed
from and abstracted away from Islam. The same young man, who, unlike
the other members present, had attended an English language private
school, remarked:

> And apart from the Qur'an, the point is that the Arabic language is the lan-
> guage of my country [*lughat baladi/*]and there must be belonging and mem-
> bership in it [*intimaa' biiha*]. This is something that belongs to me, like my
> country [*watani*]. The Arabic language is considered something from our her-
> itage [*turaathna*] like the Pharoanic heritage. It has the same destiny [*liiha nafs
> il-taqdiir*]. When we look at it that way, I must like it.

Everyone present expressed strong agreement with this assessment. Note
that the terms "*balad*" and "*watan*" are used interchangeably, whereas the
former generally denotes a locality like a village or a country and the latter

denotes "nation." Recall that a member of the family living above Nadia also characterized his failing the Arabic language exams as "failing in the language of my country" (*lughat baladi*). I asked the group what was meant by "*watan 'arabi*" and whether it meant the same as "*il-qowmiyya*" (pan-Arab nationalism). The old man responded "yes, all of it, Saudi Arabia, Kuwait, the Emirates, the Gulf, and so on." Classical Arabic is thus thought of as an imperative for the unity of Arabs and for the goals of a pan-Arab nation. Such views are widely prevalent among Egyptians. The language of this nation could not privilege one national vernacular over another because the dialects are different and would hamper not only communication but unity. At school, in the context of classes in religion, grammar, literature and history Egyptians repeatedly hear that the language of the Qur'an is "*al-lugha al-'arabiyya*." They are also taught that this is the language of Arabs and of the Arab nation. The ambiguity of Classical Arabic goes hand in hand with the ambiguity of Arab (Muslim or anyone who speaks "Arabic") opening possibilities for mutable inclusions and exclusions based on different identities and political objectives.

So far, we have discussed aspects of the social reproduction of Classical Arabic in the sphere of religious activities. We have also mentioned a number of its phonetic and grammatical features. But what does the other language that is also said by most people to be Classical Arabic—the one that is not "*'alaa ṭuul*," or direct from one person to another—look like? What kinds of processes have been involved in engineering contemporary versions of Classical Arabic? Which institutions and individuals are devoted to its production and reproduction? What kinds of constraints are authors under in using "Classical Arabic"?

A number of sites can be examined in search of answers to these questions. I have chosen to explore the emergence of "Classical Arabic"—its "modernization" and "renovation"—in the popular print media. The next two chapters are devoted to analyses of the written forms of nonreligious Classical Arabic. In chapter 3, we will follow the path of a written piece to its eventual printed form.

Chapter Three

❧

Text Regulation and Sites of Ideology

As a magazine corrector during Nasser's reign, I was afraid of getting in real trouble. One day, just before the magazine was about to be submitted to the printers, I found a curious phrase in an article. It said "the coming revolution" [al-thawrah al-qaadima]. I was puzzled because we just had a revolution. It took me a while to realize its potential danger and so I changed it to "the present revolution" [al-thawra al-qaa'ima].

—Hamid, professional copyeditor,
from interview in Cairo July/7/1996

The idea that a piece of writing reflects the exact words of *an* author—that the words "belong" to her as an individual writer—persists, despite Roland Barthes's declaration two decades ago that the author is "dead" (Barthes 1977). Barthes in part declared this death because what is written according to him is invariably multiple quotations from what has been said or written before. But instead of concluding that the author is therefore dead, one may give up the idea that what readers read is the result of the genius of a single individual, dead or alive. The quotation above shows that what may come to be attributed to an author is rarely the result of her individual output alone. According to the copy editor (they are called "correctors" in Egypt) working under Nasser, he was as responsible for those dangerous words as the author. By changing one consonant—a /d/ to a glottal stop—the corrector believes that he saved himself and the author from potential punishment. Later of course these same words would be attributed to a single individual—the idea perpetuated by practices such as quoting and putting only one name under a published piece.

This is a game that everyone seems to play, knowing but successfully pretending that what is printed is the unmediated result of a single individual's work. There need not be any political repression and strict censorship for these kinds of interventions to occur. Robert Gottlieb, the former editor-in-chief of Alfred Knopf, made quite substantial changes in the writings of such famous writers as Joseph Heller, Doris Lessing, Cynthia Ozick, Le Carré and Toni Morrison (among others). Le Carré confides that in his "most autobiographical novel," *A Perfect Spy,* Gottlieb "pointed out the places where he felt that the fiction became so autobiographical that it became embarrassing—where he felt that I had really spilled into private experience and had thrown away the mask. . . . *What we left on the cutting room floor still makes me blush"* (MacFarquhar 1994: 189, emphasis added). Michael Crichton rewrote entirely *The Andromeda Strain* as was requested by Gottlieb, and when it was finally finished, the editor told him: "Dear boy, you've got this ending backwards." Crichton changed the ending and believes that Gottlieb was "absolutely right" (Ibid: 191). On the role of editors, Crichton has said: "I think every writer should have tattooed backwards on his forehead, like *AMBULANCE* on ambulances, the words: *everybody needs an editor* (Michael Crichton 1994). Gottlieb has "fixed more sentences than most people have read," told writers to forget about certain books, to cut hundreds of pages, to change names of characters, endings, cut or re-order chapters, suggested ideas for books to various writers, rewritten entire pages and fought over punctuation. Almost all the writers he has edited believe that he made their books better. In the case of the mass-printed "Wicked Bible" of 1631, which became infamous because the seventh commandment was printed as "Thou shalt commit adultery," it may have been simply the fault of the compositor who dropped the "not" from the commandment, as Elizabeth Eisenstein (1998) argues.[1] However, the example still shows that between what is written to what is printed much can and does happen, often of some considerable consequence.

Along with Gottlieb, all the writers he has edited have come to believe that the editor and his interventions must be invisible. After his second novel, Joseph Heller was interviewed by the *New York Times*. In that interview, Heller talked about "Bob's [R. Gottlieb] value" to him as an editor. He recounts that "The day the interview ran, Bob called me and said he didn't think it was a good idea to talk about editing and the contributions of the editors, *since the public likes to think that everything in the book comes right from the author.* That's true, and so from that time on, I haven't" (Ibid: 186, emphasis added). In Gottlieb's own words:

> The editor's relationship to a book should be an invisible one. The last thing anyone reading *Jane Eyre* would want to know, for example, is that I have con-

vinced Charlotte Bronte that the first Mrs. Rochester should go up in flames. . . . I don't want to know that. As a critic, of course, as a literary historian, I'm interested, but as a reader, I find it very disconcerting. (Ibid: 186)

Readers may or may not find this kind of information disconcerting. One could argue that in this age of "expose it all," readers may in fact find the details of editors' contributions very intriguing indeed.[2]

A number of French medieval historians known as the New Philologists take the scribe as their "hero," rather than the author, because rarely does "the original" exist and all extant manuscripts are the works of scribes—with their own "corrections" and interventions (Nichols 1996, Cerquiglini 1989: 20–24; see also Eisenstein 1998: 85–86). This move—eschewing singularity and originality of texts—encourages a further revision in the way we analyze texts and their producers. If we also give up the idea of an individual author, then the scribe, the copy editor, proofreader, translator, editor—figures that I will call globally "text regulators"—may all be considered heroes or villains as the case may be.

Text Regulators

What I am concerned about in this chapter are processes of mediation involved in the production of printed texts. Analyses of the circuitous route from a written piece to its printed form provide fertile grounds for addressing a number of substantial questions on the specificities of mediation and the form-ideology dialectic. Through an examination of the institution of "correction" (*tashih*), I will show that in Egypt as well, printed pieces are almost always the work of several individuals. Who are these individuals and what kinds of education have they had? What are their class backgrounds and what kinds of linguistic norms have they been inculcated with? What does this aspect of print culture say about larger political issues?

A central question to emerge from the recent volume *Language Ideologies* (Schiffelin, Woolard and Kroskrity 1998) is: "Where are we to look for ideology's many manifestations in social life [?]" (Silverstein 1998: 128). Given the significance of sites of ideology, the vast scholarship on the history of print seems under mined by anthropologists. There have certainly been important studies such as Benedict Anderson's *Imagined Communities* and a few others, but on the whole this scholarship remains unengaged. Research on the social history of languages, including the history of the book, print, and reading habits (Fevre and Martin 1976, Eisenstein 1983, Chartier 1995, McKenzie 1985, Clanchy 1996) is highly relevant to anthropological inquiries on social change, "modernity," the constitution of the "public," language standardization and mediation processes involved in the form-ideology dialectic.

There are significant commonalties in aims between anthropological approaches to language and print history scholarship; for example, their shared concern with the politics of form. McKenzie defines the aim of bibliography as a "sociology of texts" (quoted in Chartier 1997: 83) that encompasses the more specific political economic analyses of various scholars (Gal 1989, Woolard 1989, Hanks 1987, Kuipers 1998, Caton 1990 and Joseph 1987, among others). In her introduction to *Language Ideologies,* Woolard states that "the point of the comparative study of language ideology is to examine the cultural and historical specificity of *construals* of language" (Schieffelin et al: 4). The language and more generally the form of printed texts is greatly mediated by such culturally and historically specific institutions such as text regulators, print shops, editing manuals and so on. Writing on "alternate sitings of ideology," Woolard lists various paths followed by different scholars. The list should be expanded to include what studies of print have examined. Language gets regimented not just in face-to-face interactions (the site of a majority of anthropological studies) but also in decisions about orthography (Schieffelin and Doucet 1998) and by the conditions of its production—many of which affect the form and language of a text.

In her influential review of anthropological theory since the 1960s, Ortner wrote that Geertzians found the "focus on symbol as *heuristically* liberating. It told them *where to find* what they wanted to study" (1984: 129, emphasis added) [note the spatial metaphor]. Heuristic ease does not justify the a-priori bounding off of the units of analysis—some of which remain as yet unclear. More recently, Silverstein and Urban (1996) criticize the "culture as text" move and observe: "[T]o turn something into a text is to seem to give it a decontextualized structure and meaning, that is, a form and meaning that are imaginable apart from the spatio-temporal and other frames in which they can be said to occur." They point out that both analysts and natives read pieces of culture as texts and argue against abandoning this sort of semiotic analysis. The problem is that the culture as text path does not lead to all the sites that we need to examine for a wider understanding of the form-ideology dialectic. We do not only want to know *why* a text has certain features in terms of composition, organization and linguistic form, but also *how* a text has come to be what it is. And that question involves an analysis of all that is involved in the production of a text. As Chartier argues:

> When the physical characteristics of extant copies are supplemented with information taken from printshop records (when they exist) and from old printing manuals, they provide the most massive—and perhaps the richest—records

for a history of the conditions and habits that governed the production of printed texts. (Chartier 1997: 83)

The notion of the "avant-texte" (pre-text) used by New Philology, as opposed to the text, is directly relevant to the concerns of anthropologists in understanding processes of standardization, how a text is meant to be read and understood, and the impact of modern publishing on written language (see e.g., Cerquiglini 1989: 23). Not all the significant social processes that are involved in the production of a text may be found in "traces" retrievable through textual and semiotic analysis. One may not recognize those traces, nor the reflections, manipulations, inclusions and exclusions that are the consequences of the conditions of production of the text in question even in a microscopic textual analysis. In other words, one would not necessarily know "where to look." As Ortner points out, the focus on symbol also has the serious shortcomings of an "underdeveloped sense of the politics of culture" and how symbolic systems get produced and maintained. How would a purely semiotic analysis lead to the many pages of *A Perfect Spy* left on the cutting room floor?

At the same time, why any linguistic production has the features that it does, as may be revealed by formal analysis, cannot be *fully* accounted for no matter how minute our analysis of the text and its contexts may be. An oral or written linguistic production is not the *mere* result of any one individual's efforts nor the mere result of any one set of institutions, ideologies or contexts. Indeed, if ideologies, institutional inculcations and historical practices were all recoverable directly from any given text, and if they had no internal contradictions, the politics of form would be a rather transparent object of study.[3] Hence, not all the linguistic features of a text can be predicted or parceled out to specific institutional constraints or ideologies. And yet all their conditions of production need study because, as was just pointed out, the question is not simply what is physically in the text but also how the text came to be what it is. This is where the works of historians can be more fully engaged by anthropologists.

Unlike spoken language, print language goes through a number of more or less documentable interventions from the time a transcript of an oral text or a manuscript of a written one is submitted to the time it is printed. These interventions vary in degree and intensity from discipline to discipline, fiction to nonfiction, publishing house to publishing house, and country to country. However, that it is considered normal for there to be some kind of intervention if some written material is to be printed, cuts across societies with different kinds of political systems. Thus, as we just saw, in the United States, with a political system and resources of publishing that are quite different from countries such as Egypt or France, many kinds of writings go through an editing process. Articles submitted to scholarly journals routinely undergo the interventions of copyeditors (whether or not they are accepted by the author), as well as pieces for popular newspaper and magazines (Cameron 1995). *The Chicago Manual of Style* (now in its 14th edition) and that of the *New York Times* illustrate how important text regulation continues to be to publishing houses.

I take the question of "sites" of ideology to involve, both "where" (e.g., the print shop) and the identification of the *kinds of mediation* involved in the production of any given linguistic text. In the case of print language, for example, I translate "site" into an attempt at identifying which institutions, histories, practices and ideologies are necessary for understanding the forms of print language. This formulation is not meant to imply that the writing of a text, before it gets published, is itself unmediated. Any linguistic production, oral, written or printed is mediated and there are overlaps in the mediating factors. My focus, however, will be on mediation processes of printed texts. From institutions to individuals to the printed text and back, there is a complex route. Articulating its path is my central aim.

"The words altered into other words"

There appear to be few historical studies of the institution of correction. (But see Cerquiglini 1989.) A rich but brief study by McMurtrie was published in 1922 and I will use it to provide a comparative basis for the discussion of text regulation in Egypt. The specialized profession of editing and correcting is probably a descendant of the activities of manuscript copiers and scribes. Correctors were supposed to be erudite, multilingual scholars the quality of whose interventions helped define the reputation of the publishing houses for whom they worked. In "The corrector of the press in the early days of printing," McMurtrie quotes Joseph Moxon who undertook probably the earliest study of correctors in 1683:

> A *Correcter* should (beside the *English* Tongue) be well skilled in language, especially in those that are used to be Printed with us, *vis.* the *Latin, Greek, Hebrew, Syriack, Caldae, French, Spanish, Italian, High Dutch, Saxon, Low Dutch, Welsh, etc.* neither ought my innumerating only these be a stint to his skill in the number of them, for many times several other Languages may happen to be Printed, of which the Author has perhaps no more skill than the bare knowledge of the Words and their Pronunciations, so that the Orthography (if the Correcter have no knowledge of the Language) may not only be false to its Native Pronunciation, but the Words altered into other Words by a little wrong Spelling, and consequently the Sense made ridiculous, the purpose of it controvertible, and the meaning of the Author irretrievably lost to all that shall read it in After times (Joseph Moxon 1683, quoted in McMurtrie 1922).

Though McMurtrie finds Moxon's qualifications to be "so numerous as to be amusing" (Ibid: 8), making the corrector into a "superman," there are nevertheless many indications that they were highly educated scholars. In many countries, publishers were required by law to correct a book before printing them. In 1539, Article 17 of the decree of François I stated that: "If the master printers producing books in Latin are not learned enough themselves to correct books they print, they are required to employ capable correctors, *under penalty of arbitrary fine*" (Ibid: 13, emphasis added).[4] Similarly, during Ottoman rule in 1727, the written permission granted to two individuals for opening a printing house required that books "pass the review of learned scholars" and that the printers "take special care to see that the copies remain free of error and depend on the noble learned men for this" (reproduced in Atiyeh 1995: 284). The "learned scholars" were actually named in this decree and referred to with much reverence.

Correctors were also feared because they could "wreak personal vengeance" and wreck the reputation of authors and printing houses. Religious texts in particular seem to have been at the center of this fear and the potential for the creation of animosity between different sects:

> The favorite method of wreaking personal vengeance in the printing offices of the early days was to change the spelling of a Latin word so as to change a serious and dignified statement into an expression the sense of which was obscene. . . . Perversion of statements of principle in works of a religious character was also a cause for apprehension. . . .
> A corrector of ill intent was flogged and driven in shame from the episcopate of Würzburg for having omitted the letter *w* from one word, thus occasioning an obscene expression (Ibid: 7, 8).

In the period between the sixteenth and eighteenth centuries covered by McMurtrie's study, some correctors became internationally famous—like other scholars—in the print offices of London, Paris, Leipzig, Nuremberg, Venice, Rome and other centers of publishing. With occasional exceptions, text regulators have now become all but invisible in the publishing process. In his essay entitled "What is an Author," Foucault states that "The coming into being of the notion of 'author' constitutes the privileged moment of *individualization* in the history of ideas, knowledge, literature, philosophy, and the sciences" (Foucault 1984: 101). He points out that "There was a time when the texts that we today call 'literature' (narratives, stories, epics, tragedies, comedies) were accepted, put into circulation, and valorized without any question about the identity of their author; their anonymity caused no difficulties since their ancientness, whether real or imagined, was regarded as a sufficient guarantee of their status" (Ibid: 109). The causes for "transgression attached to the act of writing," enumerated by Foucault, are also involved in the increasing invisibility of text regulators, for example: the emergence of "a system of ownership for texts," "author's rights," "rights of reproduction and related matters" (Ibid: 108). The author was to become an individual to be named, promoted *and* to be held legally responsible.

Insofar as the specificities of mediation processes are concerned, print scholarship points to the fact that religious and state institutions have always been powerfully involved in publishing. This involvement clearly entailed the regulation of the form and content of what got printed through owner- ship of publishing houses, printing presses, recourse to law, educational in- stitutions, the imposition of a "correct" language, the training of text regulators and at times competing ideologies with regard to linguistic norms.

Text Regulation in Egypt

To become a corrector in Egypt, one has to specialize in Classical Arabic in college. Whether one goes on to obtain higher degrees or not, the crucial stage after studying is apprenticing to an established corrector in a publish- ing house. What do these two processes involve? A degree in Classical Ara- bic may be obtained either from a state university or from the al-Azhar system, the oldest and most distinguished religious educational system in the country, founded in the tenth century and brought under state control in this century. A major difference between the two systems is that one has to take more courses in purely religious topics in al-Azhar. However, to the de- gree that the most revered texts in Classical Arabic are religious texts—used as linguistic exemplars, with the Qur'an as the highest exemplar of all (*il- namuuzag il-a'laa*)[5]—state universities cannot bypass such texts. This is part of a larger dilemma for the state—its own official language is promoted through texts and through a language whose historical custodians comprise a rival power base (Haeri 1997). I will return to the dilemma of the state later on.

A regular employee of all publishing organizations, the *muṣaḥḥiḥ* (agen- tive of the root ṣ ḥ ḥ "to correct") is a professional who is responsible for a number of tasks. Foremost among these is the correction of texts for gram- matical mistakes. He also corrects for infelicitous stylistic turns, lexical choices, at times, decisions about headlines and fixing matters related to the form of the layout of the page. In addition to solid knowledge of grammat- ical rules, many of which are memorized by correctors, they must be able to check the strength of the genealogy of any cited *ḥadis*[6] (actions and words of the Prophet Muhammad), and the accuracy of citations from the Qur'an. Hence as part of their tools of trade, correctors not only consult various dic- tionaries and grammatical treaties, but also biographical dictionaries, numerous *ḥadis* collections and Qur'anic concordances. Next the piece is submitted to the chief editor (*ra'iis il-taḥriir*) who may or may not make more changes and finally it is published. In general, there seems to be little contact between correctors and authors. The editor apparently acts as a shield to prevent potential tensions.

Before state universities emerged in this century, it is clear that anyone who received training in the classical language and became among other things a manuscript copier and/or a *muṣaḥḥiḥ* was trained by religious institutions. But in this century state universities began to produce their own graduates. Hence, there are also correctors that are either solely products of state schools, or joint products of religious and state institutions. At present correctors are part of the Journalists' Syndicate (*Niqabat al-Saḥafiyiin*)[7] and every publishing house has several correctors. The career trajectory of the oldest *muṣaḥḥiḥ* that I interviewed (I will call him Hamid) serves to bring us closer to some of the specificities of the processes of mediation.

A Lifetime of Correction

Before he began to go to school, like most other Muslim Egyptians across classes Hamid first encountered Classical Arabic through recitations of the Qur'an, memorizing its shorter *suras* and listening to other professional reciters. Hamid's grandfather and father had a printing house. His father did not attend school and could not write but taught himself how to read. Both his brothers also work in the publishing business. Hamid's formal education began with a four-day stint at a *kuttaab* school. The sheikh was not learned enough and Hamid contracted some disease from the other children and so he left that school. He signed up at another school named after its founder the wife of the king Malik Fu'ad, *il-Amira Shiyukar*. In that school he spent four years. The curriculum consisted of memorization and recitation of sections of the Qur'an, biology, dictation, calligraphy, drawing, arithmetic and geography (*tahfiiz* and *'iraaya, ṭabii'i, imlaa', khatt, rasm, ḥisaab* and *goghrafia,* respectively).[8]

After these four years he took an entrance exam and was accepted in an al-Azhar elementary school. He spent four years there and five in secondary school and became a graduate of the al-Azhar system. At that point he wanted to attend either of two colleges in the same system: the College of the Arabic Language, (*kulliat al lugha al-'arabiyya*), or the College of Pillars of Religion, (*kulliat uṣuul al-diin*). Although for his entrance exam, he received 38 and a half out of 40, he was told that he could not do so (this was not a good enough grade) but could go instead to the College of Jurisprudence, (*kulliat al-shari'a*). Hamid chose instead to enroll in Dar al-Ulum, a college of Cairo University that is a *state* university.[9]

He graduated after four years and although he expected to qualify then as a teacher of Classical Arabic at the high school level he was not allowed. Instead he was offered a clerkship in some government archives where he also would have had to know some English. Ironically, Hamid believes that the reason the Ministry of Education did not allow him to become a teacher was that he was not good enough in grammar. As he described it with a measure of resentment, Hamid began to work in his father's small printing shop. However, finding that his wife's family did not look favorably to that—they were afraid that the father and the son would one day have a family fight and the son would be thrown out "without a future"—he quit after eight months. He worked temporarily in the printing house of a bank until the popular weekly magazine *Rose il-Yussef* announced two openings for correctors. Hamid applied, took an exam in grammar, and got the job. That was in 1964. In 1991 he retired from the magazine but continues to work in a publishing house in the same capacity. His former employer at the magazine keeps asking him to return and work part-time because the younger correctors need a seasoned master to learn from. Hamid however finds his work at the book publishing house to be more rewarding.

Before moving on to Hamid's views on Classical and Egyptian Arabic, on his education and on other matters related to his approach to correction, I would like to present brief biographies of two other correctors. In this way, a comparison of different educational and generational backgrounds will illuminate important ideological convergences and distinctions.

Magdi is another corrector who I interviewed and who introduced me later on to Hamid.[10] He calls himself a member of the "middle generation" of correctors: "There are those before me and those who have come after." Magdi, who was in his late 40s, attended a *kuttaab* for two years before entering a public elementary school. After entering school, during summer holidays he went back to the *kuttaab* for short periods. His father was a farmer (*fallah*) and could read and write. His mother was a housewife and did not attend any kind of school. When Magdi was growing up, his father would ask him to pick up the Qur'an and read a particular *sura:* "Take the mushaff[11] and treat me to a recitation of the Sura of al-Rahmaan" (*imsik il-mushaff wa samma'-li surat al-rahmaan*). Magdi believes that his love for Classical Arabic is in large part due to his father's efforts. After finishing high school, he went on to Dar al-Ulum and specialized in the Arabic language, as Hamid had done. He did not however enter the al-Azhar system. Magdi works for a number of newspapers and magazines and for various publishing houses, but his regular job is at *Rose il-Yussef*. He has been a corrector for about 15 years. He speaks of Hamid as his "master" from whom he has learned a great deal.

The youngest corrector that I interviewed was in his early 30s and at the time of the interview had been a corrector for two years.[12] He was working for *al-Ahali*—a newspaper that is the organ of the leftist Tagammo' party. Unlike Hamid and Magdi, Abdo did not go to a *kuttaab* before entering the public school system. His major interest is in literature and within that, he majored in Arabic also at Dar al-Ulum. He said that his ambition was to go on to acquire a Masters or Ph.D. in literature but he called the curriculum at the university "a farce" (*muhzala*). For his exam, he had to recite from memory the writings of Ibn Arabi: "I do not study Ibn Arabi at all and [the examiner] asked me to recite to him verbatim the texts of Ibn Arabi and then explain the meaning. We do this in junior high (*il-a'daadi*), but at the university? So I left the exam and decided not to finish my degree." Abdo said that he did not plan on remaining a corrector all his life but found it more interesting than becoming a teacher. He had just been appointed a series editor for several works of fiction by a publishing company and was very pleased as this post was closer to his professional interests.

Hamid and Magdi repeatedly cite the Qur'an as the ultimate source of Classical Arabic. They discuss its richness of vocabulary and sayings (*alfaadh*), the layers of meaning that any given word can have, its powers of expression, its aesthetic qualities and so on. Abdo's views are rather different. He believes that throughout the last several centuries this language survived because of the importance of the Qur'an, and that this survival is mainly due to the faith of "ordinary people" (*il-naas il-'aadiyiin*). However, he explained that this language, "as was discovered by historians," was also in existence *before* Islam in Arabia. Therefore, Abdo believes, a nonreligious nationalist (*il-ragul il-qowmi gheyr mutidayyin,* lit. 'the nonreligious nationalist man') "who is living in the 20th century" does not find a contradiction in using and propagating Classical Arabic: "They see that this language originated in a place before it originated in religion. Religion simply acted as a freezer [*tallaaga*] for the language." At the same time, he added that "ordinary people" see a direct relation (*'ilaaqa mubaashira*) between Classical Arabic and religion. Hamid and Magdi, on the other hand, would certainly not deny that the language predates Islam, but because the Qur'an is the highest exemplar of the language it is the real source of the language for them and that is where its central value lies.

All three cite pan-Arab nationalism (*il-qowmiyya*) as a crucial value of Classical Arabic. Hamid and Magdi view *qowmiyya* as related to Islam while Abdo does not. However, they all believe that Classical Arabic is the only proper vehicle for this *qowmiyya*. Abdo went so far as to say that "*il-qowmiyya hiyya qowmiyyat il-lugha*" "this pan-Arab nationalism is the nationalism of language"—often said by those who want to downplay the importance of religion. Colonialism was also cited by all three as a reason for preserving and propagating Classical Arabic. Hamid and Magdi spoke of British colonialism and its "encouragement" (*tashgii'*) of the use of Egyptian

Arabic in order to divide Arabs and prevent an inter-Arab movement. Abdo began with the Ottomans and their attempts to "Turkify" Arabs and then moved to the British. He did not, however, mention their attempts to propagate the non-Classical languages. Classical Arabic, according to these correctors, reflects the "Arab character" (*il-shakhsiyya il-'arabiyya*). Egyptian Arabic does not do so because it is "local." Hamid and Magdi explained the intense disdain for Egyptian Arabic that continues to be exhibited by some intellectuals on the bases of religion and the *qowmiyya*. Abdo believes that in addition to these factors there is a lot of self-interest (*masaalih*) involved: "For Naguib Mahfouz, if 'ammiyya [Egyptian Arabic] expanded, there would be no readers left for him and he is afraid of that. And of course he is a nationalist writer and believes very much in the necessity of Arab unity and if the Arab nation were realized, the Arabic language [i.e., Classical Arabic] would completely take over and he would become even more popular."

The exalted terms through which Hamid and Magdi characterize Classical Arabic (e.g., "the language has left nothing out") are part of the general and dominant ideology with regard to this language. Hamid believes that the language is holy or sacred (*muqaddasa*), while Magdi explained that it is the Qur'an itself that is holy, not exactly its language, although it is the Word of God. Abdo did not speak in these terms since he does not see the Qur'an as the "origin" of the language. With Hamid and Magdi, I discussed publications on dieting, cooking, books on the "sexual deviances of female foreign singers who corrupt the Egyptian youth,"[13] children's comic strips and so on, which are all written in some version of Classical Arabic. I asked them whether these were appropriate usages for the language. Hamid responded that all "serve the language" (*yikhdim il-lugha*), and that there is nothing wrong with such uses. He explained that he sees "serving the language" as similar to praying, like serving God. The mere fact that "you can put this language into any use" shows its power. He further disagreed with labels used by some intellectuals to characterize "modernized" versions of Classical Arabic such as "contemporary Classical Arabic," "simple Classical Arabic," "the Classical Arabic of newspapers" and so on. He insisted that there is just one Classical Arabic: "There is only one fusha" (*fiih fusha waahid*)—a view shared by Magdi. For Abdo, a main value of Classical Arabic is that it has been amenable to innovations (*ibdaa'*) and has produced many talented writers of fiction. The term *ibdaa'* is a central trope of much writing by contemporary intellectuals.

Gatekeepers and Heterogeneity

In the professional formation of these gatekeepers of Classical Arabic, can we distinguish between the impact of state and religious institutions? A crucial concurrence that emerged in their discussions centered on the legitimacy of *heterogeneous* forms of prose and of appropriate domains of usage. They underlined the importance of tailoring language use to the reader and to the topic so that the "people" understand what they are reading—what is proper for the sports section is different from what is appropriate for the editorial. Thus, although the language has its revered canonical models whose close study was at the center of their education, it must be made to fit (within various limits) the "contemporary age and the purpose" of writing. I would argue that this acceptance of heterogeneity is in large part a result of processes set in motion by state institutions that began in earnest in the early decades of the twentieth century. Religious institutions, writers and readers conceive of Classical Arabic as a vehicle that preserves the past and the Islamic tradition. Whether they teach religion or medicine, there is one central paradigm. Therefore, the language need not be responsive to alternative paradigms. For these correctors, Classical Arabic is both a vehicle that looks to the past and preserves its glories, and is a carrier for a variety of worldviews. The state has played a major role in the diversification of the gatekeepers of Classical Arabic. To the degree that it has managed to produce, through its own colleges and universities, teachers and professors of Classical Arabic, it has changed the traditional gatekeepers of the language. It has also decreased its historical reliance on the graduates of religious institutions of learning such as the al-Azhar. The state has not wholly supplanted the old gatekeepers, but has managed to create diversity within them.

Recalling that Classical Arabic is the medium of education, for any given subject such as geography or history teachers and students must first master the language in which it is written. There is and has always been a continuous shortage of teachers of Classical Arabic. The curricula of state universities and teacher training colleges (e.g., Dar al-Ulum) aim to produce a cadre of professionals who are not religious scholars with specialties in, say, literature or the sciences, as it had been the case with the sheikhs of al-Azhar. In this century, particularly since the 1930s, women have entered universities and the work force in increasingly larger numbers. We have therefore teachers of Classical Arabic who are no longer male sheikhs, but women and men with different kinds of educational training received from state universities. To what degree Egyptian Copts have been allowed to participate in this process of diversification remains a question. The other category of gatekeepers that the state has managed to diversify, though to a lesser degree, is of course all kinds of text regulators including correctors. Both graduates of the al-Azhar system and those of state universities may become correctors. However, women correctors and Copts seem to be quite rare. Hamid told me that "we [correctors] have nothing against women, but there are no women in this profession that I know of." Professional use of

Classical Arabic therefore continues to index "Muslim men," but now they are not solely trained by religious institutions.

Since opening its own institutions of learning in the middle of the nineteenth century, the state has also played a role in processes that brought Classical Arabic into new domains of usage. Its educational institutions (military, medicine, engineering, etc.) were in need of teaching material. These contexts of use and the ensuing translations of texts from European languages had transformative consequences. The express aim of the Language Academy in Cairo (founded in 1932) was to help coin new terms using Arabic roots and if that were not possible, then to "Arabize" them. The biggest anxiety of most intellectuals in this connection seems to have been a perceived lack of "scientific" and "modern" terms in Classical Arabic. It is not only educational institutions that affect the form of a language or bring it into new domains. Virtually any institution that in one way or another must use the official language of the country has an impact. For example, state-owned, private or foreign companies all have been using Classical Arabic in their product brochures or advertisements. All these activities continue to result in the heterogenization of Classical Arabic. In Bakhtin's words, the "spheres of activity" for Classical Arabic expanded, and as I argued earlier, so have the gatekeepers of such spheres.

Because my focus is on the role of state institutions in mediating the forms of Classical Arabic, a number of other developments that are very important will be at this stage left out of the discussion. For example, what is referred to as the Arab Renaissance (al-Nahḍa) was a literary-political movement that began in the late 1800s and continued through the early decades of the twentieth century (Antonius 1946, Hodgson 1974, Gershoni and Jankowski 1986, 1995). This movement's central focus was on the "renovation" (taḥdith) and revitalization of Classical Arabic. It was the impetus to a great upsurge of short story writing, plays and somewhat later of novels. Many European literary works got translated. As an increasing number of people began to write for diverse and varied purposes, consciously attempting to mold and adapt the language to new contexts, the forms of acceptable "Classical Arabic" expanded. In part due to the results of the efforts of this movement, Classical Arabic came to be "modernized" in the view of some writers and intellectuals.

In the same period, a number of Egyptian women founded newspapers and magazines (some in French) and began to participate in the space of print in a variety of national and international debates. In this way, Classical Arabic came to be used and experimented with by a great number of actors in diverse arenas. Although historians and political scientists rarely fail to mention just how "important" Classical Arabic has been for the cultural and political life of the Arab world, this is generally as far as they have gone. Countless questions remain unanswerable because of this lack of attention. Thus, although the foregoing is too brief a description of the social and political processes that have had an impact on Classical Arabic, a satisfactorily detailed treatment would have to await basic historical research (see chapter 4).

Mediation as Appropriation and the Dilemmas of the State

The kinds of mediation that I have analyzed result in various "appropriations" ("secularization"? "modernization"?) of Classical Arabic. They take place at the level of institutions, in the figure of text regulators and on the level of the language itself. The diversification of the gatekeepers of a form, through a variety of means, including the changing curricula of study and control over the creation of different professionals, is a kind of appropriation. In this case, appropriation signifies processes that alter or diversify the legitimate gatekeepers of any given form, and of its domains of use. But can the state appropriate Classical Arabic in the sense of creating alternative authoritative sources for it? Does its power to train professional gatekeepers translate into the authority of an arbiter who defines correct usage? I would argue that the state has to struggle for this authority. The correctors that I interviewed continue to consult grammatical treaties dating from no later than the fifteenth century, for example: Sharh Qatr il-Nada from Ibn Hisham (1359), Sharh Ibn 'aqiil (1367), and al-Ashmuuni (1494).[14] These are highly celebrated and renowned works written by religious scholars. Their close study is required both within al-Azhar and state universities. Although there exist several grammars written by nonreligious scholars in recent decades, none enjoy the same reverence and are hardly consulted. The same goes for dictionaries and of course for Qur'anic concordances and the many indexed collections of *ḥadis*. All three correctors told me that no manuals or stylebooks exist to guide correctors.[15]

As a cultural and political movement and as a central component of the modern Arab identity, pan-Arab nationalism is opposed to colonialism and the West, not Islam. As we saw with the correctors, for some nationalism and Islam are intertwined (Hamid and Magdi) while for others like Abdo, they are separate. Under Sadat and Mubarak, the state has sought to bask in the glory of both. Classical Arabic is a symbolic capital that is hard to forego. As its official language, the state has an interest in perpetuating the exaltation of Classical Arabic, but it would also stand to benefit from a weakening of the connection between this language and Islam. The antecedent claims of the religious establishment over the official language of the state and the historical embeddedness of the language in Islam continue to pose a variety of dilemmas for the state. The social reproduction of language that takes place at state institutions is such that *both* the Classical Arabic of Islam and the Classical Arabic in whose formation the state has had a major role must get reproduced and represented. The degree of emphasis can change—at present, the link to Islam is strongly highlighted. (See chapter 2 and chapter 5.)

The Role of Language in Constructing Social Relations

Text regulation, as was mentioned earlier, is largely an invisible and a behind-the-scene series of activities. So are the professionals who engage in it. In Egypt, it is also not a high-paying profession. Hamid, who appeared to be a sought-after corrector and who had worked with major writers, lived in a very modest apartment in a lower-middle-class neighborhood of Cairo. Outside of the publishing industry, no one had heard of him. Yet, in the space of print, Hamid has more power (in his structural position) than whomever he happens to be correcting. But the main source of this power surely does not reside in him.

A doctoral student of sociology at Cairo University who comes from a very famous and rather wealthy family told me that she employs a corrector both for her dissertation and for whatever she wants to publish. Newspapers and magazines routinely publish interviews with literary figures, actors, politicians and so on. In the majority of cases, these interviews are in Egyptian Arabic. Either the corrector or the editor first translates sections of interest into some version of Classical Arabic. Magdi explained to me in detail that in these translations he is very careful to convey the same "feel" (*ihsaas*) as in the original. Where he finds he cannot do so, he leaves the phrase in Egyptian Arabic and puts quotation marks (*tanṣiṣ*) around it. However, an interview with an important writer or politician almost never has any phrases in Egyptian Arabic, while one with actors or sports figures may well include some. So, the practice is not always followed. In any case, it is the corrector, the translator and/or the editor who decide what word or phrase conveys the same "feel" and what does not.

In 1996, in his yearly televised meeting with a select group of Egyptian intellectuals,[16] the president of Egypt answered most questions in Egyptian Arabic even when the question was asked in Classical Arabic. The next day, all newspapers reporting on the meeting on their front pages had translated the President's answers into Classical Arabic (see al-Ahram March 1, 1996, al-Ahraar March 1, 1996).[17] Moreover, depending on the political interests of the newspaper, not only was the order of presentation changed, but certain topics were entirely dropped while different emphases were put on various aspects of the discussion. With respect to these kinds of changes as well as with respect to the translation into Classical Arabic, the ultimate authority of course does not lie with any editor or corrector, but some representative of the office of the president. In any case, it was frequently observed by a variety of people that "he didn't answer in Classical Arabic because he couldn't," that is, "he does not know it well enough." It goes without saying that many of these people themselves cannot speak Classical Arabic, nor would they have necessarily understood him had he done so. But the expectation is that the president of the country must know the language very well.

What makes it possible for power not to work in a linear manner in the case of print language? Why is it that the space of print and the existence of an official (standard) language allow such constructions of social relations?[18] Where do text regulators get their power and authority from? The answer partly leads to the same reasons why some variety becomes a standard language in the first place—speech habits of powerful groups (e.g., Queen's English), or from associations with religion, literature, cultural and commercial centers—and so on. But this cannot be the whole answer. The writers that Robert Gottlieb edits, as those that Hamid corrects, are on the whole highly educated people who know how to write not only correctly, but well. Why do they need someone to watch over them? It is easier to answer *who* prompts the watch than why. The authority behind correctors is the authority of Classical Arabic itself, bolstered somewhat paradoxically through state institutions. In the hierarchy of Classical Arabic, the writer and the text regulator, the former is there to "serve" the language and the latter to make certain of the quality of the service. The only authority that is unquestioned belongs to the language.

The Qur'an and the centuries-long exaltation of its language as the Word of God, the performance of daily rituals that are in Classical Arabic, the hyper-consciousness of its rules and codification manuals all make clear to every generation that the language "belongs" to no one and that as the Word of God it must be preserved. Hamid, like many others, told me that his central objection to a hypothetical situation in which Egyptians would have a choice of writing either in Egyptian or Classical Arabic is that it will result in a decreasing understanding of the Qur'an. "And at that point," he added: "you might as well take the Qur'an and put it in a museum." So it is not just that Classical Arabic temporally precedes its users but that its authority does not entirely depend on them. At the same time, if they are going to use Classical Arabic, they must serve the language and the public by using it correctly. Like the use of other written languages, the use of Classical Arabic is a performance that is cleaned up and rehearsed backstage by a host of figures. Where Classical Arabic plays a role in the construction of social relations, it mediates in ways that at times override other bases of power.

As I argued in the introduction, if a language is considered to be the Word of God then its users are its custodians, not its owners. If so, the right to change it, mold it, translate it, negotiate its boundaries and so on is always contested. Part of the analytic difficulties that surface in relation to the language situation in the Arab world have to do with the fact that officially the same language seems to be treated in a number of simultaneously contradictory ways. Recall our discussion in chapter 2 on the distinct experiences of people with Classical Arabic in the sphere of religious activities as opposed to all other spheres. There are strong political interests in not disambiguating the status of Classical Arabic. Insofar as text regulators are concerned, there seems to be more negotiating room with nonreligious uses of the language. There is a broad division between that which belongs to the domain of religion and that which belongs to all other domains (textbooks, newspapers, fiction, etc.). The two are not treated equally. In *The Future of Culture in Egypt*, Taha Hussein, one of the most prominent intellectuals of Egypt and the Arab world and a very prolific scholar, wrote against the monopolizing efforts of *al-Azhar* with regard to training language teachers and stated: "[W]e face the dreadful prospect of Classical Arabic becoming, whether we want it or not, a religious language and the sole possession of the men of religion" (1938: 86). There is an irony, intended or not, in putting the matter in the future tense ("becoming") as if in the preceding centuries this had not been the case. But more to the point, there is also an explicit duality in this and other writings pointing to the Classical Arabic of religion and the Classical Arabic of everything else.

Clearly, a language need not be considered sacred for different users to contest changes and innovations in it. Written, standard varieties always have a variety of gatekeepers, and state institutions (educational, legal, financial) have an interest in having "one standard everywhere." But in the nexus of state, nation and language, the construction of the latter as belonging to and defining the nation is more difficult and complex if it is a sacred language and if, by definition, no one's mother tongue. A standard language that is promoted and enforced by the state, and whose "correctness" is taught at its educational institutions, is also defended in a variety of ways from changes. But allegiance to this language, its past and its rules can be constructed as allegiance to the nation. This is not quite possible where the language is embedded in a religion and not in a national territory. This argument is indebted to Anderson's thesis in *Imagined Communities*, but in Anderson's brief treatment of Classical Arabic, one is surprised to find that he equates it with the European vernaculars (1991: 75).

That equation is not only problematic for all the reasons we have so far discussed. It is also inaccurate because "print capitalism"—the engine that, according to Anderson, drove the spread of vernaculars and formed imagined national communities—has not been operative in Egypt in exactly the same ways as in Europe. As has been pointed out by Raymond Williams,

Pierre Bourdieu and others, in capitalist economies the market helps reduce censorship and the reader emerges through the market. The interventions of editors like Gottlieb, unlike Hamid, are oriented also strongly toward a market logic and a crucial test for the editor, the author and the publisher is the sales figures. I do not mean to imply that renowned editors and the publishers they work for have exactly the same concerns and interests. Often enough they do not. But in the decisions of publishers, sales figures and "what the market wants," so to speak, are very important considerations and can override the desires of editors.

In Egypt, the government tightly controls the market through a variety of means. First, it owns the largest publishing company in Egypt, *al-Hay'a al-Miṣriyya al-'aamma lil-Kitaab,* whose resources and sheer number of publications dwarf all other publishing houses. (See chapter 5.) Second, it oversees what gets published and routinely censors what it does not like. And third, publishers (of books, magazines and newspapers) in Egypt must both obtain a permit to operate in the first place, and some receive subsidies. Even the availability of paper and its price depends on the government. At the same time, Gottlieb's authors are also not completely free. It is true that, on the whole, in the United States state institutions and the market do not censor the content of what gets printed. But not only is there systematic text regulation, as was discussed at the beginning of this chapter, but also decisions with regard to the kinds of books "the market wants," "the kinds of writings that sell," groups of readers targeted for various reasons, the whole packaging of a book—in all these marketing decisions the author must negotiate and compromise with the publishers. If the market, through the shorthand of sales figures, helps reduce content censorship, it also takes away some of the freedom of the author—encouraging certain kinds of topics, certain kinds of writing—and requires the intervention of a whole host of managers and editors. Perhaps for these reasons one might say that the author is dead, but it is empirically more justifiable to conclude instead that the author is not alone and not entirely free. There is therefore also a contradiction between the modern author and the modern text due to the mediations of the market.

I interviewed a number of publishers in Egypt in part in order to get a sense of the degree to which their survival depended on their sales. None were willing to share this kind of information. When asked how they managed to stay in business while constantly complaining "no one in Egypt reads," they responded that they mainly rely on book fairs outside of Egypt and on library acquisitions, particularly in Europe and the United States. In the network of author, text regulator, publisher and reader, the state is powerfully present as it oversees that network and its relations to the market. (See chapter 5.) So in the case of Egypt, one might speak more accurately of mediation-oversight rather than just mediation. Modern standard languages in Western market societies are used to produce common literacy and a mass public. In Egypt, such a public is more successfully created (still with state oversight) through non-print media that are overwhelmingly in Egyptian Arabic. But mastery of a mother tongue that is not used for writing is not considered to render one literate. Both the very authority of Classical Arabic and lack of good public education hamper mass literacy in the official language. For most Egyptians, gaining enough proficiency in the language in order to acquire the authority to use it is an enormous investment.

I set out in this chapter to explore the specificities of mediation processes, to map out some of the sites where various ideologies have significant implications for the language of print and to achieve a clearer picture of the role of the state and its institutions. The specific practices of text regulation and the views of correctors provide insights into how prevalent cultural understandings of Egyptian and Classical Arabic (with its contemporary versions) are produced and reproduced institutionally on a daily basis. I also aimed to indicate that Classical Arabic, as a language of print, is comparable to other languages in certain respects. Texts that are the joint production of different people with varying degrees of power and knowledge cannot be analyzed as if language in all its social contexts can equal the unfettered utterances of any single speaker/writer. That most of what gets printed has more than one author, so to speak, has both cultural and political implications. In the next chapter, we will examine how the language of newspapers was developed by various writers and journalists in the late 1800s when there were few established models of newspaper writing in Classical Arabic.

Chapter Four

Creating Contemporaneity

Struggles with Form

When in 1876 two Syrian-Lebanese brothers put out the first issue of the newspaper al-Ahram ("the Pyramids"), they began to face, along with many other writers, the challenges of transforming Classical Arabic into a medium fit for a wide readership and responsive to the exigencies of "news." In the pages of their newspaper, merchants wanted to hawk their wares, to introduce their products, praise them and persuade readers to go over to their stores. They had to make sure to describe their locations well. Was Classical Arabic a language in which one gave street addresses? Elite families wanted to announce their parties, celebrations, funerals and gratitude to each other for favors rendered. Importers of creams and potions for the common cold, for digestive disorders, fatigue, anemia and loss of hair sought to convince readers of the wonders of their concoctions. But they also were eager to reassure potential customers that the products were easy to use, instructions were included in the box and that buyers could go to any pharmacy and just ask for them. In what language were these instructions written? Recently graduated physicians wrote letters to the public, stating that they had acquired their training at a "famous university in Berlin" and would be available everyday at such and such a time and would also agree to do house calls. They usually added at the end of their personal ad that they were ready to treat the poor for free. Weather reports began to be included in the inside pages but probably those who cared most about the weather were peasants [*fallaḥiin*] and not urbanites who read newspapers. One could (can) hardly find a peasant for whom a weather report in Classical Arabic would not be "funny" whether or not he could understand it (Cf. Issue of Jan. 1, 1899). A whole series of new functions and demands were being created during these decades—and the newspaper illustrates a number of these—to which Classical Arabic had to be adapted.

Al-Ahram's variety of columns rapidly increased. The first issue had an untitled editorial in which the founding of the newspaper was announced, along with one titled column called "Various Happenings" (*ḥawaadith mukhtalifa*), in which news of Britain, Austria, Lebanon and Russia were provided. Another column started a series on the history of the Pyramids (*taariikh ahraam al-giiza*). The newspaper was at that time published once a week on Saturdays. Soon other kinds of news and columns followed. In 1880, an issue had a brief column with the heading, "A Joke" ("*nukta,*" al-Ahram 4/15/1880:3). Had Classical Arabic functioned before as a language for telling jokes? For literary satire yes, but for jokes of the kind exchanged in the course of personal interactions it is doubtful. There was a search for personalizing this impersonal language—rendering it congruent to new functions and contexts. Some court cases were reported on, local news (*ḥawaadith daakhiliyya*) acquired its own column, public announcements and advertisements (both called "*i'laan*") publicizing sales of land, opening of translation offices ("from French, Italian and English into Arabic") and new improved train locomotives. Here and there, brief reports of general interest were included: Under the heading "Rare" (*naadira*), a 15-year-old British girl was praised for crossing the English channel. Some issues included a letter from important personalities including sheikhs of al-Azhar, who praised the newspaper for the important service it was providing to the nation. The stock market of Alexandria acquired its own column, and prices of cotton, seeds and beans were reported on, as were exchange rates under the heading "kambio." News from around the world was taken and translated from the *Times, World, L'Independence Belge,* Reuters and "an Italian newspaper."

This chapter attempts to articulate the kinds of problems with form that nonliterary writers confronted. It will explore continuities and changes in language ideology(ies), forms of writing and the implicit and explicit presence of Egyptian Arabic in the elevated space of print. The language situation in Egypt both at present and in the past shares features with those in other parts of the world. At the same time, the choice of a sacred language as the primary material for the development of a contemporary and modern language makes it both different and very complex. As may have been clear by now, my inquiries into some of the implications of this situation have been guided in part by the works of Bakhtin and his circle (Bakhtin 1981, 1986; Voloshinov 1986). Bakhtin's search for the ways in which stable types of speaking and writing develop (which he calls genres) leads to concepts that are particularly apt for my own analytic purposes. For example, he does not rely on formal linguistic differences between ways of speaking (or writing) in order to distinguish between them but on "spheres of human activity" that are related to or give rise to specific usages. The object of analysis is not the language produced by the speaker/writer alone, as though she were "the first" to open her mouth "in the silence of the universe." Instead, in Bakhtin's framework linguistic usages are joint productions of speakers/writers and hearers/readers past and present. And depending on which genres they use, they face various degrees of freedom and constraint. In chapter 2, we looked for spheres of activity in trying to understand the ways in which Classical Arabic is present, used and viewed in the lives of different kinds of people. We saw that the central sphere of activity in which Classical Arabic is used for those who do not regularly read or write is the performance of religious rituals. The genres within those rituals (such as the daily prayers) consist of utterances that are already set. They can only be changed within a very narrow range.

In this chapter, we examine a very different sphere of activity, which is that of newspaper writing. Unlike prayers, those wishing to write for newspapers had no established models to follow. Classical Arabic had rarely been used for such a purpose. Hence, writers both had to create something new and were also constrained by many factors in that creation. This tension was (is) a "struggle" between the "authoritative word" and the "native word" (our "kith and kin"), between "one's own word" and "another's word" or the "alien word": "Our speech, that is, all our utterances (including creative works), is filled with others' words, varying degrees of otherness or varying degrees of "our-own-ness," varying degrees of awareness and detachment" (Ibid: 89). But struggles that are behind concrete linguistic usages are not all equal. If the "other's word" does not belong merely to one's contemporary, but to a divine text, to revered ancestors and to a time when everything was perfect, its appropriation must overcome a number of fundamental contradictions. Recognizing a hierarchy of struggles against the other's word, Voloshinov states:

> [The] grandiose organizing role of the alien word, which always either entered upon the scene with alien force of arms and organization or was found on the scene by the young conqueror-nation of an old and once mighty culture and captivated, from its grave, so to speak, the ideological consciousness of the new-comer nation—this role of the alien word led to its coalescence in the depths of the historical consciousness of nations with the idea of authority, the

idea of power, the idea of holiness, the idea of truth, and dictated that notions about the word be preeminently oriented toward the alien word (Volosinov 1986: 75).

The orientation toward the alien word in Egypt seems to have historically excluded vernacular Arabic as a medium of writing. It was neither holy nor authoritative. Newspaper writers in nineteenth-century Egypt were faced with the task of writing in Classical Arabic in genres and about topics that were new to the language. The decline of written production in that language in the preceding centuries and the existence of Egyptian Arabic as the language of life and social interaction had made Classical Arabic detached from most spheres of activity—it no longer was produced as utterances except within religious rituals and for a very small circle of scholars. Moreover, while every writer inevitably assimilated and appropriated the language to various degrees in the act of writing, its glorified status created obstacles in that process:

> The word in language is half someone else's. It becomes "one's own" only when the speaker populates it with his own intention, his own accent, when he appropriates the word, adopting it to his own semantic and expressive intention. Prior to this moment of appropriation, the word does not exist in a neutral and impersonal language. . . . And not all words for just anyone submit equally easily to this appropriation, to this seizure and transformation into private property: many words stubbornly resist, others remain alien, sound foreign in the mouth of the one who appropriated them and who now speaks them; they cannot be assimilated into his context and fall out of it; it is as if they put themselves in quotation marks against the will of the speaker. *Language is not a neutral medium that passes freely and easily into the private property of the speaker's intentions; it is populated—overpopulated—with the intentions of others. Expropriating it, forcing it to submit to one's own intentions and accents, is a difficult and complicated process.* (Bakhtin 1981: 294, emphasis added)[1]

Classical Arabic was exalted because it was sacred, but the more it would come to be used by an increasing number of writers in contexts that were new to the language the more its sacredness would be diluted. This is particularly true of journalistic writing, which deals necessarily with more mundane matters (as opposed to literature or philosophy) and is carried out under short deadlines. The expansion of contexts would lead inevitably to domains in which Egyptian Arabic had been used for centuries. But this de facto language of contemporary life was ruled out as a medium of writing. There was a historical understanding, accumulated practice, an agreement and an injunction against writing in the spoken language. Therefore, one had to make the written language more natural without slipping into Egyptian Arabic. Yet, if Egyptian Arabic were to be kept out of the space of print then Classical Arabic had to be pulled down, as it were, from its lofty heights. One had to undo the formality and stiffness that was braided into its grammar and lexicon. How does one force a grandiloquent, oratorical and highly literary language to become an *unaffected* medium for reporting on the mundane affairs of the world, for commercial advertisements, for expressions of charged emotions or for seeking help in finding a missing child who had left home to fetch a kilo of grapes, wearing a striped shirt? If the historical and ideological reasons against using Egyptian Arabic in print were not the result of any one group's conscious decisions, that there was a choice to be made became an object of fierce debates among Egyptians that began in the last decades of the nineteenth century and that has continued with various degrees of intensity to the present.

It must be needless to stress that the problem was not that Classical Arabic lacked the means for describing those and hundreds of other matters. On the contrary its extremely rich lexicon, its many genres of poetry, the practice of writing commentaries on previous works which would get published and become books of their own, the great attention paid to grammatical analysis and particularly to the arts of rhetoric (*balaagha*) made it in fact an inexhaustible resource for linguistic experimentation. But the decline in its use in the previous centuries meant that it did not "grow up" with Egypt and its inhabitants. The point bears emphasis. Classical Arabic did not lose its contemporaneity or touch with Egyptian society because it was a language of high culture and religion. Any language that is not spoken for centuries becomes distant and stiff. Had it not seen a decline in use in the centuries preceding the nineteenth, and had education been more widespread, writers in that century would have found a far more agile and suitable form more easily adaptable to their needs. Insofar as Egypt is concerned, the gap between Classical and Egyptian Arabic probably always existed because no form of Arabic had been spoken there before the arrival of the Muslim armies in the seventh century. At the time, Egyptians spoke Coptic and later the form of Arabic that emerged was not Classical Arabic. When in the 1800s, Classical Arabic began to be used by a larger number of people and for diverse purposes, it was already an aloof language, detached as it were from the needs and necessities of lived experience. But it was also not anyone's private property to do with it as they pleased. Making it one's own was and remains a very difficult and complex struggle.

I will argue that the critical and paramount struggle for writers was finding the means to render Classical Arabic into a language of contemporary life. In comparison to Egyptian Arabic, the language had always been considered as far superior in every way, but in this crucial respect, it lacked what the lowly vernacular possessed: contemporaneity. Although contempt for the vernacular as a medium of writing was and continues to be strong (mixing it with Classical Arabic would make the latter impure), it is the cause of important structural influences in that language today. In chapters one and three we posed the question of whether the status of a language as its users' private property is one of the implicit assumptions behind our understanding of a "modern language." To the degree that Egyptian Arabic has acted as a conduit for rendering the classical language both contemporary and more accepting of variation, the latter has quietly become somewhat more of a private property. The specific struggles that we will examine are in the realms of syntactic changes, the ways in which the speech of others are reported in newspapers and lexical borrowings. The first two are mainly struggles between Classical and Egyptian Arabic, while the latter is a struggle with European languages. The major source of examples for this chapter is the al-Ahram newspaper. I have examined issues chosen at random at three to five year intervals, from 1876 to 1996, the time of my last fieldwork. I have paid closer attention and examined more issues published during the first several decades. A number of other newspapers and magazines will also be used as sources.

The Western Family Tree and the Exuberance of Influence

The new functions mentioned at the beginning of this chapter were not new to Egyptians and to their mother tongue but to Classical Arabic. What was new were advances in the sciences and technology that had prompted the creation of specific vocabulary and styles of writing. Many historians speak of Egypt "awakening" to the "modern" world first as a result of Napoleon's invasion in 1798 and then Egypt's colonization by the British beginning in 1882. And the shortcomings of "Arabic" are taken as a direct reflection of Egypt's backwardness. In the mirror of Classical Arabic, they saw Egypt's incapacity to deal with the world created in part by European colonization. But in so far as the many and various communicative needs of Egyptians in the nineteenth century were concerned they did have a language that had in fact grown up with them that, like any other mother tongue, reflected the plurality of its speakers and their communicative needs. Hence, it bears emphasis that the problems of using Classical Arabic to deal with nineteenth-century life in Egypt did not entirely overlap with those of Egypt's inhabitants.

Neither French nor British colonialism prevented Egyptians from writing in their mother tongue. Nor did they directly impose the choice of Classical Arabic. Already before the British took over Egypt the volume of writing in Arabic had increased tremendously. The number of newspapers grew exponentially before and during colonial rule—Hartman's 1899 study cites 168 newspapers, only a few of which were in foreign languages. A comparison of number of books published in the early decades of the 1800s with the later ones also shows a great increase in writing activity in Arabic:

Table 4.1 Number of Books in Arabic Published Since the 1820s

Decade	Number of Books
1820s	105
1830s	358
1840s	404
1850s	443
1860s	1,391
1870s	1,597
1880s	3,021
1890s	3,086
Total	10,405

Source: Nosseir 1990:m

   Although for higher education the British encouraged the use of English, they did not (and probably could not) seek to impose that language at all levels of education. The curricula at the *kuttaabs* were expanded to include subjects other than religious teachings, but both there and at elementary schools the language remained Arabic. In Heyworth-Dunn's 1939 study, republished in 1968, of the history of education in Egypt, we read of three reports prepared variously by Egyptian and British commissions discussing literacy problems. One commission, noting that the graduates of Egyptian schools cannot read or write in Classical Arabic, "declared itself incompetent" and recommended the formation of another committee. The other two suggested the teaching of "vulgar Arabic" as opposed to "Koranic Arabic" as the only solution to the problem. For this and similar reasons, colonial rule was accused by some as desiring to eliminate Classical Arabic by encouraging the writing of the spoken language (Said 1964). But the historical and ideological understandings against the vernacular and for Classical Arabic long predated colonialism. During British colonial rule, much of secondary and professional training was conducted either in French or English (see also Starrett 1998: 31). In this sense as well as others, Classical Arabic was undermined. But there was the problem of the lack of availability of teaching material (e.g., in medicine, chemistry, engineering) and of technical terminology in Arabic. Such needs resulted in many translations and the production of bilingual dictionaries that addressed the lexical needs of specific fields or professions. At the same time, Classical Arabic continued to be the major medium of education for a majority of the population (Heyworth-Dunn 1968).

Colonial rule and its consequences weakened the image of Arabic as a "perfect" language. It continued to be viewed as a "miracle" but also somewhat paradoxically as "backward" in comparison to English and French. Unlike the latter, Arabic was perceived as a language unfit and unequipped for dealing with the modern world, with the progress of science and advances in technology. Writers spoke a language that had contemporaneity (Egyptian Arabic), wished for another that had the easy modernity of European languages, and wrote in one that lacked both but was revered. But the overwhelming political, economic and cultural dominance of colonialism were experienced and interpreted as threats that could not be combated with a language that lacked a civilizational backbone. Their mother tongue was not the language of a large and successful empire that had nurtured countless achievements in the sciences and the humanities, nor one that played any role in the establishment of a world religion. This "weak" language represented Egyptians and other Arabs as though they had achieved little in the course of the past centuries, since there was nothing written in vernacular Arabic to prove otherwise. It would be as though Egypt would choose to represent itself not through its magnificent Pharaonic monuments but through its simple peasant mud huts. For religious and nonreligious intellectuals, Muslims and non-Muslims, Classical Arabic represented a greater hope with which the increasing moral and cultural dominance of European colonialism could be resisted. Here was a language that had ample resources—in the form of grammatical treaties, dictionaries, concordances, towering writers and thinkers and eloquent poets. Why could it not be renewed and rendered capable of dealing with the modern world?

Many linguists and historians seem to believe that that renovation was only possible through changes that came from European languages (Stetkevych 1979, Hittie 1970, Vatikiotis 1991). In fact, the received wisdom is that the sources of most changes in Classical Arabic during these decades are the European languages—especially French and English. Scholar after scholar has attributed actual or perceived changes as being due to the great efforts at translation from foreign languages into Arabic and to Egyptians being sent abroad to study. The great Arabist Jaraslav Stetkevych states that:

> The generic concept of Western languages, as an influencing factor upon Arabic, is therefore not a vague, undisciplined generalization but a linguistic and cultural reality. . . . While retaining the morphological structure of classical Arabic, syntactically and, above all, stylistically it [modern Arabic] is coming

ever closer to the form and spirit of the large, supragenealogical family of Western culture bearing languages. . . . (Stetkevych 1970: 119, 121)

Yet, apart from lexical borrowings and calques,[2] admittedly not unimportant, there are rarely any syntactic preferences or changes that are not already available in Egyptian Arabic. It is as if for such scholars, vernacular Arabic simply did not exist, or was at best, wholly immaterial. Attributing syntactic patterns to "thought habits," Stetkevych finds that as the grammar of Classical Arabic increasingly moves toward European patterns, Arabs also become more European: "The modern Arabic mind [is] . . . an offshoot of the modern Western mind . . . retaining fewer and fewer of the rigidly Semitic thought-habits . . ." (119). He then goes on to imply that "live speech" does not involve "thought":

> The future of the Arabic language will thus not lie in artificial compromises between the two native linguistic sources of classicism and colloquialism, which work against each other, but rather in a straight line of development out of a classical Semitic morphology towards a new, largely non-Semitic syntax which will be dictated by habits of thought rather than habits of live speech. *Only then, in possession of a language by which to think,* will the Arabs be able to overcome the problem of conflicting colloquialism and classicism. (122–123, emphasis added)

Stetkevych seems to believe that Classical Arabic had been at some point a language with which one could "think" but that later it declined, and with the onslaught of European modernity, became outdated. In the interim, the Arabs apparently possessed no language with which they could do any thinking, particularly because the vernaculars are not "culture bearing" as European languages are. The problem is that many Arab intellectuals agree(d) to one degree or another with versions of such a view. They may not have agreed that their mother tongue was not conducive to thinking, nor that all that was happening in their societies came from a "straight line" through Europe. But they did believe that Egyptian Arabic was not a medium for serious writing and creative work generally. There continues to be an agreement on this point. The idea is that Classical Arabic is the repository (*makhzan*) for "knowledge" and "culture." Equally importantly, the recovering of the classical language became intimately tied with the discourses of "progress" and "modernization."

Most Egyptians who wrote at the time knew their mother tongue better or at least as well as another foreign language. Among the upper classes, there were those whose mother tongue was Turkish, but such people did not comprise the majority of writers (and they also spoke Arabic). As education

expanded and newspapers not only hired various people to write and correct for them, but also became social spaces to which "ordinary people"
also wrote and got published, the assumption that knowledge of a European language was shared by all who wrote is not warranted. Syntactically
there are many similarities between Egyptian Arabic and French and English (e.g., in word order and absence of cases, among others). Thus at
best, one can conclude that the sources of syntactic changes are all of
those languages. A study of books published in Egypt during the nineteenth century cites the cumulative total of all books to the end of the
1890s as 10. 405, of which only 7.73 percent were translations (Nosseir
1990). This figure is far lower than one is led to believe by the many historians who have commented on the importance of translations to linguistic change. Certainly quantity alone does not determine degree of
influence, but it does matter. There has been an ideological interest in not
professing the profound actual and potential influences of Egyptian Arabic in the development of a contemporary Classical Arabic. Linguists as
well have exaggerated this influence. In a study of newspaper language in
Egypt, while the author Nabil Abdelfattah finds ample evidence that
changes were coming through the filter of Egyptian Arabic, he repeatedly
attributes them to European languages (1990). The interest to ignore the
influence of Egyptian Arabic is shared, albeit for different reasons, between some Arab and non-Arab scholars. Arab scholars who viewed European influence in a negative light, used linguistic changes as
disheartening proof of the corrupting influence of Europe. Those who
wished for even more Europeanization commended the changes but still
saw them as coming from foreign languages. Non-Arab scholars have also
been keen on propagating, celebrating and hence exaggerating European
influence. A "Europeanized" Classical Arabic was perceived, it seems, as a
necessary step in bringing the Arab world into the welcoming arms of the
modern European family.

Writings on Language

Very early on, linguistic difficulties and disagreements became a topic of a
remarkable number of articles. There was a major concern with the "corruption" of the Arabic language as spoken by many people, lexical borrowings from foreign languages, grammatical and spelling mistakes, the dire
absence of useful books and manuals for teaching and writing correctly, the
quality of education and lack of appropriate teaching material, particularly
for Classical Arabic language classes. In 1882, an article with the title "The
Arabic Language and Success," written by one of al-Ahram's editors, reflects
a number of enduring concerns and quandaries:

Indeed it is the case that the spoken Arabic language has been subject to decay and corruption [*khilal wal-fisaad*], to the extent that one fears the loss of the glorious language of our ancestors [*lughat agdaadina al-sharifa*]. Many words which appear to be Arabic have been subject to distortion and corruption. . . . Many foreign words have entered our speech masking the ability to trace them to any known language. Many Arabs [*abnaa' al-'arab*] when hearing Classical Arabic texts assume they are texts in a strange language [*ghariiba*]. There are many differences and distinctions in the languages of our people and their terms to the extent that each group [*qowm*] or people have their own distinctive language. I shall not hesitate to add that the number of spoken Arabic languages approximates the number of their speakers. Given these conditions, it will not be long before our ancestral language loses its form, God forbid [*laa samah allah*], unless we awaken from our negligence and inattention. (al-Ahram, 1/19/1882: 1–2)

The article goes on to speak of language as the fundamental national [*al-jinsiyya*] bond, which, if weakened, debilitates the nation. It cites another newspaper's suggestion that the spoken language should become the written one [*lugha al-kitaaba*] but disagrees, stating the belief that the spoken language should conform to the written language:

How can *we give permission to ourselves to replace our glorious language* with another when it is the most noble of languages [*ashraf al-lughaat*],[3] the most eloquent in words [*afsah-haa lafzan*], the most elegant in style, and the most conducive to creativity [*badii'an*]. *How can we support a weak [rakiika] spoken language which will eliminate the sacred original language* [*al-lugha al-asiila al-muqaddasa*]. Another noble writer preceded me in pointing out and clarifying these facts. He proved and substantiated the necessity of relying on the Eloquent Arabic Language [*al-lugha al-'arabiyya al-fusha*] which is contained in and transmitted to us through the books of knowledgeable olden writers [*al-afaadiil al-qudamaa*]. There is no doubt that the majority of Arabs [*abnaa' al-'arab*] support this position. . . . It is no surprise that effort and exertion has to be expended. . . . This requires detailed research by literary people [*udabaa'*] since it is the only way to true success. The writer, though aware of his limitations and shortcomings, is not ashamed to dwell on this noble issue. He can only ask for forgiveness if he fails and thank God if he succeeds. (al-Ahram 1/9/1882: 2, emphasis added)

Thus, one could not "permit" oneself to replace the glorious language because the historical constructions of the language did not allow it to be treated as a possession that could just be discarded. This was a perfect language that had to be recovered. And the greatest threat to its "elimination" came primarily, not from the outside, but from the spoken languages. These had to be made, through exertion and effort, to conform to the written language.

This article seems to have been a response to another with exactly the same title that had been published in November 1881 in the then-prominent magazine called *al-Muqtataf*. In that article, the argument had been made that modern sciences should be written in 'ammiyya and that in Egypt, the differences between speaking and writing was a "cause of our being behind [the times]" (*'illat ta'akhurna*). It further had attributed the success of Europeans to studying the sciences (algebra, philosophy and biology) in their own languages (al-Kumi 1992: 212). Another article that advocated writing in 'ammiyya appeared later in the same magazine. Its author had signed his name as "The Possible" (*al-mumkin*), "perhaps due to fears about public opinion" (213). But the "invitation to 'ammiyya,"[4] as such ideas came to be called, caused far more controversy when a British irrigation engineer by the name of William Wilcox joined the fray. He became the editor of a magazine called al-Azhar in 1893. In the same year he organized a conference in which he gave a speech on the merits of writing in 'ammiyya in terms very similar to the earlier article in *al-Muqtataf*. He encouraged the submission of articles by Egyptian engineers in 'ammiyya and announced a competition for the translation of his own speech at the conference into 'ammiyya: "[He] who presents to us this speech in the current language of Egypt, if it [is] very successful, we will give [him] four sterling pounds" (al-Kumi: 214–215). To this day, these and similar stories about Wilcox are mentioned as examples of how the "invitation to 'ammiyya" was an explicit policy of British colonialism to weaken Egyptians and Arabs in general (see al-Qahira #163, 1996: 55).

In 1907, a writer by the name of Khalil al-Khouri wrote an article entitled "The Arabic Language and The Foreign Element" (*al-lugha al-'arabiyya wa al-dakhiil*). It was published on the front page in the editorial column:

> If a writer uses a word not in accordance with the customary rules of language and in violation of the rules of analogy [*al-qiyaas al-lughawi*], he should be not be criticized [*takhta'a*] nor accused of wrong-doing. If he were one of the most eloquent writers we would accept his terminology especially if writers are in need of it. If he violates the standards and improvises [*irtigaal*] the terminology, the general opinion [*al-ra'y al-'aam*] is that this is not allowed to late-comers [*muta'akhir* i.e., modern writers] unless they are well-versed in the language without external foreign influence. . . . Some say that improvisation is impossible for the late-comer. . . . (al-Ahram, 2/28/1907:1)

Contemporary or modern writers[5] (*al-muta'akhiruun*) therefore lacked authority to improvise. The previous article quoted above, cites "*al-qudamaa*" as the source of such authority (the ancient/old scholars)—in opposition to "*al-muta'akhiruun.*" Al-Khouri also echoes the complaint with regard to foreign borrowings. Once it is arabized (*mu' 'arrab*), it becomes difficult to tell whether a word is or is not of foreign origin: "Also the Arabs were not used to recording language and listing foreign terms as was the case among foreigners [*al-faranga*]" and therefore dictionaries cite some words as though they were of Arabic origin when they are not (al-Ahram, 2/28/1907: 1). To substantiate his claim, he provides examples of a few Greek words in current use in Arabic that everyone thinks are Arabic in origin. Settling disputes about the status of a word required the use of dictionaries. But, as the author indicates, this was often not a possibility, which resulted in endless disagreements on word origins.

But the author finds the whole controversy unnecessary because the needs of writers and whether an "improvisation" becomes popular or not should be primary concerns. He reminds his readers that "developed nations" do not worry so much about such matters:

> We do not see that developing modern terms and scientific phrases would be an obstacle to the pursuit of our work if we introduce them at schools. Initially they might appear foreign and different to our tastes and ears, but soon their foreignness will disappear. *This is what developed nations do. They do not stumble at the level of words and terms.* (al-Ahram 2/28/1907: 1, emphasis added)

He goes on to try to convince those who resist foreign borrowings by arguing that what they consider "foreign" is in fact a body of knowledge to which "our ancestors" contributed and therefore it is neither "foreign" nor a "borrowing":

> Now we have no recourse but to seek contemporary sciences [*al-'uluum al-'asriyya*] from Western peoples [*al-umam al-gharbiyya*] because our truths and valuable possessions are dispersed in their lands, protected in their homes. In this search, we are demanding a stolen right and a lost good which the spirit of our ancestors are crying for bringing back and utilizing. . . . The Arab countries from East to West cannot reach this goal without Egypt because Egypt is the bedrock of literary people [*udabaa'*]. . . . Our ancestors cooperated for the sake of science and did not shy away from seeking wisdom from other nations, so what is our excuse today to seek knowledge from a people and follow their steps, especially since the source of their advancement and the origin of the sciences are those of our ancestors who added to their skills and texts of diverse bodies of science from the Greek, the Indians, the Romans, the Syriacs and combined all this in an Arabic frame which is without fault or deficiency. We should go back to how we started. (al-Ahram 2/8/1907: 1)

Of the many published and long running debates on foreign borrowings, this is perhaps one of the most eloquent arguments put forward by an Egyptian intellectual whose exhortation to "go back to how we started" is not a plea for returning to the "pure" and perfect days of the ancestors. The ancestors, he argues, were more concerned with advancement than with purity.

While the author calls for acceptance of improvised words and usages, he goes on to state "But the new usages that contradict the syntax of the language [*tarkiib al-lugha*] should not be allowed at all." Structural, syntactic changes seem to have been deemed as far more serious and fundamental than lexical ones. His article is a programmatic one and among his suggestions, he argues for a change in the kinds of textbooks available:

> We have to start in the schools at all their levels because it is here that the foundations are laid. Through schooling, you read the books and see the shortcomings which bespeak the reasons for the retardation of language. Many schools aspired to using it [the Arabic language] as a medium of instruction, but have confronted many problems which resulted in abandoning it. I do not mean this to include the grammar and rhetoric [*balaagha*] texts. What we are lacking are the science texts of industry, agriculture and literary novels which allow the readers to move from illusion [*wahm*] to truth [*yaqiin*]. . . . What I have noticed of many of our reading text books is an excess of obscurity on the pretext and assumption by the writer that this facilitates comprehension and enlightens the mind. However, this is a mistake we have to avoid by paying attention to the rules of language *and training the students to speak in the fusha language according to their individual capabilities.* There is a need for establishing another committee in charge of summarizing the old texts and presenting them in *contemporary forms [qawaalib 'asriyya]* . . . (emphasis added)

He bemoans "an excess of obscurity" and calls for preparing old texts in "contemporary forms" but it is unclear what exactly that would entail. Presumably, the contents of those texts would remain the same; and if one is not supposed to change the syntax either, how would they be rendered contemporary? Perhaps like many other writers, he believed that an updating of vocabulary alone would suffice. This was in fact a very prevalent view—at the same time as this writer and others in the pages of al-Ahram called for a "simpler" and "clearer" language, and for manuals of correct writing as opposed to the old grammar books, the main focus was always on the lexicon. Additions to and renovations of the lexicon, along with "training students to speak fusha" were seen as the only necessary solutions to the linguistic problems.

But self-expression in the Arabic language continued to be a problem and again, in 1912, in a lengthy editorial article on language, one writer declared that "There will not be any literary person East or West of the earth who can deny the decay that befell our language to the extent that the tongue and pen of the novice among us stutters whenever he wants to express what is on his mind and his heart about this civilization and its secrets" (al-Ahram, 6/7/1912). We will return to language debates later on. What is significant at this stage is that there was clearly more acceptance of foreign borrowings than of writing in Egyptian Arabic. Borrowings would come from "developed nations" and would help Egypt advance. Thus the threat from the vernacular came primarily from its potential influence on the *syntax* of Classical Arabic—precisely what was the least acceptable of all changes.

Local Correspondents: Cracks in the Fortress of the Case System

Al-Ahram like other newspapers provided a social space for an increasing number of people who wanted to communicate their thoughts on a national level. Some readers wrote letters complaining about something that had happened to them that they believed was of general interest. A supervisor (*mulaahidh*) from the province of Daqhaliya wrote to the "Honorable Editor of al-Ahram" in 1907 describing his efforts to convince his son to become a policeman (*kunstabel*). He begins his letter in this way: "I have a son who is eligible to serve at the police academy. I was the first one who urged him to enroll in that school for love of serving the country [*hubban fi khidmat al-watan*]." He goes on to say that some people tried to discourage his son from this service but he was able to overcome their influence. He attempts to persuade his son (and perhaps the reader) with one final argument that touches on the presence of foreign policemen and the language problems this may cause : "Then I told him to look at you my son as a constable on the street is more agreeable to me than seeing an Italian constable who if he called me in the middle of the street, I would not understand what he says" (al-Ahram, 8/2/1907:2). This possibility for "ordinary" Egyptians—in this case a provincial supervisor—to write and be published on a national scale was unprecedented. Far more than the translations of medical or engineering manuals from foreign languages into Classical Arabic, it is this spread of writing—with all the uncertainties of the writer and the evident awkwardness of the language—that simultaneously propagated "Classical Arabic" and brought it closer to the vernacular.

A whole column appeared a few decades after the founding of the newspaper with its own name "Min Zakiibat al-Bariid" ('From the Letter Bag'), in which people wrote to the editors asking various questions and to which the editors responded briefly and often with humor. Another column was introduced that was called "Where art thou going this night" (*ayna satidhhab al-leyla, or ayna tidhhab al-leyla*),[6] where various happenings such as films, concerts and plays were listed. Was there a wish that readers at some point would cease to perceive the sentence and its vocabulary as "formal"? What does it take for "thou" to be read as "you"? In the Arabic example, the verb "*dhahaba*" 'to go' is not one that would be used by any person describing his or her "going" somewhere. In the spoken language, the verb is "*raaḥ*." The point is that Classical Arabic lacks a colloquial style of expression. In any case, as such events began to occupy more space in the newspaper, brief descriptions of singers and actors were given. The names of some musical albums were phrases taken from some songs. Frequently such phrases were in Egyptian Arabic and these would see the light of print without translation.

By the end of the second month of operation, al-Ahram had its own correspondents sent to different parts of Egypt and, less frequently, to other parts of the Arab world. It is one thing to *translate* news releases from, say, Reuters or some other news agency and quite another to have Egyptian correspondents write their own reports. Did they translate what they eyewitnessed and what others told them into Classical Arabic before filing their reports? Did they get "corrected" and copyedited? If so, who where the correctors and what kinds of education did they have? The correspondents of al-Ahram who were sent to various locations at times wrote back reports in which they approached their topics through a description of their own activities. They referred to themselves, where they had gone, what they had seen, and to whom they had spoken. In such descriptions, the syntax and lexicon of Egyptian Arabic are more frequently present than in other kinds of writing. This was probably both a conscious and an unconscious move on the part of the writers. In April 1889, a correspondent was sent to the province of Munufiyya and, from his report, it appears that he (almost for sure a "he") was interested in its local administration and state of agriculture:

1. wa 'inni aqtaṣir fii haadhihi al-risaala 'alaa sharḥ ḥaalat bandar munuuf al-ladhi waṣaltu
And I summarize in this the-letter on the description of situation port munuuf that arrived (I)

ilayhi li'an haadha al-bandar min ahamm al-bilaad
to it because this the-port of most important towns

'And I limit myself in this letter to the description of the situation of Munuf Port to which I came because this is one of the most important towns (locations)'. (al-Ahram 4/20/1889:65[7])

The canonical word order of Classical Arabic is verb-subject-object (VSO) and in fact most sentences in most articles in al-Ahram had this construction. Moreover, in the majority of cases, when it comes to writing, the verb that begins the sentence is in third person singular, e.g., "Went to London today the Minister of," "Met today in the parliament members of," and so on. The sentence above could have been written with that word order, or with other more classical syntactic constructions. But it has the canonical word order of Egyptian Arabic (and other vernaculars), namely, subject-verb-object (SOV); and its subject is "I"—the author of the report—a rather rare co-occurrence of the most personal pronoun of all, "I," followed by a sentence in Classical Arabic. Note that this "I" is not an illustrious poet, theologian or mathematician, but a far more "ordinary" individual whom no one has heard of.

At times, the syntax of some sentences used elements that are either more common to Egyptian Arabic, or would be considered "bad" Classical Arabic. In June 1900, a reporter was sent to Sanbalaawin, a port in the Delta. He begins his report in this way:

2. haadhihi hiya al-marra al-'uulaa allati zurtu fiiha haadha al-bandar fa-wa-jadtu(hu) baladan
this (is) the time the first that (I) visited in it this the port and found it town

> ṭayyibat al-hawaa' wa al-shuruuṭ al-ṣiḥḥiyya fiiha mutawaffira wa akhlaaq 'ahlahaa
> good of weather and the conditions of health in it plenty and temperament residents-its

> fii muntahaa al-riqqa . . ."
> in maximum gentility

'This is the first time I visited this port and I found its weather good and conditions for health plenty and the temperament of its people of utmost gentility.' (al-Ahram, 6/13/1900: 1)

This sentence has both syntactic elements and an idiomatic expression borrowed from Egyptian Arabic. These features provide it with a more vernacular rhythm. For example, after "*haadhihi*" 'this' at the beginning of the sentence, there would not normally be any pronoun acting as a copula (the verb 'to be') in Classical Arabic: "*hiya*" (lit: 'she'). The presence of that pronoun in that function is, on the other hand, very common in Egyptian Arabic. Similarly, the verb "*zaara*," 'to visit' does not normally take the preposition "fii," 'in' in Classical Arabic but it does in Egyptian Arabic. The very last phrase, "*wa akhlaaq 'ahlahaa fii muntahaa al-riqqa*," contains the very current idiomatic expression "*fii muntahaa al-riqqa*," 'in utmost gentility/refinement' that is still in use today (where "riqqa" would be pronounced with a double glottal stop and not with /q/).

As can be gleaned from the examples cited from correspondents' reports, in such usages, it is difficult to completely keep out either the syntax or the lexicon of Egyptian Arabic. And yet, many chose to write in more impersonal ways and without preambles. In fact in the same issue as the one containing the second example sentence above, another correspondent sent to Alexandria wrote in this manner:

3. ḥadatha qabl ẓuhr al-yawm ḥaaditha haa'ila wa dhaalik 'an al-saqf al-hadiidi
Happened before noon today accident terrifying and that on the roof the iron

fi warshat al-sikak al-ḥadiidiyya . . .
in workshop of roads the iron (al-Ahram, 6/13/1900: 1)

'Happened before noon today a terrifying accident and that (was) on the iron roof of the railroads workshop'

Thus it is not the case that such contexts, purposes, "one's intentions," topics and so on *necessarily* lead to the use of elements or syntactic constructions belonging to Egyptian Arabic. But they provide sites where the use of a language that is less aloof to the individual and his or her *habits of description and narration* are more difficult to suppress. Each writer faced a number of simultaneous struggles: adapting the language to one's needs, the commitment to its preservation, but also the image of self he would like to project and the degree of knowledge and mastery of the language. One had to prove oneself as a writer. And if at that time, newspaper writers were corrected by correctors, most probably the latter were trained by religious institutions because they alone were producing graduates with specializations in Classical Arabic. This was perhaps another kind of struggle that some of these writers faced.

Although the language of editorials is often far more careful and bookish than other columns, the editors at times wrote parts of their columns in forms that are close to dialogues—referring to themselves, readers, what they had already discussed in previous issues and so on. Dialogue is the site par excellence for the use of Egyptian Arabic because it was and is the de facto language of social interaction. Under the heading "The Cultivation of Cotton," one editorial column begins with:

4. mawḍuu' qulnaa fii kalimatina wa 'arafaha al-qurraa'
topic said-we in word-our and found-it out the readers

'The topic we gave our opinion on and readers got to know it' (al-Ahram 3/24/1900: 1).

Or, another column written by the editors under the subheading "Governmental Rights" (huquuq al-dowliyya) starts with:

5. takallamnaa 'alaa haadhihi al-mas'ala fii 'adad 'ams wa qulnaa 'inna al-ingiliiz
(We) talked on this the problem in issue yesterday and said that the English

qabaḍuu 'alaa arba'aṭi bawaaxir amrikiyya . . .
arrested four steamships American

'(We) talked about this problem in yesterday's issue and said that the English arrested four American steamships' (al-Ahram 1/3/1900: 1)

Both of these sentences have a rather informal style because of their Egyptian Arabic word order. The first one has the decidedly vernacular expression *"qulna fii"* (lit: 'said in', i.e., 'talked about'). The second sentence has the preposition *'alaa* (on, about) following the verb *"takallamna,"* whereas in Egyptian Arabic, it would be *'an* (on, about). In addition, the form of the verb would be *"itkallimna."* Otherwise the structure and most words are close to or the same as in Egyptian Arabic.

The fact that newspapers wrote for large audiences, needed for direct and up-to-date language, employed writers that were not literary personalities and provided narrative sites that promoted the use of Egyptian Arabic all contributed to the emergence of sentence structures that relied less on the case system and more on word order. That is, sentence structures became closer to Egyptian Arabic and the use of more familiar and current vocabulary increased. In today's journalistic writings, we find side by side, depending on the kind of newspaper, column, writer and expected readership, both kinds of word order. More generally, we find syntax that is closer to or farther away from Egyptian Arabic. Often in the same article, we find both so that there is not always a consistency to the style of writing. Two studies have carried out statistical analyses of word order in newspapers and their results are useful to examine. Parkinson (1981) found the following distribution:

Table 4.2 Egyptian Sentence Structure (subject-verb-object) in:

Front page news	5%
Middle page news	15%
Editorials	39%
Short stories	39%
Political speeches	48%
Headlines	92%

Source: Parkinson 1981: 28–30

In all categories save "Headlines," the Egyptian Arabic word order is used less than 50 percent of the time. Abdelfattah compares the frequency of subject-verb-object (SVO) sentences (Egyptian Arabic word order) in issues of al-Ahram from 1935 and those published in 1989.

Table 4.3 Comparison of SVO Word Order in Percentages

Category	1935	1989
Straight news	15	6.4
Editorials	32	43
Society	17.5	41
Sports	29	37
Women	n/a	49.5

Source: Abdelfattah 1990: 76

In all but "Straight News," the use of Egyptian sentence structure has increased. This confirms my argument that the native language has a decided influence and is difficult to fully suppress. Nevertheless, that structure is still not dominant. Changes have taken place but they are not uniform nor permanent. They are clearly held in check through a variety of means. Depending on the writer, the kind of publication, the topic and so on, Egyptian and/or Classical word order are used equally or with one dominating the other. One of the most crucial repercussions of a change in word order would be that the case system could be quietly dispensed with. Were sentences to have the SVO word order of Egyptian Arabic, the need for identifying which noun is in the nominative case (and therefore the subject) and which is in the accusative would disappear. This identification is in fact discussed to this day (among others by the correctors I interviewed) as a difficult task for the average reader. Recall that such cases are short vowels that are mostly *not* indicated orthographically—hence it is up to the reader's level of knowledge of the language. And many sentences are longer than just those three parts of speech containing adjectives, other nouns, genitive phrases and so on—let alone some stylistic embellishments—all of which make its correct interpretation a difficult task for many people. However, attempting in as much as possible, to construct sentences with word orders closer to those of Egyptian Arabic would make that task far easier. And with that word order the vocalic cases could still be claimed to be there for those who were missing them.

The Role of the Reader

The influence of Egyptian on Classical Arabic is nowhere more directly apparent as in phonology. This is in fact the case with the influence of almost all vernaculars on Classical Arabic. When an Egyptian or Lebanese reads Classical Arabic out loud (for example in news broadcasts), the hearer can immediately tell where the speaker is from. The reason is that unless the speaker makes a very special effort (depending on the occasion), Classical Arabic is most often read with the phonology of Egyptian Arabic. It is like reading a language with an accent that belongs to another language. Long before the 1800s, Egyptian Arabic showed a number of phonological divergences from Classical Arabic. Some of these are shown in the table below:

Classical Arabic	*Egyptian Arabic*
[j] /wajad/	[g] /wagad/
[th] /ḥadiith/	[s, t] /ḥadiis/
[q] /qahwa/	['] (glottal stop) /'ahwa/

When Egyptians read (and less frequently speak) "Classical Arabic," it is acceptable to pronounce the [j] as [g]. The grapheme (symbol) representing these two phonemes in writing is the same—both are written with the same symbol. Therefore, in sentence 2 above, the verb 'find' in Classical Arabic would be pronounced with a [j], (*wajad*) while if read with Egyptian Arabic phonology, it would have a [g]. This is not as strange as it might at first appear to readers of European languages: In most languages, the same letter can be read (pronounced) in a variety of different ways. In English, the letter 't' is pronounced differently depending on whether it occurs at the beginning of a word (e.g, teacher) or in between two vowels (e.g, water), but one uses the same symbol for both. Or one writes "night" but reads "nait" or "nite" due to sound changes that have occurred in the English sound system.[8] In the table above, the change from [th] to [s] is also an acceptable pronunciation while reading in Classical Arabic (e.g., hadiis instead of hadiith). The most unacceptable one is the last. That is, all [q]'s must be pronounced as such. It is likely that if a sentence has a word order close to or the same as Egyptian Arabic, and if it contains cognates, readers would read such portions of the text through the filter of their mother tongue's phonology.

An oral version of Classical Arabic with such features (somewhat Egyptianized) became widespread through radio broadcasts in the early decades of the twentieth century. The founding of the pan-Arab radio station "*sowt al-'arab*" ("The Arab Voice") and the broadcasting of the speeches of such powerful figures as Abdel Nasser in the 1950s—speeches that were mostly in Classical Arabic and that made very effective and strategic switches to Egyptian Arabic[9]—helped create an oral version of this language that varied in the degree of its adherence to the phonological and syntactic rules of the language.

Struggles to make Classical Arabic a more natural language of contemporary life have resulted in the less consistent reliance on the case system. This is the most major "change" that the language has seen, which is a direct influence from all forms of vernacular Arabic—none have a case system. This is accompanied by other linguistic transformations that take place in the act of reading and the spread of nonprint media in which the status of Egyptian Arabic has been elevated, as it has come to dominate most of the programs. Newspaper language contains also many foreign lexical items, particularly borrowings from English that have been on the rise in the last few decades.

Ways of Reporting Speech: Negotiating Boundaries between Egyptian and Classical Arabic

Newspapers are in the business of representations—representations of themselves as institutions, of the nation, of the government and of the people they report on. So much of "news" consists of what others have said, suggested, implied and so on. Regardless of what happens and in what domain—international politics or gossip about famous personalities—different people say things about what has happened or what someone else has said. Therefore, the news media are centrally involved with the reporting of the speech of others. How was this speech handled in newspapers? How were the boundaries between Egyptian and Classical Arabic negotiated? Assuming safely that most Egyptians regardless of education or class spoke varieties of Egyptian Arabic, was their speech quoted without changes? Was it allowed to get close to the elevated language of the one doing the reporting? Examples of reported speech show the difficulties in accommodating, at one and the same time, incompatible, paradoxical and ambivalent ideologies with regard to both languages, their relationships to culture and "Culture" and to the writers' past and present. Of the variety of struggles reflected in the language of newspapers, ways of reporting the speech of others show both a remarkable consistency across decades and some interesting changes. In his landmark study of reported speech, Voloshinov (1986: 123) writes "We would even venture to say that in the forms by which language registers the impressions of received speech and of the speaker the history of the changing types of socioideological communication stands out in particularly bold relief."[10] We will examine examples of various kinds of reported speech below in order to gain insights into how the two languages and the boundaries between them came to be viewed.

Both in writing and in oral exchanges, a number of formulas that I call "distancing frames" are used to keep the Classical Arabic of the Qur'an separate from any other form of speech. For example, a quote from the Qur'an is often preceded by a distancing frame such as "*qaala allahu ta'aala*" ("Said the Supreme God"). This is then followed by some quotation from the Qur'an. After finishing the quotation, there are other formulas again to distance it from the stream of other forms of speech, e.g., "*sadaqa allahu al-'aziim*" ("the Great God spoke the truth"). Such frames are often more elaborate in print and aided by calligraphic quotation marks that are exclusively used for the holy book. Such practices have been followed for centuries, though the zeal with which quotations from the Qur'an are set apart has varied in different political climates. In nonreligious writings from the 1940s and 50s, one can find examples of quotations without diacritics and calligraphic symbols. At present, particularly in newspapers, such examples are far more infrequent.

As far as the speech of others was concerned, the most prevalent way newspapers adopted for reporting the speech of others was to translate into Classical Arabic. This was the case whether the speech translated was originally in some Arabic vernacular, or in any of the foreign languages belonging to the rest of the world. This is still the central practice in journalism—what others say gets translated into the accepted medium of print. As such, the content of what is said is taken into account—not the how but the what (Voloshinov: 120). Individuals of diverse backgrounds whose different manners of speech is a central part of their identities get represented as though they all spoke some form of Classical Arabic. A language that is not spoken but treated as though it were does not evoke specific flesh-and-blood individuals. But readers know that the individuals reported on do not speak like that, and so do the writers. Therefore, the absolute majority of cases of reported speech in newspapers to this day is carried out through *indirect* reporting. That is, what is said is reported on indirectly where indicators of the original utterance's time and person are changed by the reporter or the reporting utterance.[11] A study of Moroccan newspapers also found a preponderance of indirect reporting (Fakhri 1998). Let us look at a number of examples of indirect discourse. The general pattern is to use a "verb of saying" (e.g, say, declare, announce, state, etc.) followed by "'inna" ("that") or one of its variants, followed by the reported sentence:

Al-Ahram 8/5/1876: 3

6. fa *ajaaba'anna* faransaa laa tatadakhal fi'liiyan bil-ḥawaadith al-ḥaaṣila . . .
[subject of verb: a French politician]
'And [the French politician] responded that France does not actually intervene in the events that have happened . . . '

7. wa *qaala* ba'duhum '*inna* al-haram al-'adhiim . . . [subject of verb: scholars of the Pyramids]
'And said some [of the scholars] that the great Pyramids. . . . '

Al-Ahram 2/7/1900: 1

8. *qaala* muraasil gariidat al-istandard fi baaris '*inna* al-khiṭṭa allati. . . . [subject of verb: the correspondent of the newspaper *Standard*]
'Said the correspondent of the newspaper Standard in Paris that the path that . . . '

9. fa *qaala* lahu (luh) '*inna* al-ingliiz yastahiqquun laqab "sallaabiin wa luṣuuṣ wa quṭaa' turuq" wa ta'ajjaba min duwal 'urubba kayfa lam tataḥaalaf 'alaa in-gilterra [subject: a Dr. Lids, who sent a letter to al-Ahram from Berlin describing a conversation he had had with someone]. 'And [Dr. Lids] said to him that the English deserve the title "plunderers and thieves and road robbers" and [was] surprised that European governments do not band together against Britain . . . '

Al-Ahram 7/16/1912: 1

10. wa alladhiina ya'rifuunahu yaquuluun '*inna*hu kaana al-ajdar bihi . . . [subject: "those who know Mahmoud Showkat Basha" Minister of War]
'And t[hose] who know him say that he was trustworthy . . . '

11. wa la-rubbama qaala al-qaa'iluun '*inna* tilka ḥaajat maḍat [subject: "the sayers," i.e., those who talk]
'And perhaps some said that this was a thing of the past . . . '

Al-Ahram 2/22/1920: 4

12. *qaalat* jariidat al-taimz '*innahu* yaẓhar al'aan 'anna . . . [subject: the *Times* newspaper]
'Said the *Times* newspaper that now it appears that . . . '

Al-Ahram, 9/26/1940: 1

13. fa qaala '*inn* al-ḥarb hiya allatii [subject: an Egyptian politician]
'And said that the war is what . . . '

The practice of translation and the overwhelming numerical dominance of indirect reporting continue to the present, with the same linguistic means. It matters little whether the entity to which the speech is attributed is a person or a news agency or a government organization. It also matters little whether the person is a foreigner or a local. There is little point in providing more examples from the period between 1940 and 1995–96—the time of my last research. Insofar as indirect discourse is concerned, not much has changed:

14. yaquul al-duktoor abu farḥa *'inna* al-mutakhaṣṣiṣiin . . . [al-Ahram 5/10/96: 11]
'Says Dr. Abu Farha that the specialists . . . '

15. yaquul qaaḍi madiinat manchester alladhi samaḥa li-baaraat al-madiina bi-fatḥ 'abwaabiha . . . *'inna* . . . [al-Ahram, 6/12/96: 17]

'Says the judge of the city of Manchester who allowed the bars of the city to open their doors that . . . '

But, as we just noted, both the translation into Classical Arabic and the implications and outcome of indirect reporting result in a stilted and affected language: "The analytical tendency of indirect discourse is manifested by the fact that all the emotive-affective features of speech, in so far as they are expressed not in the content but in the *form* of a message, do not pass intact into indirect discourse. They are translated from form into content . . ." (Voloshinov 1986: 128, emphasis added). So there is a double operation of "depersonalization": translation (sometimes from "Arabic" into "Arabic") and indirection. This is also what Voloshinov calls the "referent-analyzing" mode of reported speech as opposed to "texture-analyzing" (130). Personalizing the written language, carried out at times very consciously and at times not, clashed with the constraint of keeping Egyptian Arabic or at least blatant forms of it out of the space of print. In indirect discourse, the myriad problems of boundary negotiation are bypassed. Such a strategy does save space and in that sense is more economical. But it also avoids the problems of the proximity, juxtaposition or intermingling of the two languages. I believe this is a central reason for its numerical preponderance.[12]

There are, however, some changes that can be seen in newspapers from 1996—ways of reporting speech that probably only began to be used in the 1970s and 80s. One significant change has to do with translating the other's speech into Classical Arabic but quoting it as *direct speech*. That is, the references of the original utterance to time and person are left unchanged and no "inna" is used after the verb of saying. Moreover, the colon is used to signal direct speech:

16. wa qaala muḥammad ragab:
And said Muhmmad Ragab
laa yumkin 'an takuun hunaak fagwa bayn al-maglis wa al-ṣaḥaafa allatii . . .

not possible for be there divide between the parliament and the press which . . .

'and said Muhmmad Ragab: there should not be a divide between the parliament and the press which . . . ' (al-Ahram, 6/9/1996: 13)

17. wa taḥaddatha muṣṭafa kaamil muraad fa-qaala: 'agibtu li 'amr haadha al-qaanuun
And discussed Mustafa Kamil Murad and said: (I) was surprised about the matter this law

'And engaging (in the debate) Mustafa Kamil Murad said: I was surprised about this law' (al-Ahram, 6/9/1996: 13)

Unlike the examples of indirect speech where no claim is made that the words are exactly those of the person being quoted, this kind of reported speech does make that claim. It is not that in this moment in time no one ever actually speaks in Classical Arabic but the circumstances under which the use of that language for social interaction are acceptable are still quite limited. It is likely that in fact the two individuals quoted above did speak exactly the words attributed to them, but the overwhelming preponderance of both direct and indirect speech in Classical Arabic shows that al-Ahram and most other newspapers continue to routinely translate what others have said.

Who Can Say Things in Egyptian Arabic in Print?

What happens when interviews with famous personalities are carried out, or press conferences and other important meetings must be reported on? Newspapers had to devise ways of representing the speech of different people in ways that were plausible and congruent to their status. That is, the language attributed to various figures had to show some differentiation that would reflect individual hierarchies. But because no one normally speaks Classical Arabic devising ways of differentiation is difficult. And since Egyptian Arabic is officially viewed as lacking in status, it is treated also as monolithic, lacking in stylistic resources that would show hierarchies of class, education and so on (Haeri 1996). Of course, like any mother tongue, Egyptian Arabic shows precisely that kind of real-life differentiation. It has been spoken for centuries and its urban variety spoken in cosmopolitan Cairo enjoys both national and regional prestige. Still, most prominent personalities cannot be represented as having spoken in that language. One solution to the problem can be explored in comparing the representation of the words of four famous personalities: the president of Egypt, the novelist Naguib Mahfouz, the famous international actor Omar Sharif, and the most popular and prolific Egyptian comedian Adel Imam.

In a three hour televised meeting with writers and intellectuals in 1996 (mentioned briefly in chapter three), the president of Egypt stood behind a podium and answered questions on privatization, the general economic status of the country, industrial production, press freedom, Islamist opposition groups, relations between Egypt and other Arab countries and so on. Participants who were themselves respected personalities would stand up and politely pose their questions in a rather solemn Classical Arabic. The president, however, responded almost entirely in a very jaunty and informal Egyptian Arabic whose juxtaposition to the Classical Arabic of the questioner was particularly striking. There were no more than a handful of brief phrases in Classical Arabic that were used by the president. The next day, al-Ahram (as well as other newspapers) reported on the meeting extensively on its front page. Every time the president was quoted, the quotation was in Classical Arabic. In the entire article, al-Ahram did not attribute one word, phrase or sentence to him that was in Egyptian Arabic. Every paragraph and almost every sentence starts with the by now established journalistic practice of beginning with a verb in third person singular past, e.g., "Announced" "Said" "Reassured" "Emphasized" and so on (which strongly marks a sentence as belonging to Classical Arabic) followed by the subject *al-ra'iis* "the president." The translation, which also contains several examples of indirect discourse, is at points so different from the original that it is difficult to match with the written transcript of the session (which I had watched and tape-recorded). One of the closest matches arrives, not surprisingly, when the president uses a phrase in Classical Arabic embedded in a sentence that begins in Egyptian Arabic:

President: da ihna nihmid rabbina bi-kul haazihi il-zuruuf il-sa'ba . . .
'why we thank our God (rabbina) that with all these difficult circumstances . . . '

Al-Ahram: wa qaala al-ra'iis: wa nihmad allah 'anna(hu) bi-kul haadhihi al-zuruuf al-s'aba . . .
'And said the President: and we thank God (allah) that with all these difficult circumstances . . . '

In the original, the demonstrative "*da*" ('this') is used idiomatically to add emphasis. This is only done in Egyptian Arabic and therefore it is sliced out, as is the pronoun "*ihna*," which is "*nahnu*" in Classical Arabic. The word "allah" replaces "*rabbina*" (lit: God-our) because the latter is perceived to be too vernacular. And the Classical Arabic relativizer "that" is added to make the sentence even more distant from Egyptian Arabic.[13] There are very few sentences that are word-for-word translations. Here is another example of a translation that comes a bit close to the original:

President: ana ḥariis ʿalaa ḥurriyyat il-ṣaḥaafa . . . bass ana ʿaayiz il-ḥurriya il-mas'uula . . .
'I am desirous of the freedom of the press . . . but I want responsible freedom . . . '

Al-Ahram: wa ḥowl ḥuriyyat al-ṣaḥaafa qaala al-ra'iis mubaarak: 'innani maʿa ḥuriyyat al-ṣaḥaafa . . . walaakan ḥaadhihi ḥurriyya taltazim bil-dastuur wa taḥtarim al-qaanuun . . .
'And on freedom of the press said President Mubarak: That I am for freedom of the press however this freedom must be mindful of the Constitution and respectful of the law . . . '

In any case, the president, who spoke almost entirely in Egyptian Arabic, comes across as not having uttered a word in that language. Yet, almost everyone, even those who did not watch this particular program, knows that unless he delivers written speeches, the president speaks in Egyptian Arabic almost exclusively. Who then is the translation meant for? Voloshinov argues that reported speech always assumes the existence of a third party in addition to the author and the one whose speech is reported—the reader or the hearer. So perhaps that translation is meant for other Arabs—serving the cause of pan-Arabism—and the rest of the world. If it is also meant for Egyptians, as is possible, then it seems that a national game of representation is taking place in which everyone knows the secret but pretends not to. It could be argued, as is routinely done, that books and newspapers in one "dialect" would not be understood anywhere else in the Arab world; hence the need for Classical Arabic. However, this seems to be far less of a problem when Egyptian movies and television series are exported—although even here at times subtitles in Classical Arabic are used. On the other hand, one may ask whether all print media are addressed to non-Egyptian Arabs and whether this choice only has to do with communicative needs, as this very prevalent explanation implies. But if this choice simply had to do with such needs, why is a language used in which only a minority is proficient?

In order to find variations in the ways in which reported speech is handled we have to look beyond al-Ahram. Compared to other newspapers and magazines, it allows the least use of Egyptian Arabic—a significant statement by a semi-official organ of the government (though these days a few advertisements with brief phrases in Egyptian Arabic are published). The other three interviews mentioned above were published by the popular weekly magazine *Rose il-Yussef* (founded in 1925). Two of the correctors discussed in chapter 3 worked for this magazine. *Rose il-Yussef* is a very glossy magazine, full of color advertising, and by many accounts it has become more sensationalist over the years. It is staunchly anti-religious and frequently has photos of scantily clad foreign female actresses and models on its cover, in its efforts to combat religion. However, it also covers most hot political issues extensively and has a number of respected intellectuals who write for it regularly. We turn first to an interview with Naguib Mahfouz (April 29, 1996: 40–42). It is entitled "I and the Copts" (*ana wal-aqbaat*) and is characterized in the running headline as a conversation (*ḥiwaar*). In the article, Mahfouz is asked to discuss his recent attempted assassination by *"al-irhaab"* "terrorism," his milieu when he was growing up and his views on the emergence of "religious orthodoxy/fanaticism" (*al-taʿṣṣub al-diini*), on Copt-Muslim relations, democracy, Arabism and so on. The interview covers three 8 x 11 pages and has a few small pictures. Hamid, the corrector who was introduced in chapter 3, told me that this interview was in Egyptian Arabic. Again, however, it appears as a translation in the magazine. Still, here and there, interspersed throughout the article there are phrases in Egyptian Arabic attributed to the novelist. Here are the examples of the six phrases that I could find:

naas rafḍiin al-mugtamaʿ	'people rejecting the society'
nisaq fii miin?	'who should we trust'?
eeh illi biyiḥṣal da?	'what is that happening'?
wa geeh min een?	'and where did it come from'?
wa izzayy?	'and how'?
zayy il-wabuur	'like the train'

In comparison to the president of the country, the widely respected and famous novelist can be represented as having spoken a few brief phrases in his mother tongue, although as a writer who has spent his whole life writing in Classical Arabic he probably knows the language far better than the president. Still, most of the interview is in Classical Arabic, alternating between a style that is as close to dialogue as one can get in that language (like a more faithful translation of the original) and phrases in very formal Classical Arabic (e.g., *fa maadha sanatafawuḍ ʾaydan*).

The third interview we will examine is with the famous Egyptian actor Omar Sharif (January 15, 1996: 62–63), who played most memorably in *Dr. Zhivago* and *Lawrence of Arabia*. Hamid told me that the interview was conducted in Egyptian Arabic (both journalist and actor spoke in Egyptian Arabic) in Austria by a Coptic journalist. Later, someone at the magazine listened to the recording, chose certain sections and translated them on paper into Classical Arabic. Next this piece was submitted to a typist who typed it on a word processor. The typed version was submitted to a corrector. The final version was handed over to the editor. The interview is less than one page and begins with a question about the actor's illegitimate son by an Italian journalist and moves on to similar topics. Before analyzing the language of this piece, it is necessary to gain a better understanding of the attempts that pioneered this kind of writing. In the context of the *Nahda* movement, the writing of fiction (short stories, plays and novels) confronted writers with the question of how to handle dialogue. Some chose to write their dialogues in Egyptian Arabic whose sight in print caused great uproar. Many writers wanted to write on matters that did not involve dialogue and yet they wished for a larger audience and a "simpler" language. Of the many efforts at simplification (*tabsiit*), the most significant seems to have been pioneered by Abdullah Nadim (1845–1896) who was a controversial journalist, satirist and reformer (Chejne 1969: 90). He founded two journals, one called *al-Tabkit wal-Tankit* (1881) and the other *Majallat al-Ustad* (1892). He began by writing in "ornate prose" and became increasingly dissatisfied with its various limitations. He then set out to write in such a way that "the learned would not despise and the ignorant will not need to have interpreted" (in Cachia 1990: 48). To describe how he translated this aim into a new kind of prose, the linguistic categories of "function words" versus "lexical words" (also referred to as "closed class" and "open class" items) will help. Function words have a largely grammatical role (prepositions, articles, pronouns, etc.). Lexical words are those that also have a semantic content, like nouns, verbs, adjectives and so on.

The genealogical relation between Classical and Egyptian Arabic made it possible for Abdullah Nadim to take maximum advantage of cognates—lexical items shared between Egyptian and Classical Arabic. But the two languages also share some function words. Given that it is in the area of syntax where the bridging of the two is the most difficult, if one could construct sentences solely or largely with the aid of *shared* function words and cognates, the resulting prose would be the biggest reconciliation that any writer could hope for. It would then be up to the reader to read the text either in Classical or in Egyptian Arabic. Of course at times a cognate in Egyptian Arabic might not be in current use or it might have a different meaning, and the many structural differences between the two languages do not allow easy resolutions through shared function words.

Returning now to the interview, we note first that unlike in the interview with the novelist, phrases in Egyptian Arabic are here put in quotation marks. So one reads the actor speaking in Classical Arabic, and then a quotation mark appears with Egyptian Arabic inside. There are five such quotations. The section that is particularly interesting for our purposes is a rather long answer that can be read in either language:

Interviewer: It is clear that Omar Sharif is a very moody person!
Omar Sharif (in Egyptian Arabic): na'am ana mizaagi *g*iddan . . . *læw* 'umt *min* il-nowm *wa* sinna *min* asnaani tu'lim*ni* "*ab'a mish 'aawiz ashuuf ḥadd*"

Yes I'm very moody . . . if I woke up from sleep and one of my teeth were hurting "then I don't want to see anyone"

The phrase in quotation marks is entirely in Egyptian Arabic and cannot be read any other way.

Omar Sharif (in "Classical Arabic"): na'am ana mizaaji *j*iddan [or mizaagi giddan] . . . læw *q*umt min
*a*l-nowm wa sinna min asnaani tu'lim*a*ni "*ab'a mish 'aawiz 'ashuuf ḥadd*"

Words that are italicized are shared function words. Boldface and italics together indicate Egyptian Arabic only. Note that text regulators are playing a little game with the reader. They put the last phrase in quotation marks to signal that what is inside it is Egyptian Arabic, as though what is outside is indisputably *not* Egyptian Arabic. As Magdi (the second corrector, introduced in chapter 3) had explained to me, where the translation into Classical Arabic would lose the "feel" of the original, he normally chooses to leave the phrase or word untranslated but puts quotation marks around it. In the case of this phrase, there are no cognates and, had the verbs "want" and "see" been rendered in Classical Arabic, Omar Sharif would have ended up sounding more like a preacher or a scholar; more like one, that is, than would be judged warranted by text regulators. Such examples show a maximum blurring of boundaries between Egyptian Arabic and Classical Arabic.

We turn finally to our last example—an interview with Adel Imam whose popularity as a comedian is unparalleled (March 11, 1996: 63–65). This interview is supposed to give Imam a chance to defend himself against accusations that he had advocated artistic exchanges with Israel. The four line running headline is in Classical Arabic: "We are not in need of presenting this conversation with Adel Imam . . . but we only say that it is his right, our right and your right to clarify (for him) . . . what transpired around his comments at the Book Fair. . . ." The questions posed to the actor are in Classical Arabic, but all his answers are in Egyptian Arabic—perhaps edited but not translated. In fact, in this interview one has to search with a fine comb tooth for any phrases in *Classical* Arabic. I found five:

lam tad'uu 'alaa maa'ida al-mufawiḍaat	'I did not invite anyone to the negotating table'
ana lastu siyasiyyan muḥtarifan	'I am not a professional politician'
wa lan ad'uu hadd	'and I will not invite anyone'

laa aṭlub shay'an   'I don't ask for anything'
inta la tastatii' 'an   'you can't order anyone'
tu'mur ḥadd

Other than these five phrases, the entire two-page interview represents the actor's words in Egyptian Arabic. The juxtaposition of the language of the questions and the answers is again remarkable. These four examples of reported speech show a definite hierarchy. The president of the country is not supposed to utter a word in the vernacular, the novelist a few more, the actor who has not lived in Egypt for most of his life and is considered somewhat aloof and Westernized can be represented as speaking both. And it would probably be too much to represent the comedian as speaking anything other than his mother tongue, not only because that is how everyone knows him from movies and the media but also because it seems to be judged as appropriate for a comedian *not* to speak in Classical Arabic. What this examination of newspaper prose shows is that things have both changed and remained the same. They have changed in that here and there a full text in the vernacular can get printed. And they have remained the same because the language ideology that does not consider Egyptian Arabic as serving the aims of representation is still in place with all kinds of text regulators busily trying to vary the amount that should be allowed in the final publication.

Summarizing our discussion of reported speech, we note that the most frequent strategy is translated indirect discourse. Where transcripts of interviews and meetings are published, depending on the journal, the interviewee and who the audience is thought to be, the amount of Egyptian Arabic is varied. However, questions are never published in that language. The correctors told me that those who read news and interviews with actors, as opposed to pieces on intellectuals, do not mind reading Egyptian Arabic. Beyond interviews, the language that still dominates the space of print is Classical Arabic—in various degrees of older or newer styles, with Egyptian word order or its own, with idiomatic expressions translated from other languages and from Egyptian into Classical Arabic, with heavy or lighter vocabulary. Contrary to the official al-Ahram, other news media show more acceptance of the Egyptian language in print. In certain contexts, the boundaries between the two are not strictly kept and in fact can become blurred, but otherwise the struggles between the two "words" continue in a variety of ways.

Guarding National and Linguistic Borders

Al-Ahram in part financed its operations by publishing advertisements. Their number greatly increased in the span of a few months since its first issue and the last page came to be devoted almost entirely to this purpose. The seriousness and formality of the language of advertisements shows great uncertainty in ways of reconciling the most profane of activities (selling) with the venerated lineage of Classical Arabic. An advertisement for cigarette paper "Bon Duc Alfa et Camelia" (the name was written both with Latin and Arabic orthography) has a caption under two small pictures of the package that reads:

> 'inna alladhiina yuriiduuna 'an yidakhanuu ma'a muhaafizat-hum 'alaa siḥ-ḥat-hum 'aleyhum 'an yasta'miluu waraq siigaar bun duk alfa wa kamilia (al-Ahram 6/13/1900: 3)

> 'Verily all those who want to smoke while guarding their health, it is incumbent upon them to use the cigarette paper Bon Duc Alfa et Camelia'

The phrase "*inna alladhiina*" is one that begins a great number of verses of the Qur'an. For anyone with some familiarity with that text, it is impossible to miss the association and resonance. Yet, here were the "Nanopolo Frères" based in Alexandria selling cigarette paper and using, knowingly or not, one of the most famous phrases of the Qur'an in their sales pitch.[14] Not all advertisement writings showed such direct links to the language of the Qur'an but similar phrases were present in many of them. At the same time, advertisements of industrial machines for trains and agriculture were replete with foreign vocabulary: *betrol, makana, budra, bantometr, lokomibil, eksbres, fotoghrafi* (petrol, machine, powder, pantometer, locomobile, express (train), photography, respectively). Commercial uses of Classical Arabic provided one of those novel contexts that contributed to diluting and lessening its sacredness.

Judging from the names of the companies or store owners publishing advertisements in the early decades of al-Ahram, it appears that they were all either entirely foreign-owned or partly: Among them Allen Walderson and Company, based in Alexandria, Edmond Yusef Florent based in Cairo, Transatlantic Fire Insurance Company of Hamburg, Germany, Farmacia A. Niccola, Mrs. S. A. Allen's Hair Restorer, Maison G. Zananiri and Credit Lyonais. In the texts of their advertisements, one finds examples of lexical uncertainty. For example, in street addresses, there are several terms for "in front of": *izaa'a* (8/4/1884: 4), *'amaama* (7/31/1884: 4), *muqaabil* (7/31/1884: 4), *muqaabila* (7/17/1890: 2); similarly for "prices," we have within the same issues *athmaan* and *as'aar.* There is not much to be surprised about with regard to lexical uncertainty when it comes to a new activity (advertising) and new usages. One can probably find similar examples in many other beginning newspapers around the world. Mentioning the names of such companies and their ownership is not meant to imply that they alone suffered from lexical uncertainty. The rich lexicon of Classical Arabic simply provided too many choices.

But one wonders about the degree and the ways in which commerical activities contributed to the creation of new functions for the hoped for modernized Classical Arabic. Certainly, in terms of the introduction of lexical borrowings, such companies and their activities—specifically preparations of brochures, advertisements, instructions for use and so on—have been a major conduit for foreign vocabulary. But commercial activities do more than that. In the processes that were set in motion in the 1800s, which expanded the domains of use for Classical Arabic and effected a number of renovations and transformations, economic, commercial and educational institutions have played key roles. Insofar as advertisements and brochures can serve as evidence, companies introduced foreign borrowings and made attempts at finding Arabic equivalents.

Commercial activities involve both written and oral exchanges and Classical Arabic was one of the languages of written transactions. But, as a language of the market, it co-existed with vernacular forms and in urban centers with other languages like Greek, Turkish and probably the European languages that such communities spoke in addition to their mother tongues. With colonial rule began Egypt's increasing integration into the world capitalist economy—an economy that brought with it its own languages. Both the use and the value of knowledge of Classical Arabic declined as a result for it was certainly not and not allowed to be the language of that expanding economy. The preoccupation with a lack of modern vocabulary and the alarm at the rapidity and volume of foreign borrowings prompted the founding of the Cairo Language Academy in 1932. The Academy was to stem that tide and help find Arabic equivalents by drawing on the vast lexicon of Classical Arabic and using its triconsonantal root system. Where Arabic equivalents were not possible to find (or agree on), they had to try to "Arabize" (*ta'riib*) the form of the borrowings to render their phonological forms to conform to Arabic. Arabization was seen as a compromise in the struggle between Classical Arabic and European languages. A great number of French-Arabic, English-Arabic, and Italian-Arabic dictionaries were published. In the realm of formal vocabulary, Arabization has succeeded (see also Abdelfattah 1990). We have a great many terms in the political domain such as:

al-dimuqratiyya	'democracy'
imbiryaliyya	'imperialism'
istraatijiyyah	'strategy'
biristiroika	'perestroika'
diblumasiyya	'diplomacy'
diktaturiyya	'dictatorship'

And there are many more such terms. Where the Academy has tried to coin words in more common domains, such as household objects, it has invariably failed. For example, it coined words for telephone, television, video, and so on. None are used. Egyptians use /tilifon/, /tilfiziyon/ and /fidiyo/. Examining the pages of al-Ahram today, one can find numerous foreign borrowings in many semantic domains. Some continue to complain and official organs such as the al-Ahram attempt to make more use of Arabizations rather than straight borrowings (i.e., without changes to make the word sound more Arabic). But almost everyone knows that the tide of borrowings is very difficult to stop.

The Language Academy was also charged since its inception with producing a comprehensive dictionary of modern Classical Arabic. But decisions about which words can be "discarded" have proved so contentious that only one volume has seen the light of day. In analyzing the language of newspapers, Parkinson (1991) noted that some authors use words from just about any epoch in "wanton disregard for the modern nuances and meanings the word has developed over the intervening centuries, and on the assumption that how modern users feel about a particular word has no bearing on its correctness or lack thereof in a particular context." He goes on to discuss the work of the Language Academy and finds that:

> Even the Arabic Language Academy, whose mission is to modernize fuṣha, has published a dictionary recently with an absolutely confusing mixture of archaic, classical, and modern meanings under almost every entry, with no marking whatsoever on which are likely to be understood by modern readers, and which are entirely out of date . . . (Parkinson 1991: 36)

The same complaint was forcefully made at a conference on language in 1996 in Cairo by a famous linguist and lexicographer. The Language Academy is clearly unsure of its authority to come up with a dictionary of "modern" usage. In one of its sessions in 1988 which was devoted to media language, it warned of: "[G]rave consequences of the incorrect use of Arabic in media language and recommended that colleges of journalism all over the Arab world incorporate into their curriculum the study of the grammatical as well as the phonetic system of the Arabic language. The Academy also recommended the hiring of more language correctors in both the electronic and the print media" (Abdelfattah 1990: 46). The Academy has clearly had far less influence than it would have liked. While its debates on what is "old" or "new" and on borrowings and Arabization continue, most writers particularly in the media, do not wait for a conclusive set of results.

Grammar and Iconicity

A great deal of linguistic engineering can and has been done with regard to Classical Arabic. There are, however, grammatical features that are difficult to change. Every time a sentence uses a relative pronoun (e.g., who, when, that, etc.), every time a verb is conjugated for person, number and gender, every time negation is used, the forms signal a formality that cannot be hidden or easily transcended. In these aspects of grammar (as well as others), Egyptian Arabic and Classical Arabic differ greatly. For example, in the vernacular, there is only one relative pronoun: "*illi*," and it is the same form regardless of number and gender. In Classical Arabic, however, the form of the relative pronoun depends on the number and gender of the subject. For third person masculine singular, it is "*alladhii*"; for feminine "*allatii*"; masc. plural: "*alladhiina*"; and so on. Similarly, personal suffixes attached to verbs are different in the two languages (see table 1.1 in chapter one). The more convoluted and obscure aspects of Classical Arabic grammar have been successfully dispensed with in most contemporary writing, but such basic features or necessities cannot be negotiated or thrown out. Even with regard to the case endings, correctors repeated over and over that "there is nothing" they "can do"—they "cannot touch them." No matter how hip certain kinds of writing attempt to be, the presence of such grammatical particles (the function words or "closed-class items") bring in a formality and officialness that clash with the breezy, colloquial style that some authors wish to achieve. One cannot just bestow a casual, colloquial style to a language that no one resorts to in oral conversation when speaking in that style.

But it is not just a question of formality. Pieces of grammar can acquire iconicity as sounds (Jakobson 1971a,b; Caton 1987). Verses of the Qur'an that are memorized and recited over and over in the course of one's life clearly contain all kinds of grammatical particles like suffixes and prefixes. To the reader and reciter who is not proficient in Classical Arabic, these forms are sounds that become iconic in that their forms come to stand for or invoke religion, its language, world and rituals. For example, one of the most popular chapters of the Qur'an among Muslims worldwide is the Sura of Yasin (36: 22) which is often characterized as the "heart of the Qur'an" ('*alb il-qur'aan*). It is therefore widely memorized and recited. Many verses in this sura end in words that rhyme and the part that rhymes is often a grammatical particle. Below are examples of verse endings in verses 6, 7, 8 and 9 from the Sura of Yasin (they are transcribed in their pausal forms in order to lessen the complexity of detail for the reader):

Qur'an	Egyptian Arabic	Gloss
ghaafil<u>uun</u>	ghaafil<u>iin</u>	'heedless'
<u>la</u> yu'min<u>uun</u>	<u>ma</u> yu'min<u>uush</u> / ma biyi 'aaminuush	'do not believe'
mughmihuun	no longer used	
<u>la</u> yabsar<u>uun</u>	<u>ma</u> yishuf<u>uush</u> / <u>mish</u> shayf<u>iin</u>	'do not see'

What is underlined signify function words of both languages. The particle "uun" can either make a noun plural or serve as marking a verb for third person plural masculine. Even if everyone knows their functions, they are not part of the grammar of Egyptian Arabic.

When the Sura of Yasin is recited or heard, "uun" is primarily a string of sounds, but when it is read or heard in a sentence in newspapers or books, it is not part of a rhyme or a recitation, but a grammatical marker whose function needs to be understood. The same argument can be made about a host of other differences between the two languages. It is precisely this difference between Qur'anic and contemporary Classical Arabic that makes the latter for many people not "simpler" but "difficult," "frightening" and at times even pretentious (recall our discussion in chapter 2). At the same time, the role of vocabulary aside, the enduring resonance of such grammatical particles and what they have come to be associated with (i.e., the Qur'an) can make *contemporary* Classical Arabic sound like an imitation always in the shadow of the real thing. It seems plausible that writers and intellectuals who have argued in the course of the twentieth century for dispensing with certain aspects of Classical Arabic grammar including the case system (Frayha 1955, Musa 1964)[15] were aware of the power of its sounds to invoke religion and hence to prevent contemporary Classical Arabic from ever becoming an independent linguistic variety.

In a novel published in 1994 by Fathi Imbabi and entitled *The Killing Fields* (*maraa'ii al-qatl*), the author has written a postscript on the "Grammar of the Modern Arabic Language" (*nahw lugha 'arabiyya gadiida*). In a lengthy discussion of the position of various groups with regard to the language question in Egypt (*ishkaaliyat al-lugha*), Imbabi states that although "ideological, political, Arabist, and religious" factors are very important in the debate, he wishes to present an argument outside such matters. In his own novel, all dialogues are in Egyptian Arabic. He criticizes those who write dialogues in Classical Arabic: "[D]uring the writing of a literary text, the writer translates—and I mean translates—how he believes any given character might speak in the classical language." Imbabi makes a distinction between what he calls "*al-'arabiyya al-kilasikiyya*"—"Classical Arabic"—and "*al-lugha al-fusha al-'arabiyya al-hadiisa*," "the modern Classical Arabic language," arguing that the latter is the "legitimate daughter" of the old Classical Arabic (Imbabi 1994: 412). Of particular interest in Imbabi's discussion for our purposes is that he makes a list of grammatical particles or function words of Classical Arabic that should be dispensed with in writing. Among these, he lists the case endings and the plural feminine relative pronoun "*allataan*" (sing. "*allaati*") and proposes that only the masculine singular "*alladhii*" be used, rather like "*illi*" is used in Egyptian Arabic regardless of number and gender. While Imbabi states that he makes these suggestions because they are "logical," "economical" and easier on the tongues of Egyptians, his list indicates an acknowledgement of that which has so far eluded resolution or simplification.

One can change the word order of sentences and attempt to use up-to-date vocabulary. Very archaic structures and phrases can be shunned. One can even try to avoid here and there certain conjugations and the use of relative pronouns, as the example of Omar Sharif's interview showed. But grammatical particles—building blocks of sentences—cannot be avoided beyond a certain limit. Recall our discussion of Abdullah Nadim earlier in this chapter and his efforts at writing in such a way that the boundaries between the two languages could be blurred. Although such efforts can be realized here and there and continue to be seen in various kinds of writing, our analysis of newspaper prose shows why they cannot always be sustained. Hence, in many novels, the narrator's voice is in Classical Arabic and dialogues are in either language or a strange mix of both. And even this "resolution" has at times resulted in characters speaking in ways that are utterly artificial.[16]

Old, new, archaic and contemporary words occur side by side with grammatical engineerings that resist at least in part, as Bakhtin would say, the "will of the author" and "put themselves in quotation marks against his will." In short, while the Classical Arabic of the present is different from that of a century ago, it is, in ways that I have tried to indicate, a language with an uneasy relationship to its past, its genealogy, to the vernacular and hence also to the contemporary world. There are a number of writers who are considered to write in very fluent and "natural" Classical Arabic. Taha Hussein is a prime example. He is perhaps among a handful who do not translate while they write. But probably for many, writing requires a translation of the "self" into forms of writing that still show ongoing struggles between the "alien" word and their own. And in that act of translation, as with all translations, something gets lost.

In chapter two, as we saw, most people said that they do not like to read, even those who had had a college education and worked in libraries. They characterized the language of books as complex and difficult and gave this as the main reason for their lack of interest. Returning once more to the autobiography of Leila Ahmed, she states: "I have yet to hear or read any piece of Arabic poetry or prose by a modern writer that, however gorgeous and delicate and poetic and moving, is not also stilted and artificial" (Ahmed 1999: 283). This may not be the case for those who have a very high level of proficiency in the language and regularly read and write in it. But the very existence of another language (Egyptian Arabic) that serves even professional writers the minute they put their pens down, and the parts of Classical Arabic grammar that cannot be avoided, gotten rid of or somehow negotiated away keep the written language rather "alien" and too ponderous for many readers.

Chapter Five

⌒

Persistent Dilemmas

Pleasure, Power and Ambiguity

A century and a half after initial attempts at the modernization of Classical Arabic began, the language question remains a potent and highly contentious issue in contemporary Egypt. In the 1990s, not only could one find articles on this topic in the pages of al-Ahram and other publications on a weekly basis, but whole issues of journals were devoted to the subject (*al-Qahira* 1996, No. 163, *Qadaya Fikriyya* 1997 No. 17/18, among others). In the pages of such publications, heated debates on language are carried on. Recurring themes include the "isolation" of the intellectual who writes in fuṣḥa, the capabilities of 'ammiyya (or their absence) as a language for critical thought, the necessity of Classical Arabic for unity, the failures of pan-Arabism, fuṣḥa as the language of power and 'ammiyya as that of the "masses" (*il-sha'b*), linguistic modernization and simplification and so on. Beyond publications, other cultural activities also centered on language issues. In January 1996, there was a large and lavishly funded weeklong conference on "the Arabic Language and Scientific Culture" sponsored by the Ministry of Culture. Many papers and discussions in that conference were devoted to different aspects of the language question. Other conferences included "the Problematic of the Translation of Theatrical Texts" into Arabic (January 16–17, 1996), another on the poetry of the most famous 'ammiyya poet, Beyram al-Tonsi (March 25–26, 1996), and one on the fiction of Edward al-Kharrat (March 30, 1996), a Coptic Egyptian novelist who writes in fusha—all addressed the language question in different ways.

Contemporary uses of Classical Arabic have established themselves and become routine in newspapers, literary and social scientific journals and in fiction. There exists a heterogeneity of language and style, far more so than a century earlier. If this were merely a situation representing differences between speaking and writing, or one that concerned only *linguistic* matters, one would reasonably expect that the language question would have gone away by now. On the contrary, it continues to play a crucial role in most political and cultural debates dividing and uniting Egyptians and Arabs across a wide spectrum of ideologies, confronting them with a series of complex and persistent dilemmas.

This chapter is devoted to the views of writers, poets, journalists and publishers that I have interviewed.[1] It also explores the roles of intellectuals and state institutions in cultural production. We begin with the question of the relation(s) between political ideology and choice of language of writing—on what basis do writers make that choice? Our discussions so far should have made it clear that there is no linear or predictable relation between choice of language and political ideology. One may be a secular intellectual and write in fusha. (In fact, this is the case with most such intellectuals, including feminists.) And, as we will see, many people believe that there is really no choice to be made—the language of writing and of critical thought is simply Classical Arabic. Even so, few people have just one clear and unchanging position with regard to the many complexities of the language question. For example, depending on whose writing is being discussed or which aspect of the language situation, the same person simultaneously asserts that there are many different kinds of fusha and many "levels," and at another point, the assertion is made that there is really "one fusha." This is one of the clearest indications of how that question operates in an arena of multiple ambiguities. Still, language and ideology *are* related to each other and the question remains how that relation is constituted for Egyptian intellectuals. What factors intervene between political ideology on the one hand, and language ideology on the other?

Reading in Classical Arabic: A "Space of Pleasure"

I interviewed a poet and a literary critic who writes in fusha and whose first book of poetry (published in 1995) received wide attention in the press.[2] Iman Mirsal was in her late 20s at the time and well connected to the artistic milieu. As I took weekly lessons from her in Egyptian literature, I got to know her rather well. She offered one of the most enlightening explanations that I have heard for how Classical Arabic can come to represent desired and alternative worlds and how this fact promotes the development of a positive personal relationship with the language. She told me about her first encounters with fusha:

> Fusha entered my life before elementary school because my father wanted to teach me the Qur'an in order for me to do well in school. The basic idea was that the child who learns the Qur'an when he is 4 years old will do well in school after that. At that age he took me to a kuttaab. . . . After that, education was in fusha from the beginning.

Mirsal was a very good student both in learning and memorizing the Qur'an and later on at school. She took great pleasure in reading, so much so that, for her, fusha became a "space of pleasure" (*makaan il-mut'a*). She began reading early on in second and third grade—"short books in simplified fusha" of Arab history, children's stories and stories about the life of the Prophet Muhammad: "[T]his is the first relationship I made with something that I love in this world—this act of reading. And reading, its place is in fusha." She remarked that there was no television or video player in her house and that perhaps, had there been other sources of entertainment, her relationship with the language may have been different.

As she grew older and became interested in finding out about romantic love and sexuality, she could find poetry and fiction and other writings in fusha on such subjects but nothing in 'ammiyya. At the same time, people around her did not talk about such matters, particularly because as a young woman she was more frequently excluded from such domains than the men of her generation.

> social life did not offer to us [women of her generation] anything on the subject of love or sexuality or anything of the sort, it was not open to these topics . . . there were no individuals at home or friends who were telling you these [love] stories or experiences so that you could say "oh good, someone else also feels that way too."

In this way, the only space in which matters of love seemed open to articulation and exploration was that provided by writings in fusha, "when we fell in love at first, it was through the love stories that we read in fusha." Growing up as a woman, Iman explained that one was constantly told what was improper—"'*eyb*" or "shameful"—behavior for a woman: "'*eyb* if you talk in a loud voice, '*eyb* if you talk on the street, '*eyb* if you sit like that, and '*eyb* and '*eyb*. . . ." This space of shameful behavior is in the world of 'ammiyya, the everyday language through which crucial aspects of one's socialization take place. In this world, if it is shameful to talk in a loud voice for a woman, then how much more shameful it would be to confess one's love to a man who was not one's husband? "But then," Iman recalled, "you read in a love story about the woman who writes a letter to her lover and says to him 'I love you and miss you' and so on *in fusha*." So what seemed forbidden and shameful in 'ammiyya at least became a possibility in fusha—the possibility of a different world—a modern world not easily accessible in 'ammiyya.

This is a very illuminating explication of the kinds of relationships that can develop between individuals and the language of writing. It also provides a partial explanation for the surprising fact that there are far fewer 'ammiyya poets among women in the Arab world and why Arab feminists have chosen to write in Classical Arabic (apart from those who write in English and French).[3] While in speaking, women generally have been shown to rely far less on Classical Arabic than men, in writing that difference disappears (see Daher 1987, Haeri 2000). In any case, as we will see, Mirsal's views are echoed by other writers—Marxists, secular pan-Arabists and so on—because the vehicle of these new and alternative ideologies has also been Classical Arabic.

Mirsal made the point that her experience in developing a love of reading might be "unusual" (*shazza*): "This would be different for people who do not like to read or write; whose consciousness [*wugdaan*] gets formed based on 'ammiyya heritage." Mirsal's experience with the language began with Qur'anic Classical Arabic, as is the case with most other people. However, the personal relationship she developed with fusha came about, as she explains, through readings of texts that were nonreligious and whose language was "simplified" representing versions of contemporary Classical Arabic. Many of the books she read for pleasure were not school textbooks.

Public Schools and the Reproduction of "Classical Arabic"

Based on Mirsal's experience, and the experience of other writers who speak of their love for Classical Arabic,[4] we examine again the question of whether the educational system teaches and reproduces that "simplified" and modernized Classical Arabic. Does its choice of texts and themes allow the building of similar positive relationships with the language? The answer that I can provide to this question will only concern the situation at present. A historical study of textbooks would be highly illuminating but is outside the scope of this book. What needs to be kept in mind is that, historically, with the appearance of nonreligious public schools in the early decades of the nineteenth century, state institutions had to commission new textbooks for many subjects. The writing of such textbooks or their translations from foreign languages necessarily involved some new ways of writing, just as the appearance of newspapers led to a search for suitable journalistic genres.

Therefore, state institutions have played a major role in the struggles for making Classical Arabic simpler and more contemporary.

In chapter two, we investigated the school experience of different individuals and their encounters with the language of textbooks. Here we will directly analyze the language and content of grammar textbooks. It is important to begin by noting that there is not just one educational system in Egypt. In addition to public schools, there are religious ones (*kuttaabs*) and higher religious learning can be pursued within the al-Azhar mosque-university system. There are also private Islamic schools and private foreign language ones. The former are usually expensive and rather recent. Foreign language private schools, many of which are missionary schools, have been operating in Egypt for more than a century (Heyworth-Dunn 1968). By most accounts, public education in Egypt is in dire need of an overhaul. Not only does it require far more funding and resources, but also many educators, teachers and students complain about the content and language of the textbooks. There exists a large literature on the educational problems of Egypt and other parts of the Arab world, written mostly by Arab linguists, educators and other professionals.[5] The distance between the mother tongue of students and the language of education is seen by some as one of the causes of persistently low literacy rates (53.7 percent for adults and 68.3 percent for youth).[6] While I was in Egypt, one of the biggest and, it seemed, continuing controversies concerned the complaints of parents regarding the necessity of hiring teachers as private tutors for their children. Demand for private tutors had increased tremendously in part due to a loss of confidence in the quality of teaching. Of course less well-to-do families could not afford this luxury—they would either give up or pool neighborhood resources to hire a tutor who would simultaneously teach several children.

At state schools, as in schools within the al-Azhar system, Egyptian Arabic and other vernaculars are explicitly denigrated, associated with ignorance, illiteracy, backwardness and so on. This is the case despite the fact that in elementary school and in later stages, oral interaction such as lectures are mostly in that language. In interviews with high school students, I was told about how teachers reprimand them in different ways for their use of Egyptian Arabic. A particularly memorable story that I heard in this respect was recounted by one of the correctors whose career and views were discussed in chapter 3. In secondary school at al-Azhar, he had a teacher who would walk into the class and upon hearing students talking to each other in Egyptian Arabic, would declare: "my ears do not allow the language of donkeys" (*uzunii la yismaḥ kalaam il-ḥamiir*). Again, similar to the practices of the al-Azhar, public schools also teach pupils how to pray (in Qur'anic Arabic) in part through manuals published by the Ministry of

Education, as was mentioned chapter 2. The teaching of religion has been an important part of state efforts particularly since the 1950s to gain increasing control over the al-Azhar and the religious establishment in general (Starrett 1998).

In middle school (*a'daadi*), the serious and more systematic study of grammar begins. If textbooks on grammar for seventh graders are any indication, no explicit distinctions are made between religious or Qur'anic Classical Arabic and the contemporary language. The beginning textbook for seventh graders dated 1993–1994 (to my knowledge it has not changed in content),[7] begins with an introduction apparently addressed to teachers. The first line reads: "Thanks be to God who honored the Arabic Language with the Nobel Qur'an, and prayers and peace upon its Messenger Muhammad, speaker of the clear Arabic language. . . ." The introduction goes on to say that the book is a result of the program arrived at by the Permanent Committee on the Development of the Arabic Language. The language of the introduction is what some Egyptians refer to as "heavy" (*ti'iil*) Classical Arabic.[8] One sentence that is a paragraph long starts with "And this book" as the sentential subject, and goes on to enumerate various matters: " . . . and took care to offer to the student these rules [of grammar] through pleasurable stories and human values and . . . useful contemporary scientific discoveries . . . , alongside contemporary culture, and the guarding of the essence of Arab culture [*al-zaatiyya al-thaqaafa al-'arabiyya*], and [of] Islamic values [*al-qiyam al-islamiyya*] that the sons and daughters of the Arab nation are proud of." In general, the language is stilted and makes use of highly marked Classical Arabic grammatical particles (i.e., function words).

Apart from the language of the text, the content makes it clear that the "Arabic Language" whose grammar is presented through extracts and endless exercises is the language of the Qur'an first, and then the language of the "Arab nation"—no mention is made of Egypt in this respect, or of Egyptians and of their language. Note that that "nation" was meant to include, as leaders of the pan-Arab movement had explicitly wished for, Arabs of all faiths, but here the text clearly refers exclusively to Muslims. It is also stated in the introduction that the book does not offer anything new in the "science of grammar." It is unclear what is meant by this statement—"new" in relation to what? Have there not been decades of efforts to modernize the language?

As for the lessons, the first one offers four verses from the Qur'an from the Sura of Luqman (verses 14–17) and begins with "Said Almighty God" followed by verses which appear in large quotation marks and are fully vowelled as is the case with any edition of the Qur'an in Arabic. The content is about how one should treat one's parents. The lesson is then followed by one question which tests the student on comprehension, and five exercises on grammar. The second lesson is on the pursuit of knowledge from the sayings of the Prophet Muhammad. Other lessons are on the unity of Arabs, love for Egypt, the contribution of Arabs to mathematics, more verses from the Qur'an, several old morality tales and so on. Beside lessons that are either directly on religious themes or are verses from the Qur'an, the language of lessons, their vocabulary as well as the particular grammatical constructions they are meant to illustrate are stunningly archaic, heavy and humorless. It is no wonder that the majority of students feel alienated from such classes and make up countless jokes about the language and teachers of grammar (Haeri 1996).

Moreover, while one does not expect extracts from the Qur'an to have a date, there is also no indication of dates for other texts. A few have the name of the book and its author from which the lesson was extracted. All such features combine to communicate that the Arabic language the students are studying is based on the language of the Qur'an. Moreover, as the students are not familiar enough with the grammar of Classical Arabic, almost all the texts of the lessons are vowelled, meaning that cases and their various inflectional permutations are all orthographically represented. This makes them *look* very similar to the text of the Qur'an. There are no indications or explicit discussions of contemporary or modernized versions of the language.

For middle school, I examined a number of other textbooks. They all seem to be very similar to the one discussed briefly here. In high school (*saanawi*), textbooks for literature and less so for grammar do contain some extracts of contemporary works whose language is less archaic and closer to the features and vocabulary of Egyptian Arabic than what students are exposed to in middle school. Moreover, in the rare cases where teachers would in fact lecture in "Classical Arabic," it would be reasonable to assume that this oral version is closer to contemporary Classical Arabic. On the whole, the explicit message is that this is the language of Islam and is best represented in the Qur'an, although implicitly, contemporary models are also offered in the later years of secondary education. Again, many Arab authors and educators have been urging governments for several decades to change the textbooks, to make their language easier and their contents closer to the lives and thoughts of the students. Their calls seem to have gone unheeded.

Beyond the problem of textbooks, one may inquire into the relationship between the official language of the country and the state. Why do state educational institutions (at least for pre-college levels) privilege old Classical Arabic in grammar courses? Has the government given up on pan-Arabism or is it trying to inculcate a religious version of it? In that case, what happens to its claims of modernizing Egypt? Part of the answer lies in the wider context of state desire for increasing social control. Just as teaching religion and prayers at public schools is seen as a means of bringing religion within its domain and authority, teaching the Classical Arabic of the Qur'an expands further its control. The relation between states and their official languages has generally been treated as unproblematic—the establishment, expansion and reproduction of official standard languages are seen as the prime means through which states accrue authority and gain control over the citizenry through their bureaucratic and educational institutions (Bourdieu 1991, 1982, 1977).

While in general terms such arguments may be valid, in the case of Egypt the official language simultaneously reinforces the authority of the state and challenges it. The antecedent and continuing claims of the religious establishment over the custodianship of the language, and the fact that its origin is perceived to lie with the Qur'an, render the state's relation to it ambivalent (Haeri 1997). Equally problematic for the state is the fact that not all its institutions can reproduce positive values for the official language. While public educational institutions (with the exception of higher education in such fields as medicine and engineering) inculcate positive valuations of the language, some of its economic policies marginalize the currency of the language. With the integration of Egypt into the global economy come positions, jobs and labor markets that require proficiency not in the official language of the country, but in English, French and other foreign languages.

Moreover, for at least several generations, the Egyptian upper classes have been sending their children to private foreign language schools for a variety of reasons including those very labor markets just mentioned. Hence the upper classes on the whole do not receive their education in the official language of the country. Stereotypes of the upper classes (as well as that of women in general) always include their "mixed" language, "soft" pronunciations, and their general lack of linguistic proficiency. Yet, this lack does not prevent members of the upper classes from obtaining some of the highest paying jobs and most prestigious positions inside and outside of the state bureaucracy. Where there is a need for better knowledge of the language (as is the case with some diplomatic posts), there are crash courses and private tutors, proficient assistants and secretaries that are brought in to help their superiors with better linguistic skills (Haeri 1997).

Officially, the overwhelming rhetoric of state educational and media institutions, and of public officials, is that Classical Arabic is the language of the Qur'an and of Islam. But precisely because the state controls so much of the print media through its own publishing houses it is and has been also the biggest propagator of contemporary uses of Classical Arabic. Hence, it has played a central role in the dissemination of linguistic heterogeneity within Classical Arabic. Its publishing houses produce the largest number of books in that language that are nonreligious—from children's books to comic strips, scientific books, fiction and so on. Note that such productions simultaneously aim to establish the state's claims to "modernity" and "progress."

One may characterize this dual treatment of Classical Arabic as an act of appropriation, as was argued in chapter 3. Through the dissemination of the language in modern contexts, its exclusive link with religion can get diluted, and what it symbolizes becomes diversified. In this way, two simultaneous claims are routinely made, by public officials and others, that the language is that of the Qur'an and also the language of modern life. As the obligatory language of almost all that is written and published, one encounters uses of Classical Arabic everywhere—on utility bills, on commercial products from laundry detergents to nose sprays to birth control pills and computer manuals. Such usages are not looked upon, either by Egyptians or other Arabs, as bizarre. Classical Arabic is the de facto language of such written accouterments of modernity, as it is claimed to be. The many diverse consequences of the choice of Classical Arabic as the language of the state and of writing need not be, and I believe are not all, the results of conscious decisions on the part of different governments in this century, or any particular institutions within them. The processes set in motion through that choice have been too complex for any one entity to have planned them or foreseen them all.

At present, the state's ambivalent attitude towards its official language may also be seen in its legal and cultural activities. In December 1995, the daily *al-Akhbar* reported that the state was not following the constitution of Egypt because it has lowered the minimum passing grade for "Arabic" while increasing it for foreign languages such as English and French. (*al-Akhbar* 12/19/95: 4) In addition, two of the best funded conferences that the Ministry of Culture sponsored in the first half of 1996 were a four-day international conference on the most famous 'ammiyya poet, in Egypt as well as in the Arab world, Beyram al-Tonsi, and another conference on pre-Islamic poetry. Moreover, the fact that Egyptian Arabic dominates in oral communications renders it dominant as well in the nonprint media, much of which is again under state control. Hence there is also a promotion of Egyptian Arabic on radio and television. That the dominance of Egyptian Arabic in nonprint media should not be taken for granted was made clear to me when I heard the complaints of non-Egyptian Arabs in Cairo that "there is too much of it" and too little Classical Arabic in broadcast media.

Returning to the role of public education in fostering a liking for reading and writing, based on the foregoing analysis and the experiences of individuals discussed in chapter 2, it is reasonable to conclude that on the whole students in public schools do not graduate with a fondness for reading and writing. The ways in which Classical Arabic is taught and the distance between the language of the textbooks and their mother tongue render reading and writing outside of school requirements far from agreeable and gratifying. In short, the language appears quite beyond the reach of "ordinary" people. Hence, while for the poet Mirsal and others like her *contemporary* Classical Arabic can represent, among other things, a nontraditional world where alternative behaviors and ideologies become possible, for most others it remains a rather "alien" entity. The Qur'anic version of this "Classical Arabic," though *linguistically* more distant from their mother tongue, is in fact a more familiar and congenial site and sound that does not intimidate or frighten.

Even for Mirsal, however, "Classical Arabic" remains somewhat distant. She explained that although discovering readings in fuṣḥa where romantic love is explored "without shame" was exhilarating, "the contradiction [between those feelings] and the language is always present." After all, in real life, no one talks to her lover in Classical Arabic. She clarified the contradiction further: "This means that your knowledge about society passes through fuṣḥa on the level of a cultural experience but not as an experience in your life . . . *as if culture exists in one place and the living of life in another place.* . . ." Many other people that I interviewed, as well as many Arab writers, have expressed the same thought in different ways, that the language situation leads almost to a separation between "culture" and "life" (see Afsaruddin 1997). This is also often articulated in terms of translation—one's thoughts, feelings and experiences having to be first translated into the written language, thereby creating a further distance between the individual and his/her experiences, thoughts, or feelings. Mirsal gave the example of the language of personal letters to illustrate the distance created by this act of translation between her and her self:

> Sometimes when we write a letter to a friend, some of it is in fuṣḥa and some in 'ammiyya. I have experienced [this]. And once I was very surprised when I discovered [in writing a letter] that there is something between me and my soul/mind [*beinii wa bein nafsii*] in that all the things that were in 'ammiyya were more honest [*aksar sidqan*] as if the place for the existence of these emotions were 'ammiyya not fuṣḥa.[9]

Beyond daily interactions, cultural productions in theatre and film have used Egyptian Arabic to articulate all kinds of complex and "serious" thoughts. But the number of published written works in Egyptian Arabic is exceedingly small. The exact number of short stories and novels in 'ammiyya is not available, but one novel that was mentioned to me by various people was published in 1991. It is by Mustafa Musharrafa and is called "Qantara who Disbelieved."[10] It is about the 1919 revolution in Egypt and according to the author "the events took place in one of the old popular quarters of Cairo." It was first written in the 1940s and was published in a "limited edition" in the early 1960s. No less than seven authors have written prefaces that appear one after another in this new edition of the novel. In addition to discussing various aspects of the story and the events, these authors comment on the choice of language and explain that it was necessary for it to be written in 'ammiyya. The author's own explanation appears last under "the Word of the Author." He also explains why he wrote in 'ammiyya or "its original language . . . because the language takes the reader to live in these events and it [would] lose its beauty [*bahgat-ha*] if I wrote it in any other language above the level of 'ammiyya." The authority of seven other authors and their justifications seem to have been perceived as necessary for a novel that is written in Egyptian Arabic.

Not only is Egyptian Arabic commonly banned from the space of print, but publications about its history, linguistic features, grammars and dictionaries are rarities.[11] The only comprehensive dictionary of Egyptian Arabic was published in 1986 by a publishing house in Lebanon. Like its' few and far briefer predecessors, it is a bilingual Arabic/English dictionary aimed at non-native speakers who would learn the language through their knowledge of English. To date, no grammars of any Arabic vernacular have been published within the Arab world beyond those meant for non-Arabic speakers. Hence, when so many people state that "'ammiyya has no grammar," in a sense they are right. They have never seen a book of its grammar. What role do publishers play in this imbalance? Do they refuse to publish books that are not in Classical Arabic?

The Place of Egyptian Arabic in Official Culture

It is often argued that publishers in the Arab world refuse to publish books in the vernaculars because their market would be only local—those beyond Egypt would not buy books in Egyptian Arabic because, so it is claimed, they would not be able to read it. In my interviews with a number of large and small publishers and bookstore owners, I was particularly interested in finding out how publishers see their own roles in the production of culture in Egypt and how they explain the availability of so few books in Egyptian Arabic. One small press publisher who had just published a number of translated works on postmodernity (from French into Classical Arabic) said that Egyptian Arabic should not be the language of writing.[12] For him, the choice of Classical Arabic did not have to do with religious reasons but with the fact that the language is far richer and more capable. To him, there was no special language situation to debate: "[T]his is modern fuṣha, it is like any other modern language like English or French, it exists, it is everywhere, there's not much more to talk about. (quoted also in chapter two)." The acquisition consultant (*mustashaar nashr*) of a large publishing house first told me that there *are* books in Egyptian Arabic—poetry, proverbs and plays.[13] I asked whether he would publish books in, say, history, politics or sociology in that language. He said that 'ammiyya is a "dialect" and not a "language" and therefore has no grammar. Even so, he would publish in it, "but" he added, "someone has to take the risk" (*ḥadd laazim yakhud risk*). Why this would constitute a "risk" is a question that we will return to later on in this section. It should be mentioned that publishers and acquisition consultants routinely commission different kinds of books but no one that I interviewed had ever commissioned one in Egyptian Arabic.

Il-Hagg Madbouli is the owner of the most famous bookstore and printing house in Egypt and perhaps in the Arab world. He and his brother inherited a newspaper kiosk from their father which operated in the early decades of the twentieth century when Egypt was still under British colonial rule. Their kiosk was famous for stocking newspapers from around the world. Gradually, their business took off and, after the death of their father, the brothers opened a bookstore in downtown Cairo. Il-Hagg Madbouli is a self-taught man. He began learning how to read by buying comic strips from a nearby bookstore owned by a Greek Egyptian. He believes that his success is in part due to the fact that he sought out the advice of intellectuals and of the younger generation in commissioning works within Egypt and translations from European writers. He is in some ways a cultural icon, deeply familiar with contemporary Egypt, highly conscious of his role in "building" the country and sought after by the cultural elites.

In the course of two lengthy interviews, I asked whether he agreed with the general line that publishers do not want to publish in the non-Classical languages because they would not be able to sell their books all over the Arab world but only inside one country.[14] He strongly disagreed with this reasoning. He gave the example of a book on Egyptian Arabic proverbs by Taymour Basha:

> We run out of [this book] fast unlike books in fuṣha. You find that the printing runs out in less than one year and it is printed again. See how many years this has been happening? More than 35 or 40 years and it still runs out fast. Why? Because of craving [*righba*] for 'ammiyya.

I told him that many publishers would say that such a book would not sell in the Maghrib or the Gulf countries. He responded: "So what [*iḥna malna*]? We are 65 million in Egypt, as big as the Arab region [*il-mantiqa il-'arabiyya*] and we can sell here three thousand copies in Egypt. It is not necessary for it to be related to any other country." He went on to say that if I "gave him a book in 'ammiyya today" he would "publish it tomorrow." I asked whether he would do that regardless of field or topic. He said that he would publish anything—fiction, poetry, research or historical studies. Il-Hagg Madbouli's view of the language situation was that both languages have their own place and that Egypt needs both. Having spoken to a number of other publishers and others in the publishing business before and having heard repeatedly that they would not publish books in Egyptian Arabic, I found Madbouli's answers to be less "party line" and more open than others. He said that in fact in Egypt books that are in Egyptian Arabic sell better, but there are very few such books. So I asked why he does not publish more books in Egyptian Arabic. He said because there aren't any, "people don't write them." Why not? I asked. "That is a very complicated question," he answered with a smile. He added that perhaps people do not write in 'ammiyya because they are not used to it—they would simply find the idea "bizarre" or "unnatural" [*shazza*]. I mentioned to him that one commonly hears the lament that "Egyptians don't read" and if that is in fact the case, how then do publishers survive? He responded that were it not for the subscriptions of foreign libraries and sales at book fairs, publishers would not be able to make ends meet. This is clearly part of the answer but it leaves open the question of the basis on which publishers decide to publish a book. Specifically, it remains unclear what kinds of market considerations enter into such a decision.

I made several unsuccessful attempts to interview the head of the publishers' syndicate in Egypt, the Arab Publishers' Association, Ibrahim al-Mo'allem, in order to pursue those questions. I was interested in locating some statistics on not only what gets published but also on what is read. This kind of information was hard to get from the publishers whom I had interviewed. All such questions remain unanswered in part due to lack of available statistics. In a recent article on the poor state of publishing in the Arab world and the "Death of the Arab Reader" that appeared in the *Chronicle of Higher Education* (11/10/01), Mr. al-Mo'allem is among several others who gives his views on the subject:

> No exact statistics are available, but the quantity of books published in the Arab world is small, especially relative to the region's population. . . . There are 275 million Arab speakers in 22 countries, but for Middle Eastern publishers, print runs of 5,000 are considered huge. . . . A bestseller in Egypt is a book that reaches just 10,000 copies sold, a tenth of what a bestseller in the United States might do. Only a few books make it into the stratosphere of 50,000 or more copies . . . (hereafter *CHE*, 11/10/01)

The article goes on to present publishers' opinions regarding the question of lack of readership in the Arab world:

> Mr. al-Moallem . . . says that some of the distaste for books is created by educational institutions, starting at an early age. "Textbooks in most of the Arab countries are a means of torture for students. They are very badly written, very badly illustrated, poorly printed, too long, and tedious," he says. Often, he says, the books are written by employees of the country's education ministries, which are viewed by the public as corrupt. "All of this has the effect of making students hate reading," he says. (*CHE*)

This characterization, along with the conclusion that many students end up hating reading, echoes our earlier discussions. In the same article, the managing director of Elias Modern Publishing House in Egypt states that "Culturally, people buy books to study, not to read for pleasure."

Some publishers, like Lokman Selim of Beirut, who owns a small publishing house, blame the language situation:

> Mr. Selim, like many intellectuals, wonders about the future of the Arabic language. . . ." Fewer and fewer people have an acceptable knowledge of this language, and they have very big problems reading books or having the patience to read longer sentences than what they find in a newspaper, Mr. Selim says. "I think Arabic is a dead language, and we are witnessing the birth of several Arabic languages," he says. "But because of Islam, we will continue to say that the Arabic language exists" (*CHE*)

However, the same article cites the views of a professor at the American University in Beirut, Mr. Baalbaki, who:

> doubts that Arabic as a scholarly language should be read its last rites. He notes that in the late 19th century, the Arabic language had appeared to be in a state of crisis, with some scholars demanding the replacement of Arabic script with a Latin one, as eventually happened with Turkish. "Ultimately, the language prevailed due to nationalist and religious reasons," he says, suggesting that the same foundation will keep the language strong now (*CHE*)

The same article reports the view that "Publishing throughout much of the Arab world today is dominated by governments," although it mentions Egypt and Lebanon as having a larger private publishing sector than other Arab countries. One aspect of the Egyptian government's role in publishing that is particularly interesting for our purposes is its mixed attitude towards publications about or in Egyptian Arabic. Apart from plays, most of which are meant for the stage and not for reading, poetry constitutes the only established genre in which it is acceptable to write and publish in Egyptian Arabic. But even here, there are many limitations.

The Wish for a Journal of 'Ammiyya Poetry:
Cooperation between the Public and the Private Sectors

The story of the rise and fall of a journal that was meant to be devoted to the publication of 'ammiyya poetry is highly illuminating in showing the sources of some of those limitations.[15] The journal was called *Ibn Arous* and began publication in March 1993.[16] In interviews with its founder, financier and editor, the many obstacles that confronted this project illustrate the tortuous paths that any publication in Egyptian Arabic can take.[17] Mohammad al-Boghdadi is an 'ammiyya poet, journalist, editor and publisher who had for long wanted to publish a journal of 'ammiyya poetry and criticism (*naqd*). In 1992, in a conference organized by the government owned *al-Hay'a al-Misriyya al-'aamma lil-Kitab* (hereafter al-Hay'a) publishing house, Mr. Boghdadi brought up the idea for such a journal:

> We said that there should be a forum or an independent publication in which Egyptian 'ammiyya poetry can be published. In this conference, there was the Minister of Culture, the director of al-Hay'a al-'aamma, and a great many of the most notable intellectuals and poets in addition to some of the poets of the younger generation.

Because such poetry sees occasional publication in one or two places while none of the official literary journals accept its publication, Mr. Boghdadi argued that there is a need for a special publication. Having once failed to realize the same wish, he was happy that the discussion was taking place in front of the Minister of Culture who, as Mr. Boghdadi remembered, told him: "I do not own publishing houses, I am the Minister and the Ministry does not publish journals but cultural institutes belonging to the Ministry such as al-Hay'a are charged with such publishing." The director of al-Hay'a told Boghdadi that he did not have the money or a budget but that "if the Ministry allocated a budget for 'ammiyya poetry, then I will put out the journal from tomorrow." The minister of culture responded that he did not have the money. At this point, Boghdadi told them that he was "ready as a publisher to finance the project" but he needed a permit from the High Council for the Press (*al-maglis al-a'laa lil-sahaafa*) because laws prohibit publications without government permits. The minister responded that this would be fine. *Ibn Arous* would also to get help in its distribution. Mr. Boghdadi was told that in fact this will be a "new way for cooperation between the private and the public sector in cultural matters."

Mr. Boghdadi finally obtained a permit and set out to organize an editorial board for the journal. He encountered many problems from the beginning, including the fact that some of the most famous 'ammiyya poets he asked help from either refused or wanted to be sole editors. One of the poets who refused to participate in this project believed that this would "isolate" 'ammiyya poetry and that the latter should appear wherever poetry in Classical Arabic appears—that they are both poetry and one should not separate them. This same poet, whom I interviewed, had a very hard time publishing his own poetry in any venue and had to personally finance his collections. He told me that this is only the fate of poetry in 'ammiyya because those who write in fuṣḥa do not run into so many problems in publishing their work. Nevertheless, he refused cooperation in putting out an entire journal devoted to this kind of poetry.

After many attempts, Mr. Boghdadi finally got an editorial board of seven individuals together and they began the publication of *Ibn Arous* in March 1993. The first issue received "many attacks" in the press, as well as some praise. The praise came from a female journalist who expressed dismay that such a journal is nevertheless still written in fuṣḥa, with the exception of the poetry. That is, articles on various topics, historical studies and the criticism were all written in Classical Arabic. A friend of Mr. Boghdadi who is a very famous literary critic also attacked the journal and one of the newspapers organized a whole conference, according to Boghdadi in order to criticize the "thought and the independence of the group of people" who were putting out the journal. Still, *Ibn Arous* also received a lot of encouragement from readers both inside and outside of Egypt. This positive reception along with the planning of articles and new columns created much excitement among the editors. Among the topics that the journal covered was research on all the different Arabic vernaculars "from Sudan to Iraq to Palestine to Tunisia so that different people would get to know each others' languages better and so that these languages would get closer to each other through familiarity." A column was created on this subject and it was called "The Earth Speaks Arabic" (*il-arḍ bititkallim 'arabii*). Note that the title of this column (written in Egyptian Arabic) is meant to underline the fact that the non-Classical vernaculars are also "Arabic." Categorizing the vernaculars as Arabic Languages was (is) perceived to be in need of emphasis because the common term "the Arabic Language" (*al-lugha al-'arabiyya*) refers exclusively to Classical Arabic. The journal also published research articles on the phenomenon of the duality of the language situation. Lesser known poets of 'ammiyya who had been writing since the 1950s were introduced to readers for the first time. Experimental poetry that was shunned by other publications was also published and of course criticism of the poetry and evaluations of its aesthetics and of the "genius of 'ammiyya," which some argued at times outshone that of fuṣḥa.

Each week, the journal received "at least 200 to 250" letters from readers inside and outside of Egypt. They also sent in their own poetry and the journal chose several for inclusion in each issue. But the success of the journal irritated lots of people, according to Boghdadi:

> Many of the cultural and literary authorities [*salaṭaat*] were bothered because a journal like this comes out with special effort and has an expensive cover although on the inside the paper was low quality but in the end it had a special taste and shape and smell and because of that the journal irritated many people. And when I say the elite I don't mean the national security people or government elites . . .

Apparently, the established "literary and cultural priesthood" ("*il-kahanuut*") did not like the fact that an innovative journal like *Ibn Arous* was being put out without their involvement. Consequently, the journal was attacked in the press while at the same time some of the same "priests" showed up at Mr. Boghdadi's office asking that they be appointed "editor-in-chief" or in other capacities.

Two articles that reflect such tensions ran in the first and second issue under a column entitled "The Tower of Babel." The first article had the heading "And Why 'Ibn Arous' Now?!" This article, which like all others is written in fuṣḥa, begins by arguing that "History has forgotten that [fuṣḥa] is a language that is a new-comer [*lugha waafida*] in countries that spoke another language for thousands of years. And it was difficult for people . . . to learn this new-comer language with ease." It goes on to say that even those who learn to engage in literary works in this language do not really "live it" and that in any case their readers are few. It speaks of the "true literary consciousness of the Egyptian people" that is in 'ammiyya, whereas works in fuṣḥa belong only to a group of intellectuals. In its concluding remarks, the article states, "For all these reasons, this journal comes out, not in competition with al-fuṣḥa which we hold dear and sacred [*ni'izzha wa niqaddas-ha*], not to confront it or take anything away from it . . ." The article is not signed by an individual but has the byline "Ibn Arous" (1993, #1, 4–5).

In the second issue, another article appeared under the same column with the heading "There is no Fighting between Fuṣḥa and 'Ammiyya." It is clearly intended to smooth over criticisms apparently raised as a result of the previous article and the enterprise of publishing a whole journal of 'ammiyya poetry. It has both a defensive and a diplomatic tone and speaks of "voices of kindness" that have advised the journal not to get into "side battles" which should not distract from the main goals of the magazine. The article speaks of "problems" that have arisen because some writers and intellectuals seem to believe that "there is a standing fight between us and fuṣḥa." It then goes on to reassure readers that this is not the case by praising Classical Arabic. It also does not back down from some of the earlier arguments such as connecting the "hegemony" of fuṣḥa to "political and social causes." It enlists the authority of many Egyptian poets and writers as well as an equal number of Orientalists (*al-mustashriquun*) such as Silvestre de Sacy, Edward Lane and Richard Burton—"[A]ll of whom emphasized that Egyptian 'ammiyya is not merely a dialect derived from fuṣḥa, but a complete expressive language . . . independent and distinct from fuṣḥa in its suppleness, constructions, and symbols" (1993, #2, 4–5). It seems clear that the journal could not avoid the "battle" between the languages.

In addition to attacks in the press, the cost of the journal turned out to be far greater than Mr. Boghdadi had imagined. After putting out three issues, he realized that he could no longer finance it alone. He therefore went to the minister and to the director of *al-Hay'a* and asked for help. He requested that one of the government cultural institutes (for theatre, film, opera, etc.) put an advertisement in his journal regularly so that at least half of the cost would be born by the payment for the advertisement. He was told, however, that *Ibn Arous* was really a publication of *al-Hay'a*—a public sector company (although it was Mr. Boghdadi's private publishing house that was paying for it) so that if any of its governmental sister institutes wanted to place an advertisement, they should not have to pay for it. The journal was entirely on its own when its small and private sector publisher could no longer afford to bear all the costs.

The rest of the story is similarly perplexing. Mr. Boghdadi went to see many people to ask for help, proposing different solutions for raising some money to save the journal. In the end, funds were not forthcoming and the journal stopped publication after three issues. As Mr. Boghdadi said, "this particular cooperative venture between the public and the private sector did not work out."

> The terrible reactions we got did not stop the magazine as much as the financial problem. We had the capability to withstand and confront [the attacks] but like we say in 'ammiyya, 'they left it to die on its own' in order to avoid a lot of other problems. If they had wanted to give us financial help, [the journal] was going to last and this would have then created a lot of worry ['ala']. But they left it to die so that they wouldn't even have to see themselves as responsible in its killing [*qatlahaa*] and so that there was not even the need to say [admit] *that there is an enmity between the Egyptian cultural priesthood and 'ammiyya* . . .

This "enmity" is in fact quite striking. One hears intellectuals of many political persuasions speak of 'ammiyya in terms that are reminiscent of colonial officials' attitudes toward "native" languages and peoples. It is difficult to fathom, much less explain, the contempt and disdain for 'ammiyya among many intellectuals. I asked Mr. Boghdadi to provide some background on the reasons behind this attitude:

Of course this has been going on for a long time—there is no literary award from the High Council for Culture for 'ammiyya poets. There is an award for poetry but not for 'ammiyya poets. In publishing, most journals, governmental and otherwise, publish poetry in fusha but poetry in 'ammiyya is expressly forbidden [*mamnuu'a*]. There are claims that this is against Arabism [*al-qowmiyya al-'arabiyya*], this is one side. And the other is that this [fusha] is the language of the Qur'an and maybe ['ammiyya] will destroy that language.[18]

The failure of Ibn Arous sent Mr. Boghdadi "into a major depression" because "I could see what others could not: I felt that there is a hidden tyranny [*ta'amur khafi*] without it being observable [*malhuuz*] or without anyone being able to identify the real killer. . . ." The opaque nature of the large and small political games played in the realm of cultural productions makes it difficult, as Mr. Boghdadi points out, to pinpoint exactly who (or what) keeps 'ammiyya from becoming a full-fledged language of writing. What is less opaque is that such games are so frequently played that they have become a ubiquitous part of cultural and political life in Egypt.

In any case, *Ibn Arous* was published in three issues in 1993 (March, May and June) and then ceased. One cannot say that the state was explicitly against it because the magazine received a permit. In addition, the director of *al-Hay'a* took credit for the journal through a letter published in the first issue, although at the same time his publishing house refused any financial assistance. There is a lack of straightforwardness with regard to the involvement of the public sector here. Beyond the involvement of government officials, the top echelons of Egyptian intellectuals according to Mr. Boghdadi also reacted to it with hostility. Egyptian Arabic poetry with a long history and much popularity remains, therefore, on the margins of official culture, without a regular channel for its dissemination and promotion.

Toward the end of my interview with Mr. Boghdadi, we discussed the fact that there are so few books in Egyptian Arabic. He volunteered his own thoughts on the subject saying that he too as a publisher would not publish books in 'ammiyya although he writes his poetry in it:

because language writes the history of a culture. If we write on literature or science we must write it in a language that is capable of staying the same for a long time. The language of 'ammiyya changes faster than fusha and because of this we find that, after a little while, we don't understand what is written in 'ammiyya, after 10 or 20 years . . . as long as we document scientific or historical thought or facts, for facts it is necessary that we insure stability [of language] for a longer time . . . and also fuṣḥa has its [authoritative] sources—there are dictionaries, grammars, etc. . . .

I responded that if every time people tried to create sources for 'ammiyya, publishers refused to publish them, then the situation would always stay the same. Boghdadi's answer was that publishing "in the end is a commercial project" and publishers have to think of their losses. But he added:

> It is possible for specialized institutes like universities and departments of Eastern and Arabic languages to do these kinds of dictionaries [of 'ammiyya] but then they would be entering a situation in which if they made available the rules and grammar of dialects to make dealing with them easier, [but] this would fundamentally transform matters and the Arabic Language [fuṣḥa] would be lost in the end and this is obviously a difficult equation [*mu'aadila*] . . .

Who Censors Whom and Why?

A number of publishers and writers that I spoke with mentioned censorship as a persistent problem. But discovering exactly who is censoring whom points up another arena of cultural and political games. To begin with, the government controls such a large part of the mass media, print and non-print—in production and distribution and as supplier of raw materials—that at times it ends up censoring decisions made by its own institutes. Secondly, ownership does not automatically translate into "control" so that one may be a private publisher but not have full control over decisions with regard to publications. Private publishers need government permits and rely on different kinds of governmental subsidies. At the same time, government officials can have their own private companies. Under such circumstances, the implications of ownership—what belongs to the government and what is privately owned—are not transparent. Recall that although *Ibn Arous* was privately financed, it was treated by the government-controlled publishing house as a governmental publication, in part because it helped in its distribution.

A bookstore owner told me that he was selling a book published by an author, but distributed by the al-Ahram conglomerate, which is basically controlled by the government. The bookstore owner was put in jail for several days for selling this book. He said that although he kept repeating to the judge that he was neither the publisher nor the distributor, he still got charged. In this case, for reasons that were unclear to this bookstore owner, the government went back on its decision to distribute the book and it ended up censoring both one of its own subsidies and the author. Another writer and publisher told me that some of the correctors working for *al-Hay'a* (the government-controlled publishing house) who engage in "linguistic corrections" are very "reactionary." For example, some correctors had deleted certain lines and words from the poems of several poets because the correctors "were not in agreement" with what they said. "But" he added, "these people are never asked to explain themselves or [are] pursued legally" even by the publishing house they work for. Such "corrections," which blur the line between "linguistic correction" and censorship, are apparently widespread as other people that I interviewed recounted similar stories. (See also chapter 4.) In such cases, the correctors often invoke linguistic rather than political reasons for their "corrections"—and so it may appear that no one is really doing any censoring.

The article in the *Chronicle of Higher Education* cited earlier, also mentions the following incident on censorship:

> In January, the Egyptian Culture Ministry, acceding to demands by some conservative Islamists, banned three novels that the government itself was publishing, declaring them "explicitly indecent material." The day following the ministry's edict, Ali Abu Shadi, who was the vice minister of culture, was fired for allowing the books to be published. In protest of the censorship, four editors at the ministry resigned. A group of writers and intellectuals boycotted the government-sponsored Cairo Book Fair. (*CHE* 11/10/2001)

To the outside world, this story suggests a familiar scenario—the government generally engages in censorship due to pressures from "conservative Islamists." But it must be remembered that because the government both owns and controls such a large part of the media, "it" does many things simultaneously which at times constitute contradictory acts. The government and the media cannot be separated so easily. No large arena of power can be free of contradictions except perhaps under fully totalitarian conditions. The many government owned cultural institutions fill their ranks with all kinds of people including intellectuals who believe in free speech and the exploration of political, religious and cultural taboos. In this way, books that private publishers may not publish because of financial or political considerations can get published by "government" publishing houses. Although it would not be incorrect to say that both the government and "conservative Islamists" are responsible for some of the censorship, it would be too simplistic because it would gloss over just how convoluted the situation seems to be. As in the case of the journal *Ibn Arous,* it is difficult in the end to point a finger at just one party.

Leftists, Pan-Arabists and Fears of the Vernaculars

The profound hostility toward writing in 'ammiyya has too many layers to be fully explained. Nevertheless, a number of the intellectuals that I interviewed did discuss some of the reasons, which I would like to report on in this section. Like many other Arab writers and intellectuals, Mr. Boghdadi believes that a central reason for the pervasiveness of hostility towards 'ammiyya is that it is historically associated with leftist ideologies: "This mighty opposition [against 'ammiyya] started from a long time ago because all 'ammiyya poets were revolutionaries and trouble makers [*mubridiin*] and at the same time progressives or leftists. . . ." The same point was made by Mahmoud Amin al-Alem, who is perhaps the most prominent socialist writer and public intellectual in Egypt.[19] Professor Amin al-Alem is in his 70s. He is a widely respected figure who has been active in many of the cultural and political movements within Egypt and the Arab world and has published a number of books in philosophy and literature. He is a very articulate and open man with a great sense of humor. Amin al-Alem mentioned that in the 1950s, "many of the great 'aammiyya poets like Salah Jahin, Fu'ad Haddad, Sayyid Higaab and Abdel Rahman Abnuudi emerged from inside the Marxist movement." Most were put in jail and wrote poems and songs that became famous while they were in prison. Such poets were of course not imprisoned because they wrote in 'ammiyya but because they were leftists. Yet the association between their ideology and their choice of language became established and further resonated with the older accusation against proponents of writing in 'ammiyya that they were "against religion" (Booth 1992). Thus, 'ammiyya is also historically associated with "leftist" or at any rate with nonreligious opposition groups and individuals whose views were perceived as threatening political stability in the Arab world. In Egypt, Islamist opposition groups were seen as less problematic than leftist parties by the governments of Sadat and Mubarak. Although members of both kinds of groups were censored, imprisoned and executed, a conscious decision was made to "beat" the left by allowing more leeway to the Islamists. The many consequences of such a policy (now perhaps recognized as a mistake) cannot be pursued further here. However, it is crucial to understand the fear of 'ammiyya also as part and parcel of this policy.[20]

In the 1920s and 30s, secular nationalists had advocated writing in 'ammiyya instead of fusha. They viewed both the British and the "Arab invasion" of Egypt as colonial enterprises. Such ideas were forcefully brought out in many public and published debates about the proper language for Egyptian literature. Classical Arabic was characterized as being artificial because no one spoke it and hence it could not represent Egyptians. In 1929, one social critic wrote:

National literature demands first and foremost naturalness. Is it natural in any way that we address the *fallaḥ* or the merchant in a language foreign to him! One of the most distinguishing characteristics of nationalism is the language in which the people [*qawm*] speak. If we really want to have a national literature, so we must write in the colloquial language. [21]

The problem of "naturalness" has not been resolved. In fiction, some writers write dialogues in Egyptian Arabic, while the rest of their prose is in Classical Arabic. Other writers, like Naguib Mahfouz, write dialogues in Classical Arabic but the language is often a translation from what the dialogues would have been in Egyptian Arabic. In such cases, it is difficult to pinpoint the characters in time and place because, again, no one actually speaks like that.

Since the emergence of pan-Arabism in the 1950s, some of its ideals and rhetoric continue to dominate social, political and cultural life in Egypt—a country that sought to be at the forefront of this movement in order to fulfill its role as the historical leader of the Arab world. What has been the impact of the ideology of pan-Arabism on the language question? Amin al-Alem believes that the slogan of Arab unity managed to silence the language debates: "from the point of view of language, . . . I believe that the mistake the socialists fell into at that time [1950s] was because the dominant slogan was the Arabist unity movement, the socialists tried to compete with the Arabists in their Arabism."[22] One consequence of this "competition" has been that most secular intellectuals somehow ceased to perceive the choice between 'ammiyya and fuṣḥa as constituting a central aspect of political and cultural life in Egypt—unlike those writing in the 1920s. As has been mentioned before, pan-Arabism chose to define an Arab as one who speaks "Arabic" and most of its followers wrote in the "Arabic Language." Rejecting both a religious and a racial basis for defining an Arab was expressly part of a movement that saw itself as a *modern* and progressive alternative to the colonial dictates of single nation-states and to the domination of politics by religion. Pan-Arabism championed the Arabic language, and propagated the Arabic Culture, Arab Thought, the Arab Character, the Voice of the Arab, as forms of resistance against colonialism and against Israeli occupation of Palestinian lands. Yet, it embedded an expressly nonreligious movement in the language of Islam. The movement's choice of Classical Arabic is generally explained by the argument that this language is the same across the Arab world and hence is indispensable to their unity, whereas the vernaculars' differences would only serve to create divisions. At present, the strength of the relationship between Islam and Classical Arabic is underplayed or denied by many nonreligious intellectuals with different degrees of commitment to pan-Arabism. Amin al-Alem sees claims about that relationship as "just talk": "That's just talk, it is a judgement, it is an ideology . . . In Lebanon, who revitalized the Arabic Language? Who added to it? Christians. Therefore, religion did not play a big role here. Here the pan-Arab thinking [*il-fikr il-qowmi*] is more important than religion." Indeed the great extent of the participation of non-Muslim Arabs in reviving Classical Arabic through many efforts, including the production of modern dictionaries and proposals for grammatical reform, shows the early success of the pan-Arab movement in its inclusive world view. But the enthusiasm of non-Muslims shows that religion was in fact an important factor—one could unite around a common language and hope for the fading away of the link between that language and Islam. And yet, by the time of my last fieldwork in Cairo, the explicit participation of non-Muslims in language debates seemed to have disappeared. Against the original wishes of the movement for inclusiveness, a number of factors converged to make it into a rather intolerant ideology. One was that by choosing the global category of "Arabness" and therefore Classical Arabic, it greatly reinforced the historical overlap between Islam and Arabs. The other was the continuation of colonial rule which made it easy for those in power to characterize any dissent as helping the "foreigners and their stooges." Equally importantly was the creation of Israel which solidified, more than any other single factor, the desire for a large and powerful "Arab" block to resist it. A perception of such outside threats, the desire to gain the support of Islamic nationalists and so on eroded the actual inclusiveness of the movement. That inclusiveness has survived far more in rhetoric than in reality.

Egypt has been both a leader of pan-Arabism and a site of intense resentment towards that ideology. Egyptians had to be made, often forefully, into "Arabs" because they did not historically identify themselves as such. Egypt was self-consciously a nation not only before pan-Arabism but also before becoming a colony of the British Empire. Its territorial continuity since ancient times, its unique history as exemplified in its pharaonic past and later on its Coptic language and culture, had already made Egypt into a nation for centuries. Egyptians saw themselves, their history, culture and language as specifically Egyptian and not "Arab." The version of political unity sought by pan-Arabism required an erasure of local cultural differences among Arabs. And one of the prime local differences was linguistic. Amin al-Alem told me that this was one of the most important divisions between socialists who supported a form of Arabism that would respect local specificities and the Nasserites. Even for those who fully supported pan-Arabism and its resistance to colonial rule, these changes in identity were difficult to assimilate. The Egyptian historian Leila Ahmed writes in her memoir:

> The year was 1952 . . . I remember how I hated that incessant rhetoric. Al-qowmiyya! Al-Uraba! Nahnu al-Arab! Arab nationalism! Arabness! We the

Arabs! . . . Propaganda *is* unpleasant. And one could not escape it. The moment one turned on the radio, there it was: military songs, nationalistic songs, and endless, endless speeches. . . . Nor was it only through the media that the government was pressuring us into acceptance of its broad political agenda and coercing us into being Arab. For this was the era, too, of growing political repression and of the proliferation of the *mukhabarat,* the secret police—the era when political opponents and people suspected of being disloyal to the revolution were being jailed or disappearing. In this atmosphere, being disloyal to the revolution and to the Arab cause (being, as it were, un-Arab) became as charged and dangerous for Egyptians as being un-American was for Americans in the McCarthy era. (Ahmed 1999: 245–6)

Ahmed also describes how the new definition of Arab gradually excluded non-Muslim Arabs such as Copts and Jews. At present, although many believe that the dream of pan-Arabism has either gone into hiding or has actually turned into a nightmare, calls for writing in 'ammiyya are far fainter and have a fringe quality to them. Decades of being branded as either leftists, supporters of colonialism or against Islam and Arabism seem to have made such calls far riskier than they once were. Recall that the acquisition editor of a publishing house explained that for there to be more books in 'ammiyya "someone has to take the risk." It seems to me that these were the kinds of social costs to reputation that he was referring to in that assessment. Hence there are multiple kinds of censure that are common and form an explicit part of debates on language.

Amin al-Alem believes that Classical Arabic has been modernized successfully and that its progress shows advances (*tatawwur*) in thought and culture. At the same time, he characterizes it as the language of the powerful, "not related to the interests of the people":

If by democracy we mean real democracy and not just elections so that those who are already in power reach power and domination again, if there were popular participation and everyone could take part . . . *then in that case language would be in reality connected with the people and to their interests, expertise, thoughts* . . . but . . . what we [have] is government domination of the economy, of education, of thought and therefore there is also domination of language. And therefore there are two kinds of language, the kind that is official, bureaucratic [*diwaaniyya*], whether it be *fasiiha,* or half *fasiiha* or modern *fasiiha* [*fasiiha hadisa*] and then there is the language of the street, the language of daily connection and this is the natural result of domination from the top and its relations to society.

Note that for Amin al-Alem, the degree to which some usages are fusha or "*fasiih*" does not matter because they all have the same relationship to power and they are all different from the "language of the street." I asked him why he has chosen to write in fuṣḥa. He responded with a rhetorical question: "[H]ow can you write philosophy in 'ammiyya—it does not have the tools and the vocabulary that would be necessary." He explained further that he wrote his thesis in French, but later translated it into Classical Arabic.

I interviewed a prominent 'ammiyya poet who was also my language teacher for a short period of time.[23] Zein al-Abdine Fu'ad is in his 50s and has published volumes of poetry. His views on the relations between Classical Arabic and politics are similar to those of Amin al-Alem: "The religious and political ruling classes always use fuṣḥa. The dominant religious and the political classes benefit from its existence. I am not just speaking about Egypt but about all of the Arab world. . . ." I asked him whether he thought that contemporary uses of fuṣḥa at times continue to carry associations with the language of the Qur'an, even when the content has nothing to do with religion. He responded: "it is true that the associations [*tadaa'iyaat*] of fuṣḥa, their roots or origin is the Qur'an and *if there is a [linguistic] dispute, we all turn to the Qur'an and that is a fundamental issue*. . . ." That so long after modernization efforts began, the main linguistic authority remains the Qur'an demonstrates, among other things, that no writer and no social movement, including pan-Arabism, has managed to create new sources of authority for the renovated and modernized Classical Arabic. Recall that in chapter 4, the older correctors cited fifteenth-century grammatical treatise written by religious scholars and based on Qur'anic usages as the sources they consult.

Zein al-Abdine Fu'ad told me that he and other 'ammiyya poets generally find it difficult to find publishers for their collections and often have to pay out of their own pockets. He explained why he decided not to write in fuṣḥa in these terms.

> From the time I was 17, I stopped writing altogether. I stayed for three years and did not write anything on purpose—a conscious decision I made. I decided not to write at all because I noticed that there is a difference between the manner in which I think and the manner in which I write. There is a difference that I noticed when I was 15 or 16. I started to get to know socialist thinking and see the problems of life while writing in a manner that was completely romantic [*rumansiyya*]. But these don't go together and so I decided not to write until I would be able to write like I think. . . .

Iman Mirsal, the poet we began this chapter with, explained to me that she did not confront a choice of writing language when she started to write:

> When I came to write for the first time, I had not read absolutely anything in 'ammiyya. . . . I remember the first thing I wrote when I was 12 which was

on myself because my mother had died and that day was Mothers' Day. I remember that very well and my language was the standard [uses word in English] that I knew. This was the language of the poetry that I read and so even the question of which language I should write in did not come up . . . and it still does not. . . .

At the same time, she also believes that fuṣḥa is the language of power:

> Fuṣḥa is one lump/block [*kutla*], [it is] one thing even given its levels. . . . For example, when you see a [government] clerk writing a request to some organization, you will see just how important this is to him. He might tear up seven pieces of paper, and he is not thinking that this fuṣḥa is supposed to be more "simple" or. . . . He sees that this [language] is something different, meaning fuṣḥa, and this comes from his old religious feelings and because of that, fuṣḥa is the language of hegemony or authority [*il-hiimana*] whether it is religious hegemony or governmental.[24]

Although in certain contexts and for some groups, fuṣḥa may be "one block," as Mirsal points out, she sees her own style of poetry in fuṣḥa as modern—different from what the language was like a century ago.

"Chauvinism" against Egyptian Arabic

It is not easy to sum up the ambivalent feelings of non-Egyptians toward Egyptian Arabic. At times, particularly among educated non-Egyptians, there seems to be a mix of contempt, fear and a recognition of its relatively higher status (compared to other Arabic vernaculars). In discussing the language situation with a number of Jordanians and Syrians in Cairo, I was often struck by the degree to which they disdained Egyptian Arabic. Syrians, for example, invariably stated that their knowledge of Classical Arabic is superior to that of Egyptians in part because their educational system is better. They also were surprised to find that Egyptians were proud of their language and used it "too frequently" with no apparent self-consciousness. On the subject of allowing the writing of non-Classical Arabic, non-Egyptians argued that there would be no basis in preferring one vernacular over another for a written language that would serve the Arab world. They argued against the choice of Egyptian Arabic as a (written) lingua franca. Interestingly, many Egyptians seemed to agree on both points.

That there would be no basis to choose one vernacular over another is debatable. For several well-known reasons, Egyptian Arabic has become a lingua franca in the Arab world in oral interactions. Egypt has been exporting labor, movies and television programs to the rest of the Arab world for decades. It has also been a cultural center for centuries and hence visited by large numbers of other Arabs. As a result, Egyptian Arabic has become the most widely understood of all Arabic vernaculars. Mr. Boghdadi finds "chauvinism [*shovoniyya*] and nationalism" on the part of other Arabs specifically with respect to the Egyptian 'ammiyya:

> since this is the only 'ammiyya [in the Arab world] that is understood by all Arab peoples. I mean when someone speaks Iraqi or Tunisian or Moroccan, it is rare that a Syrian can understand everything he says. But the only language that can connect is the Egyptian 'ammiyya. I believe that the screams [*na'araat*] of pan-Arabists specifically against Egyptian 'ammiyya is because other dialects are incapable of becoming channels of connection and communication. There is for example Nabatean poetry that is written in Saudi Arabia but no one can understand it except themselves and so this dialect is neither defended nor attacked by anyone because it is so limited. But there is fear of Egyptian 'ammiyya, because it is something between fuṣḥa and 'ammiyya—it is in my opinion an inhabited fuṣḥa . . .

The last statement alludes to the frequent characterization of fuṣḥa as the lingua franca of Arabs and Muslims. But it is a language that has no native speakers and therefore is not "inhabited" by speakers. Egyptian Arabic, according to Boghdadi is both a language of wider communication and "inhabited."

Conclusion

In this chapter, I have tried to explicate the ways in which different intellectuals experience and think about Classical and Egyptian Arabic. Of particular interest is that on the one hand, fuṣḥa is seen by some as a language that provides a space for modern and alternative ways of thinking and being. But on the other hand, they also see it as a language that is used by those in power for the purposes of political domination. At the same time, because Egyptian Arabic has not been allowed to become officially a language for creativity and critical thought, it can represent in contrast a "backward" and rigid world. For example, the number of published love stories in Classical Arabic exceeds by far those in Egyptian Arabic. This is of course the case for almost any subject. But at the same time, the steady expansion of nonprint media in which Egyptian Arabic dominates (e.g., movies) has made associations between that language and a wider world more established.

We also saw the profound ambivalence of most intellectuals toward both languages but in particular toward allowing Egyptian Arabic to become the language of prose writing—any writing that can be characterized as "serious"—fiction, history, social sciences and so on. And here, there seems to be an agreement between them and government cultural institutions. Even those who write their poetry in 'ammiyya, who have suffered greatly because of prejudice toward that language and articulate the political games that are played in this arena, are not convinced that the latter should become a language of writing. In many ways, the experiences and ideas of intellectuals seem to differ from those of people described in chapter 5. But there are also commonalities: that Classical Arabic should remain as the language of writing (see also Haeri 1996). The poet Mirsal likened the disjunction between the language of speaking and that of writing to "life" existing in one place and "culture" in another. I will take up the implications of this characterization in the next chapter.

Chapter Six

Conclusion

Egyptian Arabic was created by our fathers and grand-parents and we suckled it like the milk of our mothers. We learned it while we were still young and pronounced in it the first words that left our mouths. We remained speaking it throughout our lives, at home, in the field, at the factory and in offices, at the market and the university until it mixed with our blood and satiated us and we began to love it just like we love our fathers and mothers. We add something new to it everyday, and in doing so we feel that we are perfecting it—we educate it and bring it up as if it were our daughter and we grow to love it like we love our children. Our love for it is twofold: the love for our parents and the love for our children.

—Osman Sabri, 1967

I began this book with the aim of analyzing the role of language in the nexus of state, nation and religion in Egypt. I would like to end it by revisiting three of the themes that have run through the preceding chapters: the relations between language, modernity and vernacularization; the struggles to breathe contemporaneity into Classical Arabic; and some of the results of those struggles, in particular the persistent ambiguity in the status of what we have called contemporary Classical Arabic.

In the introduction, we juxtaposed vernacular and sacred languages in terms of ownership/custodianship, arbitrariness of the sign, translatability and human versus divine origin. I would like to focus first on the different property relations between speakers, their mother tongues and sacred languages. For Egyptians, there is ample evidence to suggest that they see

Egyptian Arabic as their property, as a possession. Osman Sabri, who was quoted above, was a legal advisor (*mustashaar*) to the mixed courts in the 1960s. The quotation is extracted from an article of his in which he advocated writing in Egyptian Arabic. This article was written in 'ammiyya in 1967 and reprinted in the literary journal *al-Garaad* in 1994. Note that whereas it is Classical Arabic that renders learners literate, in the case of Egyptian Arabic according to Sabri, it is the speakers that educate it— "*we . . .* perfect it." He also argues against changing and simplifying Classical Arabic because it is an "entrusted legacy" and goes on to say:

> Most partisans [*anṣaar*] of the Classical Arabic Language do not deny its difficulties and complexities and its unsuitability for expansion and for life, and they tried its simplification with suggestion after suggestion. Some even went so far as to propose getting rid of the case endings at the ends of words. . . . As a Muslim Arab I protest all such suggestions that try to change Classical Arabic to the point of destroying its historical character (101).

He further elaborates his position on the basis that the language "is not our[s] to deal with [*nitsarraf fiiha*] as we please." He does not say that the language is God's Word, but refers to "Arabs" (i.e., Peninsular Arabs) who were its "owner" (*ashaabha*—can also mean "adherents") and who had the "right of modification/disposal [*haqq il-taṣarrof*] to it."

> In so far as we are concerned, this is the language of the Noble Qur'an and of old Arab literature that is studied by specialists. . . . But if we decided to develop it and give it life, simplify its grammar and change its rules, this is a work that has no finality to it . . . and in the end we would end up with the Modern Arabic language or Egyptian Arabic . . . which is what I am inviting everyone to write in because it is ours, *it is a possession in our hands* [*milkina fii 'iidina*], we knead it and develop it according to our needs and desires and moods, *without obligation to any limits* . . . and here I ask all those who would object: "why this hypocrisy or literary cowardice?" and "why this circling around?" Is it not better and easier that we confront facts [*haqaa'iq*] and call things by their name? (101–102).

Sabri's analysis also captures the fact that while Egyptians have authority over their own language, their authority in relation to Classical Arabic is precarious and contestable. Furthermore, it seems to me that a change in the status of Egyptians from custodians to owners of the language is not merely a matter of time. That is, no matter how much time passes and how modernized Classical Arabic may become, Egyptians or other Arabs will not become its owners without a number of other radical changes that I will elaborate below.

More than three decades after Sabri wrote those lines, the question of "rights" with regard to Classical Arabic continues to be controversial. In al-Ahram of June 7, 1996, an article was published with the headline: "Award to Novel Arouses a Tempest: Is it an Author's Right [*haqq*] to Change the Rules of the Arabic Language?" (*hal min haqq al-kaatib 'an yighayyar qawaa'id al-lugha al-'arabiyya*) (6/7/1996:22). The article posed the question with respect to a novel published in 1994 by Fathi Imbabi that had just won a government prize. This novel was mentioned in chapter 4 in relation to the author's suggestions on further changes to Classical Arabic. The al-Ahram reporter shows surprise and communicates her disapproval over the selection committee's choice of this novel. She begins the article by asking whether one can separate language from the "foundation of a literary work" and goes on to cite, with a degree of sarcasm apparent in her use of exclamation marks, some of the author's suggestions for grammatical changes to Classical Arabic: "And [one's] surprise increases when we discover that those who made the selection are writers who have been able to work (*tatwii'*) with the language *without attempts to break its rules* . . ." (Ibid., emphasis added).

Many long decades of modernization and hundreds of articles and books on the subject have not yet taken the controversy out of changes to Classical Arabic. The reporter of al-Ahram interviews a few members of the selection committee who tell her that although there were reservations about this novel, they thought it was deserving of the award. One interviewer, in defending the choice, tells her that "[We] have to admit that experiments and mistakes are both tools of advancement even with respect to language." Another member of the selection committee praises the content of the novel "in spite of [the fact] that the author's attempt in linguistic renovation has not been in all instances successful." We should note that the novelist in fact does not apply most of the changes that he suggests in his postscript in the novel itself and the al-Ahram article mentions this as well.

Similar arguments about linguistic choices, particularly in prose, are also made with regard to written languages that are based on vernaculars. But what is notable in this case is that the reporter characterizes the matter in terms of a "right," as Sabri did, which she does not believe exists as she repeats the question rhetorically at the end of her article: "Is it an author's right to change the grammar of the Arabic Language and make mistakes in it and win a prize." Criticisms of innovations or choices made by authors who write in vernacular-based languages are generally not framed in terms of "rights" but in terms of bad or unwarranted aesthetic choices, or at worst, questions are raised with regard to an author's knowledge of the language and of literary standards. Why does Imbabi or any other novelist lack this right? One has rights to vernaculars but in relation to sacred languages, they can always be contested.

I suggest that the reason the language situation remains unresolved is in part because the question of the rights (*haqq il-taṣarrof*) of Egyptians to Classical Arabic is very difficult to settle. In order to settle that question, a series of other highly divisive and complex questions would have to be settled as well. Among them would be the sacred status of the *language* of the Qur'an, whether Egyptians are Arabs, and if so what happens to their own language; if they are not Arabs, then why should they use Classical Arabic? Furthermore, if Egyptians' claim to the language is mainly due to the fact that they are (in majority) Muslims, then are they custodians of this language or its owners? The simultaneous positions that the language is sacred but certain changes (which?) can be cautiously made are untenable. Who has the authority to define the limits of such changes? A sacred language cannot become a fully living language until it loses that status. Since modernization efforts began, renovated forms of the language have carried with them at every turn, all the contradictions, accusations, uncertainties and struggles that are inherent in attempts to make a sacred language contemporary. Whether one calls changes to the language "modernization," or "simplification" the point is that change necessarily goes against purity and sacredness. Put simply, Classical Arabic is not the mother tongue of Egyptians or other Arabs and, not being its "owners," their rights to the language will remain precarious. The dilemma is that were they to take steps to own it, the language would cease to be sacred. Few if any of these problems would have arisen had Classical Arabic remained simply the language of religion, while other spheres of life would be served by writing in Egyptian Arabic.

Vernacularization and Modernity

In the introduction to this book, we began a discussion of the importance of vernacularization to the "ushering in" of modernity. I would like to return now to that discussion and to Pollock's study of vernacularization in India. My central interest here is to find an answer to the question of why vernacularization should be so significant a socio-historical process. Pollock (1998: 45) points out that vernacularization in southern Asia and Europe have had similar consequences and occurred in both areas within the same time period. He goes on to say:

> with respect to the production of literary texts, something unprecedented came into being in the period between roughly 1000–1500. At different places and at different times . . . people in southern Asia began to make such texts in languages that did not travel—and that they knew did not travel—as far as Sanskrit, the language that had monopolized the world of literary production for the preceding thousand years.

Viewed through the angle of vernacularization, the construct of modernity can perhaps escape its automatic association with the particular experience of Europe and hence acquire wider applicability. Pollock links vernacularization to "changing conceptions of community" and to "transformations in cultural practice, social identity and political order" (Ibid: 47, 41). He sees a central role for vernacularization "in having "help[ed] make early modern Europe modern" (Ibid: 65). Such assertions make sense intuitively but we have yet to spell out why a vernacular language is so central to such changes. Again, there is a danger that in examining the consequences of vernacularization, we characterize them as "modern" and then define modernity based on those consequences.

Perhaps one possible way out of this is to analyze more closely the nature of vernacular languages, as we did in the introduction. What is it about vernaculars that make those "transformations" and the new "conceptions" possible? The replacement of sacred languages with vernacular ones, and the use of the latter for high and low written purposes can have the consequences that Pollock mentions because of the particular relation that speakers have with vernaculars. For one thing, they own them and have authority over them. They also treat the relation between a vernacular's forms and meanings as a matter that is in their own realm—as part and parcel of the mundane world. In that relation, the sacred non-arbitrariness of the sign is absent. Hence speakers are less constrained in their use of vernacular languages—they can define the limits in their creations and innovations, notwithstanding the fact that speakers are differentiated among themselves in terms of power and authority. I am aware that we do not normally go around discoursing about the relation between form and meaning, though in the Arab world, many people talk about that relationship with respect to the language of the Qur'an. Equally important, the change from the use of a sacred language to that of a vernacular changes a community's conception of knowledge because what comes to be created in the vernacular will also be considered as knowledge. In Egypt, Classical Arabic continues to be viewed as the prime container of knowledge—by learning it, one automatically acquires knowledge. Hence generally what is outside of it, is either of secondary importance or of none at all. Indeed, Egyptians are discouraged to produce work in their own language. In this way, vernacularization changes a community's relation to its past and present through a transformation of what constitutes knowledge.

We do not know of a single vernacular language whose speakers claim for them divine origins, though communities develop at times very different ideologies with respect to their mother tongues. A vernacular language is one whose speakers "can add something new to it everyday" because it is theirs. This is the case, in spite of the fact that speakers of vernacular-based languages may be constrained by standardization norms and inequalities of access, class, gender and so on. In these ways, Egyptian Arabic is a modern language while the modernity of contemporary Classical Arabic remains difficult to achieve. Adding, changing and subtracting are not possible, at least not without the struggles that we have discussed, if there is a belief in the divine non-arbitrariness of the sign.

In short, I am suggesting that vernacularization is essential to certain socio-historical transformations because of the contrasts between sacred and vernacular languages: differential property rights, arbitrariness of the sign, the question of origin, and the possibility of translation. Clearly, all of these features are related to one another. The argument constructed here can also go some way toward answering a larger question that was posed in the introduction: What is the role of language in the construction of different social and political orders? Without repeating all that has been said so far, we can say that language is at the heart of such constructions.

One issue that has not so far been dealt with is the relation between religion and vernacularization: Has Islam prevented vernacularization from occurring? For a number of reasons, the answer is certainly negative. To begin with, most Muslim-majority countries speak and write in their own mother tongues and in other vernaculars (see the introduction). For them, Classical Arabic is above all the language of religion and, apart from religious scholars who *may* write at times in Classical Arabic, no one writes in that language. Therefore, Islam has not prevented vernacularization in those countries. Of course apart from other differences, non-Arabic-speaking Muslims do not consider their mother tongues as both genealogically related to Classical Arabic and as corrupt versions of that language. Hence, the question of a "choice" between their mother tongue or Classical Arabic as a language of writing does not come up.

If Islam has not prevented vernacularization, has it discouraged translations of the Qur'an into vernacular forms of Arabic, which is necessary for vernacularization to take place? In India, as Pollock states, Sanskrit texts remained untranslated long after vernacularization began. Hence, vernacular translations of sacred texts promote vernacularization but are not essential to it. In Muslim countries whose official languages are not related to Arabic, the Qur'an has been translated. In Turkey, the Qur'an was translated into Turkish in the twelfth century (Holt et al. 1970: 684).[1] Translations of parts of the Qur'an into Persian are more than 1,000 years old and at present there are numerous complete translations of this text in Iran. Bilingual editions are ubiquitous and may be found in most homes. Although the question of translation has been a point of debate and disagreement since the early centuries of Islam, Abu Hanifa, who was Persian-speaking and a founder of one of Islam's legal schools, issued a fatwa in the eighth century that opened the way (Khorramshahi 1997: 619). He argued that the recitation of the Sura of Fatiha (the opening chapter of the Qur'an) for those who do not know Arabic, but who wish to pray, is allowed (Ibid: 691). A number of *hadis* and Qur'anic verses are cited in support of the permissibility of translation. The most prominent verses in this respect are: "And we have not sent an Apostle except [to teach] in the language of his own people in order to make [things] clear to them" (14: 4).[2] The other verse that is cited is "God does not demand of anyone except according to his abilities" (2: 286).

Although the Qur'an refers to its language as a "miracle," challenges readers to create writing that would rival it, and mentions a number of times that its language is "clear," nowhere does it forbid its own translation. It remains for historians to tell us when, how and why the ideology of the untranslatability of the Qur'an developed. The evidence of the achievements of early Muslim scholars in many fields suggests that for them the language was supple and pliable, not untouchable. As is well known, when confronted with words or constructions in the Qur'an that they were unsure of, such scholars sought the aid of Bedouins whose dialect was the same as that of the Prophet in order to settle such questions. This method of verification suggests that their conception of the language of the Qur'an did not preclude asking humans for clarification. And that seems to be a very long way from present-day claims.

Constructions of Contemporaneity

For the purposes of understanding and explicating some of the consequences of the language situation in Egypt, perhaps one can replace the problematic term of "modernity" with "contemporaneity." The struggles described in chapter 4 to produce versions of Classical Arabic that would be responsive to the contemporary needs and lives of Egyptians were (are) not just struggles with linguistic form but also with clashing ideas about Egypt's past and present. In using this term, I hope to better capture both what Egypt is today and what it has the potential to become—the potential to confront "its self" and narrow the many divides created by the language situation. That Egypt's relations to its self are many and that there are multiple such "selves" is evident. Yet it is still useful to examine such questions in the context of constructions of "self."

To begin, no Egyptian doubts or denies that Egyptian Arabic is her/his mother tongue. It is a language that is contemporary with its speakers in all their heterogeneity and myriad linguistic needs. Preventing it from becoming a language of writing and self-expression shows a highly uneasy relation to the self. Children grow up hearing at school and other places that their mother tongue is "weak," "corrupt," "has no grammar," is the "language of donkeys" and so on. And the language they have yet to gain any mastery over is far superior—in fact so much so that it is the language of the Qur'an. Every act of self-expression is also a translation, even when one writes in one's mother tongue. But there is a certain denial of the contemporary self in Egypt that, ironically, is obliged to translate itself into a language far less contemporary if it desires written self-expression. In print, Egyptians have to translate themselves for themselves, and they are obliged to so for the outside world.

An uneasy relation to the self is not the same as having an identity crisis. Egyptians in fact have a very strong sense of their national identity and of their differences with other Arabs. But the obligation to disown a central defining aspect of their identity—their mother tongue—when it comes to writing, to creating and evaluating what is or is not knowledge, mediates and intervenes in their relations to themselves and to the world. The censure of Egyptian Arabic from official and national culture, seem to prevent Egypt from tapping its many potentials. Egypt's constitution makes no mention of the existence of Egyptian Arabic, educational institutions do not teach it, in textbooks no historical characters seem to have spoken in this language, and in cultural productions involving print, it is shunned. For these and other similar reasons, as I have tried to indicate, Egypt has a fraught and uncertain relationship with its own contemporaneity.

Many Egyptians strongly believe in the idea of a unified pan-Arab nation and are disappointed that pan-Arabism has failed politically.[3] But what most people point to as its success is language—namely, Classical Arabic. The language alone is made to carry the flag of unity and the burden of other failures. It is as though all hope for a rescue of the political ideals of pan-Arabism depends on the language. In this way, the language and the omnipresent rhetoric about it also serve to mask the failures. And the more threats are felt from the outside (against Palestinians, Arabs and Muslims in general) the higher becomes the pitch of the rhetoric in praise and support of it. Pan-Arabism was put forward both as a modern alternative to the colonial divisions of the Arab world and against the Western model of single nation-states. It was also conceived as an alternative to Islamist political groups (not to Islam as a religion). Egyptian Islamists do not see a contradiction between being believers and at the same time pan-Arabists—in fact they see Islam as more consistent with a less territorial form of nationalism. For them, there is no question that Classical Arabic is the language of Islam and that it is believers who have its custodianship. Those who have wished to create a different world through changes to the language and to stage an "indigenous modernity" for the Arab world cannot be also its custodians.

Yet pan-Arabists chose Classical Arabic, and as some Egyptians put it, "tried to beat the Islamists at their own game." The Egyptian self had to become "Arab." To appropriate the prize jewel of Islamic civilization, the "miracle" of the religion, as the Qur'an refers to its language, and the wish to take possession of it—a language that admits of no owners and already has ardent custodians—has proved a tall order. In failing to create an "indigenous" or "Arab modernity," pan-Arabists' choice of language has been immensely consequential. As pan-Arabism changed from being an opposition and liberation movement to becoming the official ideology of the state during and after Nasser, the language question became increasingly politicized. The progressive ideals of early pan-Arabism that now remain mostly as rhetoric continue to provide a progressive cover, albeit a thin one, for governments that have proven to be far from those ideals.

The constitutions of 1923, 1956, 1971 and 1980 of Egypt all state that "Islam is the official religion of the state, and Arabic [*al-lugha al-'arabiyya*] is the state's official language." It is interesting that the two are always stated together under the same Article (in the 1980 constitution, it is Article 2). These constitutions were drawn up in very different political climates, the first one while Egypt was under the control of the British colonial administration with King Fu'ad as the nominal ruler; the second after the revolution of 1952 and independence; and the third and the fourth in the era of Sadat. That all the constitutions of Egypt eschew any mention of the mother tongue of Egyptians in defining a citizen, and that the language that is mentioned as the official one has a deeply ambiguous status, are matters with direct political consequences. It would not do to merely repeat here that the project of pan-Arabism has required the "unity" that Classical Arabic is supposed to provide to all Arabs. The constitution could have simultaneously recognized both as official languages, as the constitutions of many other countries do. By defining a citizen in part in relation to Classical Arabic, the status of the language is acknowledged in the constitution. But on the same basis, the status of being a citizen is put in doubt in the absence of any acknowledgement of that citizen's mother tongue.

Beyond its use for religious purposes, most Egyptians find speaking and writing in Classical Arabic difficult, especially given the dire state of pre-college education. The official language thus acts as an obstacle to their participation in the political realm. There is of course no suggestion here that this is the only reason for the absence of democracy in Egypt. But the language situation makes a strong comment on the nature of politics in that country. There seem to be deeply entrenched political interests in having Classical Arabic be the sole official language. But we ask again, as we did in chapter two, *which* Classical Arabic is the official language? The one that is the language of the Qur'an and of Islam, or contemporary Classical Arabic, or both? What happens to the status of non-Muslims whose religions do not have the same kind of privileged relationship with Islam? The general silence on these questions, both on the part of official institutions and on the part of intellectuals continues to be maintained.

That silence that extends to the wider implications of the language situation is maintained even in the works of Arab scholars who are constructively critical about their societies. A recent example is the Arab Human Development Report published in 2002 and prepared by a number of Arab scholars under the auspices of the United Nations Development Programme (UNDP). A full consideration of the entire report cannot be undertaken here, but I would like to comment on its treatment of the language question in the Arab world. This is a very valuable detailed report of the achievements and shortcomings of Arab societies with respect to a number of social development indices. The report discusses many important issues and does not shy away from criticism and from suggestions for improvement. However, in its extended discussion of education and literacy, the role of language is only mentioned in relation to information technology and the "digital divide." Otherwise, the relation between education, literacy and language is left untouched:

> There are many signs of decreasing internal efficiency of education in the Arab world, including high failure and repetition rates, leading to longer periods spent at different stages of education. However, the real problem lies in the quality of education. Despite the scarcity of available studies, complaints concerning the poor quality of education abound. The few available studies identify the key negative features of the real output of education in Arab countries as low level of knowledge attainment and poor and deteriorating analytical and innovative capacity (54).

Throughout this report, the authors place great emphasis on "knowledge acquisition" and somewhat less often on "knowledge production." Yet they do not seem to consider the fact that knowledge is communicated through a variety of vehicles and chief among them is language. If pupils do not have enough mastery over the vehicle of knowledge, they will perform poorly. If in their analyses, they have to worry primarily and continually about the grammar of Classical Arabic (whether the noun is in the nominative or accusative or whether the vocabulary they have chosen will pass as Classical Arabic), then indeed their "analytical capacity" can "deteriorate."[4]

In their discussion of the digital divide, among the factors listed as "significantly influencing" that divide, is language: "Most information currently available on the internet is in English, a language that most of the population do not know well" (76). But the same could be said about Classical Arabic, which is the medium of public education. This fact should be at least equally important. Last but not least, the report praises many aspects of the literacy program "medersat.com" for rural areas in Morocco and states that "The introduction of information technology as a medium helps medersat.com to build a new generation of students in rural areas *while respecting the students' culture and mother tongues, whether Arabic or Berber*" (96, emphasis added). The rest of the discussion does not touch on this issue further. Do the authors mean Moroccan Arabic or Classical Arabic? Why not disambiguate this term in a discussion that is about education and requires clarity in this respect? In English, "Arabic" is almost always used to refer to Classical Arabic. And the latter is not the mother tongue of Moroccans or other Arabs. I return once again to Osman Sabri and to one of the questions that he posed in his 1967 article: "Is it not better . . . that we call things by their name?"

"A choice between domination and domination"

In many postcolonial societies, the language people speak and write, or one of the languages, is a colonial one whose status as a "native" or "mother" tongue is rather dubious. It is one thing to claim that one owns one's mother tongue and quite another to say the same thing about other vernaculars. What happens to property rights then in cases where the vernacular one speaks is not, at least not originally, one's mother tongue? First, colonial languages like English, French or Dutch are themselves vernaculars and are the mother tongues of many people. As such, they do not have a "sacred" status and see changes and innovations within their own communities routinely. In learning them as second languages, one may be confronted with "glorious" pasts, highly revered literary texts, the "genius" or "inherent logic" of the language (e.g., "le génie de la langue française"), but not with their sacredness. There is no doubt that the imposition of a foreign language can have profoundly negative effects, as the literature on colonialism has shown (wa Thiong'o 1986). The languages of colonizers and those of God all put learners in highly unequal power relations, but one crucial difference is that in time learners can become native speakers of the colonizers' language. Many continental Indians speak English as one of their mother tongues. As the case of the success of Indian literary authors indicates, these are languages that can be owned and appropriated. Still, "Indian English" and British English are not equal in that the latter can serve as the "standard" both inside and outside of Britain. But the inequality has not prevented English from developing and being appropriated by Indians everywhere. The same could be said of Arab, African and Caribbean authors who write in English and French.

Some Egyptians refer to Classical Arabic as "imposed" by the conquering Muslim armies and hence as a "colonial" language. But even the Muslim armies did not actually speak in Classical Arabic. The various kinds of Arabic they spoke mixed with Coptic and other languages and what we now call Egyptian Arabic came into existence. In any case, if Classical Arabic was imposed, it does not have to remain so. There is no *outside* power that is any longer imposing the language. I quote again from the memoir of the Egyptian historian Leila Ahmed. After having spent some time in the Gulf, living and working there, she came to realize that "Gulf Arabic" and culture were "different from standard Arabic" and the "Arab culture of literacy":

> Ironically enough, the steady spread and imposition of this culture of literacy throughout the Arab world seems to represent a kind of linguistic and cultural imperialism . . . that is being conducted in the name of education and of Arab unity and of the oneness of the Arab nation. Steadily throughout the Arab world, as this Arab culture of literacy marches inexorably onward, local cultures continue to be erased and their linguistic and cultural creativity condemned to permanent, unwritten silence. And we are supposed to applaud this, not protest it as we would if it were any other form of imperialism or political domination. (1999: 282)

Ahmed further comments on her educational experience and its effects while growing up in Cairo in the 1950s:

> In all of Egypt there was no school that I could have attended where I could have read books and learned to write in my mother tongue. . . . There is no linguistic reason why Egyptian Arabic could not be a written language, only political reasons. . . . Whatever school my parents sent me to, Arabic or English, I would have found myself imbibing a culture and studying a language and learning attitudes that were different from those of the world in which I lived at home in Cairo and Alexandria. . . . In short, *the choice was always only a choice between colonialism and colonialism, or at any rate between domination and domination.* (1999: 283, emphasis added)

There is still no school in Egypt or anywhere else in the Arab world to my knowledge where vernacular Arabic serves as the medium of education. But there are many schools, colleges and universities in which the language of literacy is a European language.

At times, those who choose to write in the language of a colonial power even after the independence of their countries feel uneasy about this choice and are accused of not being "nationalist" or "anti-colonial" enough. Katib Yacine, the Algerian poet, novelist and playwright who was also an anti-colonial activist, wrote most of his works in French, although he directed a number of plays in what he called "dialectal Arabic" in Algeria. But when he wanted to publish the same plays, he was met with resistance. He has written a great deal on the subject of choice of language. Being dismayed with the political situation in Algeria in the 1970s, which he saw as only becoming worse later on, he blamed it in part on the "imposition" of Classical Arabic and the marginalization of both Berber and "dialectal" Arabic. In this regard, he wrote, "Algeria does not yet dare to be itself" (1994 [1971]: 169).[5] Very much the same could be said about Egypt.

Although the situations in Egypt and Algeria are different in several ways, Ahmed and Yacine also make similar points with regard to the role of Classical Arabic in undermining a plurality of traditions in their respective countries. In Algeria, a central and historical demand of Berbers has been the official recognition of their language Tamazight. This demand was voiced recently in several large-scale demonstrations by Berbers.[6] The law of Arabization that was voted by the Popular National Assembly of Algeria in 1990—the strictest such law in the Arab world—required not only the Arabization of administration and of tertiary education (by 1997), but also of all imported technology, media, billboards and road signs (Djité 1992: 15). Although there was "immediate and unequivocal disapproval" of the law of 1990 in Algeria, it stayed in place. Hocine Ait Ahmed, the leader of the Front of the Social Forces, an opposition party that has a large Berber constituency, called it the "wicked law" (Djité 1992: 27). Note that the law was imposed *after* the electoral victories of Islamists moved the government to cancel the elections. The implementation of the law seems to have run into problems and quietly postponed in certain areas. In 1998, there were renewed demonstrations by Berbers that were in part against this law which was reportedly characterized by some Algerians as a "sop to Islamic fundamentalists."[7] In the end, Tamazight was not given the status of an official language of Algeria, but was recognized as a national language.[8] Commitment to Classical Arabic is routinely used by governments to shield themselves from different kinds of criticism and to engage in exclusionary practices.

Ambiguity

As the language of religious rituals, Classical Arabic has an integral place in the daily lives of believers who find it utterly beautiful, soothing and powerful (as do in fact many nonbelievers). It is when the language is taken out of the realm of religion that its status becomes ambiguous and its politicization difficult to prevent. To make the sources of this ambiguity more precise, I compare Egyptian Arabic, Qur'anic and contemporary Classical Arabic (CA) in table 6.1.

The last column in table 6.1 attempts to capture some of the central reasons for the persistent ambiguity in the status of contemporary Classical Arabic. Every aspect of this language variety sits on the proverbial fence: its

Table 6.1 The Ambiguities of Contemporary Classical Arabic

	Egyptian Arabic	Qur'anic CA	Contemporary CA
Origin	human	divine	divine?
Ownership	speakers	God	God? the Nahda authors? pan-Arab "nation"?
Scope	Egypt	universal, pan-Muslim	pan-Arab, pan-Muslim?
Relations between form and meaning	arbitrary	nonarbitrary	??
Modern	yes	no	??

origin, and hence its past and present, its relation to users, whether it can or cannot be tampered with, and whether it is a "new" creation that is independent of Qur'anic Arabic. The question marks in the last column are points of major struggles and ceaseless debates. But the parties to this struggle are not equal. The far greater share of the burden is on those who wish to use the language of religion for creating a world where religion is not supposed to occupy a central place. In practice, what is written today is in fact different from old Classical Arabic, thanks in large part to the influence of Egyptian Arabic. But the contemporaneity of Classical Arabic is not merely a matter of linguistic change, nor is it only in the hands of those who have wished to weaken its social and historical roots.

There is, of course, Egypt outside of the printed word—in all kinds of rituals, undying epics that are memorized and performed orally, songs, dances, clothes, jokes, movies and other kinds of creativity that do not have names. But when these aspects of Egypt are written about by Egyptians, surprisingly often there is a condescension evident both in their praise and castigation. Routinely, Egyptian cultural productions are labeled as *"sha'bi"*—that is, folk or "low brow," mostly good for the illiterate poor. The language that is used by speakers to produce and construct a large part of Egypt's contemporaneity is not allowed to develop while the other language over whose contemporaneity there continue to be unending struggles remains the official language of the "Arab Republic of Egypt." There is an abiding and deeply conflicted sensibility toward just what Egypt's contemporaneity is and should be. And language is at the center of that conflict.

Notes

Chapter One

1. Hebrew went through a revitalization and is now spoken as a mother tongue. See Harshav 1993, *Language in Time of Revolution*.
2. "Arabic" replaced many local languages. In Egypt, it replaced Coptic.
3. One exception to note is that Nubians in Upper Egypt speak Nubian as their mother tongue and many are bilingual. To my knowledge, there are no varieties of Egyptian Arabic that are primarily defined on the basis of ethnicity, again with the possible exception of Nubian Egyptian Arabic. Egyptian Muslims and Copts are considered to belong to the same ethnic group.
4. Cognates are words common to two or more languages with or without small differences in their phonological forms. The term is also used to refer to languages that are cognates, i.e., share the same ancestors, like for example members of the Romance language family. In all languages, certain differences between sounds make a difference in meaning (e.g., "ten" vs. "den" in English), while other differences make no such difference. In English, there are many differences in the pronunciation of /t/ depending on where it occurs in a word (e.g., "teacher" vs. "water" vs. "Newton"). But we say that English has only one phoneme /t/ that has variants (see Crystal 1991: 258). Egyptian and Classical Arabic share many phonemes but they each have phonemes that are lacking in the other one.
5. With a few exceptions, the rejection of Egyptian Arabic as a language of writing and the preservation of Classical Arabic have generally been treated as self-evident matters in the social scientific literature. They are dismissed rather than explained by quick references to Islam and then to pan-Arabism. Recent works that do not take such matters for granted but whose primary aims lie elsewhere are Armbrust 1996, I. Gershoni and J. Jankowski 1986.
6. Diglossia refers to the co-existence, in some communities, of two languages, one that is used for writing and high culture functions, and often associated with a particular religion, and another that is the spoken language and that is generally not allowed to become a language of writing. See Marçais 1931 and Ferguson 1959a.
7. The word in Egyptian Arabic is /taḥdiis/. A note about the translation of this term is in order. In dictionaries, it is translated as "modernization, updating,

bringing up to date" (al-Mawrid 1995: 284); as "modern" and "late" or "recent" by Hans Wehr for the related word "hadith" (different from the Prophet's hadith) (1976: 161) "Renovation" and "revival" are also used in various historical works. By settling on "modernization" as a reasonable translation of the term, I do not mean to imply that the English and Arabic words denote exactly the same thing or that they have fully overlapping connotations. Nevertheless, from the writings of those who wished to make the language more feasible for new needs and functions, one can reasonably settle on this translation. Among the few historians who discuss in some detail the language situation in the Arab world, many use the term "modernization" (e.g., Hodgson 1974: 292).

8. I will not elaborate further on other aspects of reformism in the nineteenth century—there is a rather large literature on the topic. My main focus is on the contemporary language situation. For a general introduction to the topic see Hourani 1991.

9. Note that, as is the case with all vernaculars that co-exist with a classical or standard national language, the vernacular's heterogeneity is simultaneously emphasized and denied. The heterogeneity is exaggerated where it serves the idea that it causes divisions and miscomprehension or lack of comprehension, and it is denied where the question of stylistic resources is concerned. It is claimed that vernaculars lack lexical and syntactic resources whereas the classical language is "rich"—this being the proof that they are "limited" and unfit for use in multiple domains (see Haeri 1996).

10. Unlike the situation in the early decades of the twentieth century, very few individuals at present publicly advocate the replacement of Classical with Egyptian Arabic.

11. Prescriptive studies, which used to occupy the attention of most grammarians, were aimed at prescription. That is, they told readers how they should speak, write, pronounce and so on. Descriptive studies aim to describe how people actually speak. "Arbitrary" means there there is no "natural" relation between the phonological form of a word (its "signifier") and its meaning (the "signified"), hence forms can change, or die out and be replaced by new words with the same or similar meanings. This is also called the thesis of the arbitrariness of the sign (see Culler 1986).

12. For exceptions, see for example Caton 1990, Eickelman 1995 and Shyrock 1997.

13. One *can* argue convincingly that in fact they are more "artificial" than spontaneous, oral, face-to-face exchanges. But precisely because written languages are more "unnatural" and "woman-/man-made," they are highly relevant to debates on structure, agency, representation, ideology and so on.

14. Language issues figure prominently in almost all the central debates within and outside national borders—debates about "progress," "modernity," nationalism, globalization, religion, education and distribution of wealth. See Bourdieu 1977, 1991, Caton 1990, Kuipers 1998, Gal 1987, 1989, Irvine, 1989, Woolard 1989, Hanks 1987.

15. See footnote 19.
16. One major concern revolves around the question of whether there is only one kind of modernity, which is that of the West, or whether there are "alternative," or "multiple" forms based on the experiences of non-Western societies. It may be argued that searching for "multiple" and "alternative" modernities in the non-West implies that the term may be defined *objectively* according to criteria not inspired by the West. That is, the search implies that the political objective inherent in the term to create a division between the West and the rest, so to speak, may be taken out of the term. It is not my intention to resolve this problem nor to fully enter debates on modernity in particular because they rarely consider questions of language. The exception to this is Pollock's explicit discussion of language and modernity which will be discussed later in this chapter and which I will address again in the conclusion. See for example *Daedalus: Journal of the American Academy of Arts and Sciences.* Vol. 127, No. 3, issue entitled "Early Modernities," Summer 1998; Same journal, Winter 2000, issue entitled: "Multiple Modernities"; *Public Culture,* Vol. 11, No. 1, 1999, issue entitled: "Alter/Native Modernities."
17. One of the most popular television series is a program hosted by the famous Sheikh Sha'raawi. In it, Sha'raawi reads sections of the Qur'an and often translates them into Egyptian Arabic. These oral translations seem to be very well received and many people explicitly state that one of the reasons they like the program is because Sheikh Sha'raawi speaks in Egyptian Arabic. He is also characterized as being very friendly and non-intimidating.
18. Separability is perhaps a more apt concept than arbitrariness because the former is more oriented toward the views of speakers and because arbitrariness as articulated by Saussure has been persuasively challenged by scholars. See Benveniste 1971.
19. In discussions of this work with several historians of Western Europe, while some saw a number of parallels with the case of Classical Arabic, others argued that because Latin was not the original language of the Bible, it did not come to be considered as a sacred language. But it seems that this historical "fact," not necessarily known to all Christians since the original translation, did not prevent Latin from attaining the status of sacredness for most people. In many historical studies, the belief that it had that status is articulated in a variety of ways. Latin may not have had exactly the same status as Biblical Hebrew or Classical Arabic, but still it was considered sacred at least by lay Christians. Moreover, the controversy of the Reformation with regard to the translation of the Bible from Latin into the vernaculars would be quite difficult to explain otherwise, as would the decision of the Catholic Church to switch to non-Latin masses. See, for example, Clanchy 1993 and Anderson 1991.
20. His book was first published posthumously in 1913.
21. The same term is often used in reference to immoral acts such as prostitution, adultery and so on.

22. Although one can imagine that a language can become resacralized. American fundamentalist Christians seem to believe that about the English of their Bible. There is an anecdote recounted in many publications and attributed variously to some governor, preacher or Congressman. One version is as follows: "Texas once had a governor James Edward 'Pa' Ferguson, who was succeeded by his wife 'Ma' in 1924. A debate ensued. Should all those Mexican children streaming across the border go to school in English or start out speaking Spanish? Holding up a Bible 'Ma' Ferguson settled the issue in her own inimitable fashion. 'If English was good enough for Jesus Christ' she declared, 'it is good enough for us'" (usnews.com, May 14, 2001).

23. The entire discussion in this section is inspired by Bakhtin's concept of the "chronotope" (literally, time-space), and on his distinctions between genres in terms of freedom and constraint. See "The problem of speech genres" In *Speech Genres and Other Essays*, 1986: 78–81. Instead of the usual divisions of genres based mainly on formal linguistic and structural differences, Bakhtin categorizes genres according to the kind of time (hence the kind of world) that a literary work creates—for example, "adventure time," "biographical time," "novelistic time" and so on. Explaining further the significance of the chronotope, he states that:

> The chronotope in literature has an intrinsic generic significance. It can even be said that it is precisely the chronotope that defines genre and generic distinctions, for in literature the primary category in the chronotope is time. The chronotope as a formally constitutive category determines to a significant degree the image of man in literature as well. *The image of man is always intrinsically chronotopic* (1981: 85, emphasis added)

> It is not just literary genres that have chronotopes but language in general: "Language, as a treasure-house of images, is fundamentally chronotopic" (Bakhtin 1981: 251).

24. Most other Muslims (perhaps like the rest of the world) do not seem to be aware that "Arabs" do not speak the Arabic of the Qur'an. For them, there is just "Arabic"—a misunderstanding that is perpetuated by Arab and non-Arab authors who generally use just one term. The idea that "the language has degenerated" is not shared by other Muslims. The father of an Iranian friend, a pious Muslim who had memorized many parts of the Qur'an, tried to use the language to speak to Egyptians when he visited Cairo. Upon finding more bewilderment than response to his efforts, he commented with despair: "But these Egyptians don't know any Arabic!" His wife gently replied, "Perhaps YOU don't know Arabic."

25. Quoted in Chejne 1969: 165.

26. This surprising characterization of the mother tongue of Egyptians including that of the author himself was offered when pan-Arab thinking was at its peak. To my knowledge, the author has not offered a different opinion in more recent times. While a number of novelists write their dialogues in

Egyptian Arabic and the rest in Classical Arabic, Mahfouz also writes his dialogues in that language. Often, the dialogues are translations into Classical Arabic of what they would have been in Egyptian Arabic. I heard a number of discussions among Arabic speakers from different regions in which there were disagreements about whether Mahfouz's dialogues were in one or the other language.

27. From *King Lear*, 1963. New York and Toronto: The New American Library.
28. The word often connotes someone who is illiterate, gullible and superstitious.
29. Interesting facts about the social history of Classical Arabic and the Arabic vernaculars are embedded in many articles, but rarely has the topic received book-length treatments. Exceptions are the valuable studies of Chejne 1969, Stetkevych 1979, Versteegh 1997. There are also perceptive discussions of language in Hodgson's 1974 monumental historical work, *The Venture of Islam*. Still, Chejne and most historians are concerned with learned elites and do not enter into details of language use.

Chapter Two

1. Lack of attention to the role of religious rituals in the survival of Classical Arabic as a language is coupled by a paucity of studies of the ṣalaa itself. In his study of the social meanings of daily prayers in Indonesia, Bowen states: "Although central to the Muslim's religious repertoire, it is usually accorded only a brief mention in studies of Islamic communities" (1989: 600).
2. Translation from A. J. Arberry's *The Koran Interpreted*, 1996 [1955], Simon & Schuster.
3. Wagner (1993: 44) finds a similar situation in Morocco.
4. She showed me a number of the books that she had read or was reading. These were mostly on the education of Muslim children and on how to be a good Muslim. One was based on the ḥadiis (the prophet's actions and sayings) in four volumes, and one from a contemporary author.
5. Taher's older brother also works in the same restaurant where Taher sings. He has his own apartment where he lives with his wife and daughter. I did not get a chance to spend much time with him. He did not attend a *kuttaab*, and after he obtained his high school diploma he began to work in a restaurant. A number of relatives of this family—mostly first cousins—also live in this neighborhood. I spent time with one of Nadia's nieces who was studying to become a nurse, and with a few other relatives. The husband of the niece who was studying to become a nurse had also spent many years in Saudi Arabia and Iraq, like the husband of Fatima. In many ways, the daily lives of these relatives are very similar to those of the members of Nadia's family, in particular in terms of the role and place of Classical Arabic. For this reason, I do not describe their daily lives as well since it would be largely a repetition.
6. See Singerman 1995 for a detailed discussion of how important and difficult this stage is in the life of young people with limited resources in Egypt.

7. Ahmed's spelling reflects the pronunciation of the name of this *sura* in Egyptian Arabic. The spelling inside the brackets is to make clear the pronunciation in Classical Arabic.

8. The programs that are in Classical Arabic are put in bold face in order to make comparisons to those in Egyptian Arabic easier, both in terms of the kind of program and in terms of the amount of time devoted to them.

9. A similar example in terms of effect is provided by a recent headline in the *New York Times:* "Wherefore art thou Pokémon" (*New York Times* 2/13/00: 29).

10. There is an alternation in Egyptian Arabic between [l] and [n], e.g., [borti'aan]/[borti'aal] "orange, the fruit," [gornaan]/[gornaal] "newspaper." Thus, Mansour says [bundozer] sometimes and [bulldozer] at others.

11. The first term is the less technical one used by everyone, while the second is used in grammar books and in more formal contexts.

12. Hence the word /bint/ "girl" would be written as bnt because that vowel is short. The plural of /bint/ is /banaat/ containing a long vowel and so it would be written as bnat.

13. The dictionary does not list 'asr as an adjective, but the related form "mu'aasir" which it defines as either "contemporary" or "modern" as in "il-insaan il-mu'aasir" "modern man" (Badawi and Hinds 1986: 581).

14. A great deal has been written on the origins of Arab nationalism and much effort has been made to trace in time its exact beginnings. Engaging in the details of this history and the settling of which view(s) are "right" would not shed a great deal of light on what is happening at the moment. This is particularly the case because most of this history does not deal in much detail with questions of language in terms of different people's experiences.

    Whether the idea of a pan-Arab identity came from the British to serve their political ends, as Ahmed (1999) argues, or from the exposure of Egyptian intellectuals to Europe (Antonius 1965, Vatikiotis 1991), or from the literary movement of the Nahda with non-Muslim Arabs being particularly invested in removing religion as a basis for an Arab identity, or all of the above, is important but not immediately relevant to my analysis.

15. This was volunteered information as I had no idea about such an understanding nor was I at all asking about Copts.

16. How many generations have been reading their Bible in Classical Arabic? I was told by a number of Copts that the translation must have taken place early on around the tenth or eleventh centuries. Of course, this does not necessarily mean that after that all Copts began to read their Bible in Arabic. Among the manuscripts in the National Library (Dar al-Kutub), I found a Bible in Egyptian Arabic. It was published in 1926, apparently in sections. The one at the library is section 5. There are two title pages, in Arabic and in English. They read: "il-khabar il-ṭayyib bita' yisuu' il-masiih ow il-ingiil bil-lugha il-maṣriyya. Qism il-khaamis: a'maal il-rasuul, (The Good News of Jesus Christ or The New Testament in Egyptian, No. 5: The Acts of the Apostles). It is unclear who had undertaken the translation. In a search

among Christian bookstores in Cairo, I did not find any copy nor had anyone heard of that Bible.

Chapter Three

1. Discussed in Eisenstein 1998: 51–52.
2. In literary studies, the muddled status of authorship has long been recognized. The problem of "corrupt texts" and how to restore which one, for example in relation to the works of Shakespeare and Joyce, has been extensively
   written about.
3. Bakhtin's "stable types" (1986: 60) are material activities that intersect but
   rarely fully overlap with the ideology of institutions and individuals devoted
   to their production and regulation.
4. I have so far been unable to locate studies of how this institution changed in
   Europe when books began to be published in the modern national languages. In general, historical studies of text regulation seem to be rare.
5. In Classical Arabic: *al-namuuzaj al-a'laa.*
6. Ḥadiith in Classical Arabic.
7. There seems to have been an enduring struggle in that journalists did not
   want to accept correctors as members of their syndicate.
8. In Classical Arabic, /'iraaya/ would be /qiraa'a/ 'reading'; and /gughrafia/
   would be /jughrafia/ 'Geography.' Hamid used the Egyptian Arabic cognates.
9. This college produced its first graduates in 1873 (Aroian 1983: 28). It was
   founded in order to train teachers, particularly language teachers, for state
   educational institutions.
10. Interviews with Magdi were conducted in Cairo on 4/18/96 and 4/26/96. I
    interviewed Hamid again in early August 1996 at his home. Unfortunately,
    I did not indicate the exact date on the cassette tape.
11. A "mushaff" is a term used to refer to a *copy* of the Qur'an.
12. Interview conducted in Cairo on 4/23/96.
13. There were a number of books, among them one on the controversial
    "Donna International," whose supposed sexual deviance was dangerous be-
    cause as a popular singer she had the power to influence the young genera-
    tions. The quotation is taken from this book.
14. Heyworth-Dunn, in his 1939 study of education in Egypt, mentions the
    names of some of these same books which were, according to him, taught at
    the al-Azhar (see pp. 45–65).
15. In his dissertation on al-Ahram, the Egyptian daily, Abdelfattah states that
    "Egyptian newspapers rely, in place of stylebooks, on language specialists,
    correctors, whose sole function is to correct the grammatical errors of re-
    porters, without having anything to do with stylistic standardization. In the
    absence of stylebooks, inconsistencies become the norm in the spelling of
    foreign names and words. . . ." (Abdelfattah 1990: 19). There is in fact a
    style manual published by al-Ahram but I located it too late for inclusion in
    my analysis.

16. The full title of the meeting was liqaa' al-ra'iis Mubarak ma'a al-'udabaa' wa al-mufakkariin, 'the meeting of President Mubarak with litterateurs and thinkers.'
17. This example will be discussed at length in the next chapter.
18. Abdo related an anecdote about a university professor who was shocked to find out that writers such as Naguib Mahfouz must submit to corrections. In a public lecture, the professor asked rhetorically whether it would be accepted for a painter to submit his painting to someone else—a technician— to correct. Why, he asked, is this acceptable with writers who have put behind them all their "struggles" with the language? I have heard various versions of this anecdote from different people.

Chapter Four

1. From the essay on "Discourse in the Novel," in Bakhtin 1981.
2. While a word in its original form can be borrowed from one language into another, e.g., Arabic *kambiyuter'* for "computer," a calque is a kind of borrowing where each word or morpheme of the original is *translated* into the borrowing language. These are also called loan translations, e.g., /athar al-qadam/ "footprint."
3. The Qur'an refers to human beings as *"ashraf al-makhluuqaaat"*—the most noble of the species (creatures).
4. Note that the term *da'wa* "invitation" also means "proselytization."
5. The al-Mawrid dictionary defines *"muta'akhiruun"* as "later, modern authors" (1995: 949).
6. In Egyptian Arabic, the sentence would be: /raayih feen innaharda/ "going where today?"
7. At times page numbers show consecutive numbering from previous issues. Because these issues are available on microfilm, their quality and the quality of photocopying is often not very good. Hence, sometimes page numbers have been wiped off or smeared. For this issue, only consecutive page numbers could be read.
8. Also in example 2, since in Arabic orthography short vowels are not indicated, the suffix attached to the verb *"wagad"* is written as "t h" which can be read either as *"tuhu"* with Classical Arabic pronunciation or as "tu" with Egyptian Arabic pronunciation.
9. On the language of Nasser and other Arab President's see Mazraani 1997 and Holes 1993.
10. A number of scholars have argued that the book bearing Voloshinov's name as its author, namely *Marxism and the Philosophy of Language*, was in fact written by Bakhtin. I can have no personal position on the matter and therefore will continue to cite Voloshinov without wishing to discount the possibility.
11. A pair of indirect and direct examples in English would be:

Wright told reporters that they should leave him alone.
Wright told reporters, "leave me alone."

12. I searched for examples where an article quotes someone speaking Egyptian Arabic. This is rather difficult to find as such examples prove to be rather rare. One that I found was in the al-Ahram of 3/2/1956: 4. The headline is about someone who suffocated his wife. The man is then quoted (and his words are put in quotation marks) as having uttered two sentences in Egyptian Arabic and then immediately one in Classical Arabic (in boldface):

wa huwa basyah(?): "ib'aduu 'anni . . . ana ha'uul il-ha'ii'a . . . sa-a'tarif lakum bi-kull il-shay'"!
And he shouted (?): "take the [dog] away from me . . . I will tell the truth . . . I will confess to you everything"!

13. An example in English would be "The table that is in the hall." Relativizers are a major way in which sentences can be combined to make one sentence. They are also refereed to as relative pronouns, e.g., who, when, where, what and so on.

14. The closest sentence in Egyptian Arabic would be: illi 'aayiz yidakhan ḥafza 'alaa ṣiḥḥituu laazim yista'mil wara' sigaara Bon Duc . . .

15. This is the fourth printing of Musa's book that was perhaps first published in 1945 because the introduction is signed with that date. Musa begins the introduction by saying, "We all write on language now, and all of us feel the urgency (*khutuura*) of this topic, because we have concluded, from what we know of European languages, that our linguistic lateness (*ta'akhurna*) in Egypt is one of the greatest causes of our social lateness" (7). Later on, he states: "And the invitation to a contemporary language (*lugha 'asriyya*) is in its essence an invitation to contemporary life" (9).

16. See Salwa Bakr's novel "*al-'araba al-dhahabiyya la tas'ad ilaa al-samaa*" (1991). The main character is a woman named Aziza who is in a women's prison. She has an imaginary dialogue with another inmate, Umm Ragab (implied to be illiterate), and in this dialogue, Aziza starts in Egyptian Arabic and without any warning moves into sentences that have mostly Egyptian Arabic words but Classical Arabic grammar (7). I asked a number of Egyptians to read this passage and tell me what they thought of it. Everyone said more or less the same thing, namely, that "no one speaks like that." The novel has been translated into English under the title "*The Golden Chariot*," 1995, Reading, UK: Garnet Publishers. The translator states that "This novel uses colloquial Arabic to capture *the reality* of the spoken language for women in Egypt" (xi, emphasis added).

Chapter Five

1. Most of the data in this chapter is based on interviews that I conducted in 1995–96 in Cairo. The dates of these interviews are given in these notes: 2, 12, 13, 14, 18, 20 and 24. While I discuss the contents of a number of published articles, I privilege the interviews because they constitute new material and would not otherwise be available in any published venue.

2. All quotations are from discussions between March and May 1996, and from a tape-recorded interview on June 2, 1996 in Cairo. The title of her book is *A Dark Passage Fit for Learning to Dance, mamarr mu'tim yiṣlaḥ li-ta'allum al-raqs*. 1995. Cairo: Dar al-Sharqiyat lil-Nashr wal-Towzi'.

3. See M. Badran. 1995. *Feminists, Islam, and Nation: Gender and the Making of Modern Egypt*. Princeton: Princeton University Press.

4. See *A Daughter of Isis: The Autobiography of Nawal El Saadawi*. 1999. London, New York: Zed books.

5. See for example, Altoma 1970; Abu-Absi, 1984; Ibrahim, 1983; Doss, 1992 and 1996; Wagner, 1993; Ennaji 1988 and 1991; Elbiad, 1991; Djité, 1992; and Haeri, 2000, among others.

6. Statistics are taken from the Human Development Report 2000, New York, Oxford: Oxford University Press, 2000: 196. This is a publication of the United Nations Development Program (UNDP). The statistics are for the year 1998; "Youth" is defined as those between 15 and 24. It is unclear how literacy has been defined. In the more recent UNDP report, the "Youth" category is combined with adults and the literacy rate for 1999 is 54.6 percent (based on the "illiteracy rate" provided). (Arab Human Development Report 2002: 151).

7. The textbook is called *qawaa'id al-lugha al-'arabiyya lil-ṣaff al-awwal al-a'daadi* ('The grammar of the Arabic language for the first class of middle school'). It is published by the Ministry of Education (wizaarat al-tarbiyya wal-ta'liim).

8. For example, although the book has three authors and one editor, the personal pronoun "we" is never used in discussing its preparation and choice of texts and other features. This is all stated through the use of third person singular verbs, implying a third person singular pronoun that seems to refer to the book. The use of personal pronouns other than third person singular (and less so third person plural) would mark the language of the text as less formal and less classical (see chapter 4). At the same time, it is culturally appropriate to be modest and self-effacing with regard to one's abilities in the use of Classical Arabic.

9. I interpret her last remark, that those things she writes in 'ammiyya are "more honest," to be a commentary on what is more likely to happen when translation is involved, and not on the general dishonesty of anything written in Classical Arabic.

10. "Qantara" is the name of the protagonist who is a sheikh.

11. But see the research article on the grammar and history of 'ammiyya in the journal *al-Qahira*, No. 63, June 1996: 9–49. The title of the article is "The Language of Egyptian 'ammiyya: The Language of Thought and Life."

12. Interview conducted at his office in Cairo on January 26, 1996. He did not want the interview to be tape-recorded.

13. Interview conducted at his office in Cairo on July 14, 1996. He did not want it to be tape-recorded.

14. Tape-recorded interviews conducted at his bookstore in Cairo on July 16, 1996 and August 2, 1996.

15. Publishing humor pieces, cartoons and folkloric stories are far more easily allowed. There are a few humor magazines with many political cartoons. The language of all such cartoons, no matter where they are printed, is almost always 'ammiyya.
16. Ibn Arous is the nickname given to a poet who was born in 1780 in the era of the Mamluks. His story is explained on the very first page of the first issue of the journal.
17. Interviews conducted at his office in Cairo on May 5, 1996 and June 26, 1996. They were both tape-recorded.
18. He added that in the 1960s, another attempt had been made by Salah Jahin, one of the most revered 'ammiyya songwriters and poets, to publish a similar magazine but that he had not managed. He also spoke of one of Jahin's poems in which he tried to show that "'ammiyya poetry is not against Qur'an or against Arabism but that this poetry is capable of communicating the meaning and the theme to a people whose illiteracy rate [*nisbat il-ummiyya*] is above 70 percent."
19. Interviews conducted in his office in Cairo on July 17, 1996 and August 7, 1996. They were both tape-recorded.
20. See the recent article in the New York Times by Saad Mehio (*New York Times,* 12/2/2001: 15). Mehio writes that during the cold war: "The policy of using political Islam as an anti-Communist tool was a crucial reason why so much of the Muslim world came to be dominated by stagnant, undemocratic but stable . . . and adequately pro-Western governments. . . ."
21. Quoted in Gershoni, I. and J. Jankowski. 1986: 219.
22. The "mistake" according to Amin al-Alem continues in that Marxists want to fight Islamic groups by saying that the latter do not know "real Islam": "At present, some Marxists say of the Muslim Brotherhood (il-ikhwaan il-muslimiin) that they are "*muti'aslimiin*" meaning that their Islam is not correct. When a Marxist says that they are "*muti'aslim*" it means that *he* is the one who knows Islam well? Instead of saying that that thought is frozen [*mutihaggir*] and inflexible [*gaamid*] . . . so the Marxist wants to lay claim to Islam."
23. Tape-recorded interview conducted at his home in Cairo on May 29, 1996.
24. For her, though, the potential religious resonances of contemporary Classical Arabic depend crucially on the actual syntax of the sentence and its vocabulary. "You might find someone saying in a newspaper article "Verily the clerks, if they were offered the necessary conditions for work, and they will then . . . ," this immediately will have associations with the language of religion. But if someone says "The resolution of the problems of clerks after 40 years of bureaucracy and . . . this will not at all make those associations for me. For me, the word order [*tarkiib*] of the sentence is fundamental [*'asaas*]." (Interview with Iman Mirsal, Cairo, 6/2/ 1996).

Chapter Six

1. *The Cambridge History of Islam.* P. M. Holt, A. Lambton and B. Lewis. Vol. 2B. 1970.

2. Translation into English from *The Holy Qur'an: English Translation of the Meanings of the Qur'an with Notes.* Abdullah Yusuf Ali, 1992. Indianapolis: H & C International. The Persian translation is somewhat different. In English it would read as "And we have not sent a Messenger [with a message] except in the language of his people in order to make [rulings and realities] clear" (Khorramshahi 1997: 255).

3. Among other writings on the subject that were published during the period of my research in Cairo, a lengthy four-part article on the causes of this failure appeared in al-Ahram in 1996 with the title "Arabs the Enemies of Arabs?" (June 4, 11, 25, and July 2).

4. It is difficult to disagree with the assessment presented in the report that the quality of education in the Arab world is poor, though of course there are differences among countries, within fields of study and level of education. The report provides a few indices to substantiate this assessment, but at least one does not seem to support their conclusion. The "number of pupils per teacher" for secondary education in Egypt in 1995 is 20. The same table provides, for the purposes of comparison, the same data on Hong Kong and North Korea, which are 20 and 24 respectively (154). Clearly the ratio in Egypt is not so bad and not any worse than the other countries. The report seems to be following a longstanding position by many Arab intellectuals that if only the *quality* of education would improve (according to some criteria), educational problems would be alleviated. But while improvements in education are very necessary, the problems caused by the language situation will be ameliorated but not resolved by better education.

5. Katib Yacine, *Le Poète comme un Boxeur, Entretiens 1958–1989.* Editions du Seuil, 1994.

6. As reported by BBC Online on Thursday, October 4, 2001.

7. As reported by BBC Online on Wednesday, July 22, 1998.

8. As reported by *Le Monde,* April 10, 2002.

Bibliography

Abboud, Peter. 1988. "Speech and Religious Affiliation in Egypt." In *Languages and Cultures: Studies In Honor of Edgar C. Polome*, eds., M. A. Jazayery and W. Winter. Berlin: Mouton de Gruyter, pp. 21–27.

Abdelfattah, Nabil Mohamed Saber. 1990. Linguistic Changes in Journalistic Language in Egypt, 1935–1989: A Quantitative and Comparative Analysis. Ph.D. dissertation. Austin: The University of Texas at Austin.

Abdul-Aziz, M.1986. "Factors in the Development of Modern Arabic Usage." *International Journal of the Sociology of Language* 62: 11–24.

Abou Ghazi, Emad. 1996. "Observations sur la langue a travers l'etude d'actes notariés de l'epoque mamelouke." *Égypte/Monde Arabe* 27–28 (3 and 4): 147–156.

Abu-Absi, Samir. 1990. "A Characterization of the Language of Iftah ya Simsim: Sociolinguistic and Educational Implications for Arabic." *Language Problems and Language Planning* 14 (1): 33–46.

————1986. "The Modernization of Arabic: Problems and Prospects." *Anthropological Linguistics* 28 (3): 337–48.

————1984. "Language Planning and Education in the Arab World." *International Journal of Education* 1 (2): 113–132.

Abuhamdia, Zakaria. 1988. "The Arabic Language Regions." In*Sociolinguistics: An International Handbook of the Science of Language and Society*, eds., U. Ammon, N. Dittmar and K. Mattheier. Berlin: Mouton de Gruyter, pp. 1238–44.

Abu-Lughod, Ibrahim. 1975. "Arab Cultural Consolidation: A Response to European Colonialism?" *Islamic Quarterly* 19.1 (2): 30–41.

Abu-Lughod, Lila. 1989. "Zones of Theory in the Anthropology of the Arab World." *Annual Review of Anthropology* 18: 267–306.

Achard, Pierre. 1980. "History and Politics of Language in France: A Review Essay." *History Workshop Journal* 10: 175–83.

Ahmed, Leila. 1999. *A Border Passage: From Cairo to America- A Woman's Journey.* New York: Farrar, Straus and Giroux.

Allen, Roger. 1997. "The Development of Fictional Genres: The Novel and the Short Story in Arabic." In *Humanism, Culture, and Language in the Near East: Studies in Honor of George Krotkoff*, eds., A. Afsaruddin and A. Mathias Zahniser. Winona Lake, IN: Eisenbrauns, pp. 105–118.

Alrabaa, Sami. 1986. "Diglossia in the Classroom: The Arabic Case." *Anthropological Linguistics* 28 (1): 73–79.

Alter, Robert. 1994. *Hebrew and Modernity.* Bloomington: Indiana University Press.

Altoma, Salih. 1969. *The Problem of Diglossia in Arabic.* Harvard Middle Eastern Monograph Series, 21. Cambridge, MA: Harvard University Press.

———1970. "Language Education in Arab Countries and the Role of the Academies." In *Current Trends in Linguistics.* Vol. 6, ed., T. A. Sebeok. The Hague: Mouton, pp. 690–720.

Anderson, Benedict. 1991 [1983]. *Imagined Communities: Reflections on the Origin and Spread of Nationalism.* London, New York: Verso.

Antonius, George. 1965. *The Arab Awakening.* New York: Capricorn Books.

Arberry, Arthur. 1996 [1955]. *The Koran Interpreted: A Translation.* New York: Simon and Schuster.

Armbrust, Walter. 1996. *Mass Culture and Modernism in Egypt.* Cambridge, MA: Cambridge University Press.

Aroian, Lois. 1983. *The Nationalization of Arabic and Islamic Education in Egypt: Dar Al-Ulum and Al-Azhar.* Cairo Papers in Social Science. Vol. 6, no. 4. Cairo: The American University in Cairo Press.

Asad, Talal. 1986. *The Idea of an Anthropology of Islam. Occasional Paper Series, Center for Contemporary Studies.* Washington D.C.: Georgetown University.

———1993. "The Concept of Cultural Translation in British Social Anthropology." In *Genealogies of Religion: Discipline and Reasons of Power in Christianity and Islam.* Baltimore: Johns Hopkins University Press, pp. 171–199.

Afsaruddin, Asma. 1997. "Bi-l'arabi al-fasiih: An Egyptian Play Looks at Contemporary Arab Society." In *Humanism, Culture, and Language in the Near East: Studies in Honor of George Krotkoff,* eds., A. Afsaruddin and A. Mathias Zahniser. Winona Lake, IN: Eisenbrauns, pp. 129–141.

Atiyeh, George, ed. 1995. *The Book In the Islamic World: The Written Word and Communication in the Middle East.* Albany: State University of New York Press.

'Awad, Louis. 1993. *Muqaddima fi fiqh al-lugha al-'arabiyya.* [Introduction to the Philology of the Arabic Language], Cairo: Sina lil-Nashr.

Badawi, El-Said. 1973. *Mustawayaat al-'arabiyya al-mu'aasira.* [Levels of Contemporary Arabic], Cairo: Dar Al-Ma'arif.

Badran, Margot. 1995. *Feminists, Islam, and Nation: Gender and the Making of Modern Egypt.* Princeton: Princeton University Press.

Bakalla, Muhammad Hasan. 1983. *Arabic Linguistics: An Introduction and Bibliography.* Mansell: London.

Bakhtin, Mikhail M. 1992. [1986]. *Speech Genres and Other Late Essays by M. M. Bakhtin,* eds., C. Emerson and M. Holquist. Austin: University of Texas Press.

———1986. [1981]. *The Dialogic Imagination: Four Essays by M.M. Bakhtin,* ed., M. Holquist. Austin: University of Texas Press.

Barthes, Roland. 1977. *Image, Music, Text.* London: Fontana.

Belnap, Kirk and Niloofar Haeri. 1997. *Structuralist Studies in Arabic Linguistics: Charles Ferguson's Papers, 1954–1994.* Leiden: Brill.

Beneviste, Emile. 1971. *Problems in General Linguistics.* Coral Gables: University of Miami Press.

Bentahila, Abdeláli. 1983. "Language Attitudes Among Arabic-French Bilinguals in Morocco." *Multilingual Matters 4.* Clevedon: Bank House.

Birkeland, Harris. 1952. *Growth and Structure of the Egyptian Arabic Dialect.* Oslo: Dybwad.

Bohas, Georges, Jean-Patrick Guillaume and Djamel Kouloughli. 1990. *The Arabic Linguistic Tradition.* London, New York: Routledge.

Booth, Marylin. 1992. "Colloquial Arabic Poetry, Politics, and the Press in Modern Egypt." *International Journal of Middle East Studies* 24: 419–440.

Boukous, Ahmed. 1979. "Le profil sociolinguistique du Maroc: Contribution méthodologique." *Bulletin Economique et Social du Maroc* 140: 5–31.

Bourdieu, Pierre. 1991. *Language and Symbolic Power.* Cambridge, MA: Harvard University Press.

———1982. *Ce que parler veut dire: L'économie des échanges linguistique.* Paris: Fayard.

———1977. "The Economics of Linguistic Exchanges." *Social Science Information* 16: 645–68.

Bourdieu, Pierre and Luc Boltanski. 1975. "Le fetichisme de la langue." *Actes de la Recherche en Sciences Sociales* 1(4): 1–32.

Bowen, John. 1989. "*Salat* in Indonesia: The Social Meanings of an Islamic Ritual." *Man* 24: 299–318.

Cachia, Pierre. 1990. *An Overview of Modern Arabic Literature, Islamic Surveys 17.* Edinburgh: Edinburgh University Press.

———1989. "The Development of a Modern Prose Style in Arabic Literature." *Bulletin of the School of Oriental and African Studies* 52(1): 65–76.

———1967. "The Use of the Colloquial in Modern Arabic Literature." *Journal of the American Oriental Society* 87 (1): 12–22.

Cameron, Deborah. 1995. *Verbal Hygiene.* London: Routledge.

Caton, Steven. 1991. "Diglossia in North Yemen: A Case of Competing Linguistic Communities." *Southwest Journal of Linguistics* 10 (1): 143–59.

———1990. *"Peaks of Yemen I Summon": Poetry as Practice in a North Yemeni Tribe.* Berkeley: University of California Press.

———1987. "Contributions of Roman Jakobson." *Annual Review of Anthropology* 16: 223–260.

———1987. "Power, Persuasion, and Language: A Critique of the Segmentary Model in the Middle East." *International Journal of Middle East Studies* 19: 77–102.

———1986. "*Salam Tahiyah:* Greetings from the Highlands of Yemen." *American Ethnologist* 13: 290–308.

Cerquiglini, Bernard. 1989. *Eloge de la Variante: Histoire Critique de la Philologie.* Paris: Seuil.

Chartier, Roger. 1997. *On the Edge of the Cliff.* Baltimore: Johns Hopkins University Press.

Chejne, Anwar. 1969. *The Arabic Language: Its Role in History.* Minneapolis: University of Minnesota Press.

Clanchy, M. T. 1993. *From Memory to Written Record, England 1066–1307.* Oxford, Cambridge, USA: Blackwell.

Clark, Katerina and Michael Holquist. 1984. *Mikhail Bakhtin*. Cambridge, MA: Belknap Press/Harvard University Press.

Crozet, Pascal. 1996. "Les mutations de la langue écrite au XIXe siècle: le cas des manuels scientifique et techniques." *Égypte/Monde Arabe* 27–28 (3&4): 185–211.

Culler, Jonathan. 1990. [1986]. *Ferdinand de Saussure*. Ithaca, NY: Cornell University Press.

Daedalus. Special Issue on *Early Modernities*, Vol. 127, no. 3. 1998. Cambridge, MA: American Academy of Arts and Sciences.

Daedalus. Special Issue on *Multiple Modernities*, Vol. 129, no. 1. 2000. Cambridge, MA: American Academy of Arts and Sciences.

Daher, Nazih. 1987. "Arabic Sociolinguistics: State of the Art." *Al-Arabiyya* 20 (1&2): 125–159.

Danielson, Virginia. 1997. *The Voice of Egypt*. Chicago and London: The University of Chicago Press.

Dawwarah, Fu'ad. 1965. *'Ashara Udaba Yatahaddathun*. [Ten Literateurs Converse]. Cairo: Dar al-Hilal.

Dictionary of Egyptian Arabic. 1986. By El-Said Badawi and Martin Hinds. Librairie du Liban: Beirut, Lebanon.

Djité, Paulin. 1992. "The Arabization of Algeria: Linguistic and Sociopolitical Motivations." *International Journal of the Sociology of Language* 98: 15–28.

Doss, Madiha. 1996. "Réflexions sur les débuts de l'ecriture dialectale en Égypte." *Égypte/Monde arabe* 27–28 (3&4): 119–145.

————1992. Discours de réforme. In *Entre Réforme et Mouvement National: Identitié et Modernisation en Égypt 1882–1962*. Cairo: CEDEJ.

Duranti, Alessandro and Charles Goodwin, eds. 1992. "Introduction." In *Rethinking Context: Language as an Interactive Phenomenon*. Cambridge: Cambridge University Press.

Eckert, Penelope and Sally McConnell-Ginet. 1992. "Think Practically and Look Locally: Language and Gender as Community-based Practice." *Annual Review of Anthropology* 21: 461–90.

Eco, Umberto. 1995. *Search for the Perfect Language*. Oxford, UK & Cambridge, USA: Blackwell.

————1980. *The Name of the Rose*. New York: Harcourt Brace.

Eickelman, Dale F. 1995. "Introduction: Print, Writing, and the Politics of Religious Identity in the Middle East." *Anthropology Quarterly* 68: 133–38.

————1992. "Mass Higher Education and the Religious Imagination in Contemporary Arab Societies." *American Ethnologist* 19(4): 643–655.

Eisenstein, Elizabeth. 1998 [1983]. *The Printing Revolution in Early Modern Europe*. Cambridge, New York: Cambridge University Press.

Ennaji, Moha.1988. "Language Planning in Morocco and Changes in Arabic." *International Journal of the Sociology of Language* 74: 9–39.

Fakhri, Ahmed. 1998. "Reported Speech in Arabic Journalist Discourse." In *Perspectives on Arabic Linguistics XI*, eds., E. Benmamoun, M. Eid and N. Haeri. Amsterdam, Philadelphia: John Benjamins, pp. 167–182.

Farag Allah, Abd al-Rahman. 1996. "La question de la langue dans la presse Égypti-enne." *Égypte/Monde arabe* 27–28 (3&4): 435–449.

Febvre, Lucien and Henri-Jean Martin. 1976. *The Coming of the Book: The Impact of Printing 1450–1800.* London: Verso.

Ferguson, Charles. 1991. "Epilogue: Dilgossia Revisited." *Southwest Journal of Linguistics* 10 (1): 214–234.

———1959a."Diglossia." *Word* 15: 325–40. [Reprinted in *Sociolinguistic Perspectives: Papers on Language and Society, 1959–1994/ Charles Ferguson,* ed. T. Huebner. New York and Oxford: Oxford University Press.1996: 25–39].

———1959b. "The Arabic Koiné." *Language* 35 (4): 616–30. Reprinted in Belnap and Haeri.

———1959c. "Myths about Arabic." In *Languages and Linguistic Monograph Series, Georgetown University,* ed., R. Harrell, pp. 75–82. Reprinted in Belnap and Haeri.

Fernández, Mauro. 1993. *Diglossia: A Comprehensive Bibliography 1960–1990.* Amsterdam, Philadelphia: John Benjamins.

Fikr lil-Dirasat wal-Abhath. Special issue on *Taha Hussein: ma'at 'aam min al-nuhud al-'arabi.* [Taha Hussein: 100 Years of Arab Revivals], No. 14, 1989.

Al-Fikr al-'arabi. Special issue on *al-lugha al-'arabiyya wal-umma.* [The Arabic Language and the Umma], No. 75. 1994.

Fleisch, Henri. 1964. "Arabe classique et arabe dialectal." *Travaux et Jours* 12: 23–62.

Foucault, Michel. 1984. "What is an Author." In P. Rabinow, ed., *The Foucault Reader.* New York: Pantheon Books.

Frayha, Anis. 1955. *Nahw 'arabiyya muyassara.* [The Grammar of a Feasible Arabic]. Beirut: Dar al-Thaqafa.

Gal, Susan. 1989. "Language and Political Economy." *Annual Review of Anthropology* 18: 345–7.

———1987. "Codeswitching and Consciousness in the European Periphery." *American Ethnologist* 14 (4): 637–53.

Geertz, Clifford. 1973. *The Interpretation of Cultures.* New York: Basic Books.

———1968. *Islam Observed: Religious Development in Morocco and Indonesia.* Chicago and London: Chicago University Press.

Geertz, Clifford, Hildred Geertz and Lawrence Rosen. 1979. *Meaning and Order in Moroccan Society.* Cambridge: Cambridge University Press.

Gellner, Ernest. 1981. *Muslim Society.* Cambridge: Cambridge University Press.

Gershoni, Israel and James Jankowski. 1995. *Redefining the Egyptian Nation, 1930–45.* Cambridge: Cambridge University Press.

———1986. *Egypt, Islam, and the Arabs: The Search for Egyptian Nationhood, 1900–1930.* New York: Oxford University Press.

Gilsenan, Michael. 1990. "Very Like a Camel: The Appearance of an Anthropologist's Middle East." In *Localizing Strategies: Regional Traditions of Ethnographic Writing,* ed., R. Fardon. Edinburgh: Scottish Academic Press and Washington: Smithsonian Institution Press, pp. 222–239.

The Good News of Jesus Christ or The New Testament in Egyptian Arabic: The Acts of the Apostles.[il-khabar il-tayyib bita' yissu' il-masih ow il-ingil bil-lugha al-masriyya, il-qism il-khamis: a'maal il-rasul. 1926. Cairo: Matba'a al-Nil al-Masihiyya.

Grandgillaume, Gilbert. 1991. "Arabisation et language maternelles dans le contexte national au Maghreb." *International Journal of the Sociology of Language* 87: 45–54.
———1983. *Arabisation et Politique Linguistique au Maghreb*. Paris: Maisonneuve et Larose.
Gully, Adrian. 1993. "The Changing Face of Modern Written Arabic: An Update." *Al-Arabiyya* 26: 19–59.
Haeri, Niloofar. 2000. "Form and Ideology: Arabic Sociolinguistics and Beyond." *Annual Review of Anthropology* 29: 61–87.
———1997. "The Reproduction of Symbolic Capital." *Current Anthropology* 38 (5): 795–815
———1996. *The Sociolinguistic Market of Cairo: Gender, Class, and Education*. London, New York: Kegan Paul International.
Hanks, William. 1987. "Discourse Genres in a Theory of Practice." *American Ethnologist* 14(4): 668–92.
Hans Wehr Dictionary of Modern Written Arabic, 3rd edition. Ed., J. M. Cowan. Ithaca, NY: Spoken Language Services.
Harshav, Benjamin. 1993. *Language in Time of Revolution*. Berkeley, Los Angeles, London: University of California Press.
Hartman, Martin. 1899. *The Arabic Press of Egypt*. London: Luzac & Company.
Herzfeld, Michael. 1996. "National Spirit or the Breath of Nature? The Expropriation of Folk Positivism in the Discourse of Greek Nationalism." In *Natural Histories of Discourse*, eds., M. Silverstein and G. Urban. Chicago: University of Chicago Press, pp. 277–298.
Heyworth-Dunn, James. 1968 [1939]. *An Introduction to the History of Education in Modern Egypt*. London: Luzac and Company.
Hitti, Philip K. 1970. *History of the Arabs*. New York: St. Martin's Press.
Hodgson, Marshall. 1974. *The Venture of Islam: Conscience and History in a World Civilization*. 3 Volumes. Chicago: University of Chicago Press.
Holes, Clive. 1993. "The Uses of Variation: A Study of the Political Speeches of Gamal Abd Al-Nasir." In *Perspectives on Arabic Linguistics V.*, eds., M. Eid, and C. Holes. Amsterdam, Philadelphia: John Benjamins, pp. 13–45.
Hourani, Albert. 1991. *A History of the Arab Peoples*. Cambridge, MA: Belknap Press/Harvard University Press.
———1983. [1962]. *Arabic Thought in the Liberal Age, 1798–1939*. New York: Cambridge University Press.
Hudson Alan. 1992. "Diglossia: A Bibliographic Review." *Language in Society* 21: 611–674.
Hussein, Taha. 1954 [1944]. *The Future of Culture in Egypt*. Washington, DC: American Council of Learned Societies (translated from Arabic).
Imbabi, Fathi. 1994. *Maraa'i al-Qatl. [The Killing Fields]*. Giza: al-Nahr lil-Nashr wal-Towzi'.
Irvine, Judith.1989. "When Talk Isn't Cheap." *American Ethnologist* 16: 248–267.
Jakobson, Roman. 1971 [1966]. "Relationship between Russian Stem Suffixes and Verbal Aspects." In *Selected Writings, Vol. II. Word and Language*, R. Jakobson. The Hague: Mouton, pp.198–202.

————1971 [1965]. "Quest for the Essence of Language." In *Selected Writings, Vol. II. Word and Language*. The Hague: Mouton, pp. 345–59.

Karpat, Kemal. 1982. *Political and Social Thought in the Contemporary Middle East*. New York: Praeger.

Khoury, Philip. 1983. *Urban Notables and Arab Nationalism: The Politics of Damascus, 1860–1920*. Cambridge, New York: Cambridge University Press.

Kuipers, Joel. 1998. *Language, Identity, and Marginality in Indonesia: The Changing Nature of Ritual Speech on the Island of Sumba*. Cambridge: Cambridge University Press.

Al-Kumi, Abdel-Aziz Sami. 1992. *Al-ṣaḥafa al-islamiyya fi miṣr fil qarn tasi' 'ashar*. [The Islamic Press in Egypt in the Nineteenth Century], Mansura, Egypt: Dar al-Wafa lil-Tabaa'a wal-Nashr wal-Towzi'.

Leith, Dick. 1997 [1983]. *A Social History of English*. London: Routledge.

MacFarquhar, Larissa. 1994. "Robert Gottlieb: The Art of Editing I." *Paris Review* 132: 182–223.

Magli, Nasim. 1995. *Louis 'Awad wa ma'arikihi al-adabiyya*. Cairo: al-Hay'a al-Miṣriyya al-'aamma lil-Kitab.

Marçais, William. 1931. "La langue arabe dans l'Afrique du Nord." *Énseignement Public 105: 20–39*.

————1930. "La diglossie Arabe." *Énseignement Public 97: 401–9*.

Al-Mughni Plus: Active Study Dictionary of English-Arabic. By Hasan Karmi. Beirut: Librairie du Liban.

Al-Mawrid: A Modern Arabic-English Dictionary. 1995. By Rohi Baalbaki. Beirut: Dar El-Ilm Lilmalayin.

Al-Mawrid: A Modern English-Arabic Dictionary. 1996. By Munir Baalbaki. Beirut: Dar El-Ilm Lilmalayin.

Mazraani, Nathalie. 1997. *Aspects of Language Variation in Arabic Political Speech-Making*. Surrey: Curzon Press.

McMurtrie, Douglas C. 1922. *The Corrector of the Press in the Early Days of Printing*. Greenwich, CT: Condé Nast Press.

Messick, Brinkley. 1993. *The Calligraphic State: Textual Domination and History in a Muslim Society*. Berkeley: University of California Press.

El-Messiri, Sawsan. 1978. *Ibn al-Balad: The Concept of Egyptian Identity*. Leiden: Brill.

Michel, Nicolas. 1996. "Langues et Écritures des Papiers Publics dans l'Égypte Ottomane." *Égypte/Monde Arabe* 27–28 (3 and 4): 157–183.

Mitchell, Timothy. 1988. *Colonising Egypt*. Cairo: American University in Cairo Press.

Musa, Salama. 1964. *al-Balagha al-'asriyya wal-lugha al-'arabiyya*. [The Contemporary Style and the Arabic Language], Cairo: Salama Musa lil-Nashr wal-Towzi'.

Musharrafa, Mustafa. 1991. *Qantara alladhi kafar*. [Qantara who Disbelieved], Cairo: *Adab wa Naqd.*A publication of *al-Ahali/Hizb al-Tagammo' al-Watani al-Taqaddomi al-Wahdawi* [The Nationalist Progressive Unity Party].

Mustafa, Mahdi.1996. "Egyptian Arabic: Is It a New Language?" *al-Qahira: Magalla al-Fikr wal-Fann al-Mu'aṣir* [Cairo: *Journal of Contemporary Thought and Art*]. Special Issue 163: 4–5.

Nelson, Kristina. 1985. *The Art of Reciting the Qur'an*. Austin: University of Texas Press.

Nossier, Aida Ibrahim. 1990. *Arabic Books Published in Egypt in the Nineteenth Century.* 3 Volumes. Cairo: The American University in Cairo Press.

Ortner, Sherry. 1984. "Theory in Anthropology Since the Sixties." *Comparative Studies in Social History* 26: 126–66.

'Osam al-Din, Ahmed. 1986. *Harika al-targima fi misr fil-qarn al-'ashrin.* [The Translation Movement in Egypt in the 19th Century], Cairo: al-Hay'a al-Miṣriyya al-'amma lil-Kitab.

Parkinson, Dilworth. 1993. "Knowing Standard Arabic: Testing Egyptians' MSA Abilities." In *Perspectives on Arabic Linguistics V,* eds., M. Eid and C. Holes. Amsterdam: John Benjamins, pp. 47–73.

————1991. "Searching for Modern Fusha: Real Life Formal Arabic." *Al-Arabiyya,* 24: 31–64.

————1981. "VSO to SVO in Modern Standard Arabic: A Study in Diglossia Syntax." In *Syntactic Change,* Monograph No. 25, eds., B. Johns and D. Strong, pp. 159–176.

Pollock, Sheldon. 1998. "India in the Vernacular Millennium: Literary Culture and Polity 1000–1500." *Daedalus* 127 (3): 41–74.

Public Culture. Special issue on *Alter/Native Modernities.* Vol.11, no. 1. 1999. Cambridge, MA: Daedalus.

Qadaya Fikriyya. Special Issue on *Lughatina al-'arabiyya fi ma'rakat al-ḥaḍara.* [Our Language in the Battlefield of Civilization], No. 17, 18, 1997.

Rodenbeck, Max. 1999. *Cairo: The City Victorious.* New York: Knopf.

El Saadawi, Nawal. 1999. *A Daughter of Isis: The Autobiography of Nawal El Saadawi.* London, New York: Zed Books.

Sabri, Osman. 1967. "il-lugha il-'arabiyya il-hadisa ow il-lugha il-masriyya (il-'ammiyya)." In *Rihla fil-Nil.* Alexandria: Maktaba al-Arab al-Masriyya. Reprinted in *al-Garad,* 1994, pp. 79–111. Title is changed in *al-Garad* to "Fil lugha al-maṣriyya al-mu'aṣira."

————1964. *Nahw abgadiyya gadida.* [Toward a New Alphabet], no publisher listed.

Said, Edward. 1981. *Covering Islam.* New York: Pantheon Books.

————1978. *Orientalism.* New York: Pantheon Books.

Said, Nafusa Z. 1964. *Tarikh al-da'wa ila al-'ammiyya wa athariha fi miṣr.* [The History of the Call to 'ammiyya and its Influence in Egypt] Alexandria: Dar al-Thaqafa.

de Saussure, Ferdinand. 1966 [1959]. *Course in General Linguistics,* eds., C. Bally and A. Sechehaye. New York: McGraw-Hill Company.

Schieffelin, Bambi and Rachelle Charlier Doucet. 1998. "The 'Real' Haitian Creole: Ideology, Metalinguistics, and Orthographic Choice." In *Language Ideologies: Practice and Theory,* eds., B. Schieffelin, K. Woolard and P. Kroskrity. New York: Oxford, pp. 285–316.

Schieffelin, Bambi, Kathryn Woolard and Paul Kroskrity. 1998. *Language Ideologies: Practice and Theory.* New York: Oxford.

Seckinger, Beverly. 1988. "Implementing Morocco's Arabization Policy: Two Problems of Classification." In *With Forked Tongues: What Are National Languages Good For?* ed., F. Coulmas. Ann Arbor, MI: Karoma, pp. 68–89.

Shyrock, Andrew. 1997. *Nationalism and the Genealogical Imagination: Oral History and Textual Authority in Tribal Jordan.* Berkeley: University of California Press.

Silverstein, Michael, and Greg Urban, eds. 1996. *Natural Histories of Discourse.* Chicago: University of Chicago Press.

Singerman, Diane. 1995. *Avenues of Participation: Family, Politics and Networks in Urban Quarters of Cairo.* Princeton, NJ: Princeton University Press.

Starrett, Gregory. 1998. *Putting Islam to Work: Education, Politics, and Religious Transformation in Egypt.* Berkeley: University of California Press.

Stetkevych, Jaroslav. 1970. *The Modern Arabic Literary Language: Lexical and Stylistic Developments.* Chicago: University of Chicago Press.

Taymour, Mahmoud. 1956. *Mushkilat al-lugha al-'arabiyya.* [Problems of the Arabic Language], Cairo. No publisher listed.

UNDP, 2002. *The Arab Human Development Report 2002: Creating Opportunities for Future Generations.* New York: United Nations Development Programme, Regional Bureau for Arab States.

Vatikiotis, Panayiotis.1991. *The History of Modern Egypt: From Muhammad Ali to Mubarak.* London: Weidenfeld and Nicolson.

Versteegh, C. H. M. 1993. *Arabic Grammar and Qur'anic Exegesis in Early Islam.* Leiden: Brill.

Versteegh, Kees. 1997. *The Arabic Language.* Edinburgh: Edinburgh University Press.

Voloshinov, Valentin N. 1986 [1973]. *Marxism and the Philosophy of Language.* Cambridge, MA: Harvard University Press.

Wagner, Daniel. 1993. *Literacy, Culture, and Development: Becoming Literate in Morocco.* Cambridge: Cambridge University Press.

Washington-Serruys. 1897. *L'Arabe Moderne, Étudié dans les Journaux et les Pièces Officielles.* Beyrouth: Imprimerie Catholique.

Wa Thiong'o, Ngugi. 1986. *Decolonizing the Mind: the Politics of Language in African Literature.* London: J. Currey; Portsmouth, NH: Heinemann.

Weinreich, Uriel, William Labov and Michael Herzog. 1968. "Empirical Foundations for a Theory of Language Change." In *Directions for Historical Linguistics,* eds., W. Lehmann and J. Malkiel. Austin: University of Texas Press, pp. 95–185

Williams, Raymond. 1977. *Marxism and Literature.* Oxford: Oxford University Press.

Wucherking, Joan. 1984. *Historical Dictionary of Egypt.* Egypt: American University of Cairo Press.

Yacine, Kateb. 1994. *Le Poéte comme un boxeur, entretiens 1958–1989.* Paris: Editions du Seuil.

Index

DATE DUE

Printed in the United States
42668LVS00004B/1-147

9 780312 238971